JOHN BERTALOT'S
IMMEDIATELY PRACTICAL
TIPS FOR CHORAL DIRECTORS

D0595683

JOHN BERTALOT'S IMMEDIATELY PRACTICAL TIPS FOR CHORAL DIRECTORS

Cover and book design: Lecy Design

Library of Congress Cataloging-in-Publication Data

Bertalot, John
    [Immediately practical tips for choral directors]
    John Bertalot's Immediately practical tips for choral directors.
    p. cm.
    ISBN 0–8066–2810–3
    1. Choirs (Music) 2. Choral conducting. 3. Church music-
-Instruction and study. I. Title.
    MT88.B47 1994   94–24996
    782.5'145--dc20   CIP
                                                       MN

The paper used in this publication meets the minimum requirements of American Standard for Information Services–Permanence of Paper for Printed Library Materials. ANSI Z329.48–1984 ∞™

Manufactured in the U.S.A.   AF 11–28103

4   5   6   7   8   9

DEDICATED TO

The music staff of Trinity Church, Princeton:
  Robert Palmer, associate choirmaster,
  Nancianne Parrella, associate organist,
  Roberta Ellsworth, music secretary,
  Gregory D. Smith, choir librarian,

and to the successive chairs of the choirs' steering committee during my
  time here: Ann McGoldrick, Pegi Stengel May Papastephanou,
  Diane Woodside, and Cheryl Halverson,

and to the boys and girls, ladies and gentlemen of our choir programs,
  past and present,

and to the clergy and wardens of Trinity Church, Princeton who have
  been such strong supporters of the music program,

and to my professors and friends who helped to change my life:
  Harold Darke, Fernando Germani, George Guest, Martin How,
  Herbert Howells, Gerald Knight, James Litton, Hubert Middleton,
  Boris Ord, Sir David Willcocks, and Alec Wyton,

and also to the young choirmasters from many parts of the United States
  who have stayed with me, as described herein, to observe our choir
  program,

and especially to Bob from Seattle, who stayed with me while this book
  was being written and ate a lot of ice cream! He, however, is an
  experienced choirmaster, and the questions he asks in this book are
  not his, but those which I asked when I was a student. Similarly, the
  words put into the mouths of all the other persons portrayed in this
  book are mine alone.

Particular thanks to
Eberhard Froehlich for his drawings of choirdesks,
Roberta N. Ellsworth for photographs,
and to Elisabeth Caruso Gray and Nancianne Parrella
for their many practical suggestions during the preparation of this book.

CONTENTS

 PRELUDE

The phone on the music director's desk rang for the sixth time within half an hour. The choirmaster wearily got out of his chair on the far side of his office where he was trying to complete a descant on his computer for next Sunday's service. "It'll never get done at this rate," he sighed as he lumbered across the room to answer the insistent summons.

"Yes?" he said, somewhat sharply. "John," said the desk volunteer at the other end of the line in an unbearably cheerful voice, "there's a long distance call for you from Washington State on line two." The director perked up a bit—he liked long distance calls—they always held the potential for the unexpected.

"Hello, who is it?"

"John? This is Bob from Seattle. You may remember we met last summer at a workshop you led in Denver."

"Oh yes, Bob! How are things going with you?"

"Pretty well. I've just graduated from college and I've been hired as director of music for a church here. I'm starting next month, and I wondered if I might take you up on your offer to let me see you at work with your choirs before I begin. I need a musical booster shot, and you're the person to give it to me!"

"Of course, Bob, I'd be delighted to have you over here. Why don't you stay with me and we can talk shop day and night, if that's what you'd like."

"That would be terrific—thanks!"

"What sort of musical setup do have at your new church?"

"Well, my predecessor had a great program, but we're short of singers right now. My first concern is to get new people into our choirs, both kids and adults, and to revitalize the whole situation. I'm excited by the prospects," he continued, "but I'm also a little scared, because I haven't had much experience. I know you've got a big program at your church, and so I'd love to see what you do to make it so successful."

"This is a good time to come because we're just about to start our new season. You can see everything from the very beginning."

"That's exactly what I need. Will it be all right if I fly in on Saturday night?"

"Of course," said the director again, "I'll meet you at the airport."

"See you Saturday—and thanks again!"

The director put down his phone and returned to his computer with a lighter step. He loved sharing his passion for choir work with young directors and he knew that Bob would be an enthusiastic person to have around who would respond eagerly to everything he saw and heard.

"That young man will go far," he thought as he resumed his composing. "I'm really looking forward to seeing him again."

He reread a letter that had arrived in the mail that morning. It was from a choirmaster who had attended a workshop that he'd led in the summer. One paragraph in particular caught his eye.

> Your workshop gave me the tools I needed to stretch my choirs further than I ever dreamed possible. I learned more from you in that short week than at college and working in the church music field for years. You've made choirtraining an adventure to try rather than a feat to fear.

"Hmm," mused the director, remembering with pleasure the response of other choirmasters to his workshops, "let's see if I can turn Bob's apprehensions into buoyant hopes by the end of his visit here."

During the next few days the director looked over his lecture notes for the most effective techniques he had learned during his many years conducting choirs all over the world: procedures he had seen other people carry out successfully, things he had learned through trial and error, inspiring insights that had come upon him suddenly, secrets he had learned from watching some of the greatest directors, and also a few common sense matters which everyone should know but too few actually practice.

He grew quite excited as yet further ideas came to him. "I've never seen these written in any choirtraining books I've read," he said to himself. "Many of them are absolutely essential if Bob is to head a thriving choir program in his new church. I'll certainly share the Great Secret of choirtraining which I learned in Canada a few years back—how I got through so much of my musical career without knowing that secret I'll never know!

"I wish I'd known all these techniques when I began my career," he thought. "I'd have made far fewer mistakes and would have been able to achieve so much more. Oh dear, oh dear!" he sighed as he stood up, "How many opportunities slipped through my hands in those days and I didn't even realize that they were there!

"Well, Bob's not going to fall into the same holes that I did," he said, looking at an old photo on the wall of himself, in his student days, with his first choir. He hardly recognized himself in it—it was so long ago—but he was pleased to see that, as a young director, he did have the essential sparkle in the eyes as he was surrounded by a mixed bag of singers. "They didn't sing very well," he thought, "but they were all my friends, so perhaps I wasn't quite as inept as I thought I was!

"Bob is going to begin his career benefiting from everything that I've learned since those days; his people are going to love him for it, and they'll be a fine choir, too!"

♪ SATURDAY ♪

1
WELCOME

Three days later the director had a busy schedule.

In the morning and afternoon he led a Singalong Day for all the choir-girls at his church. At 10:25 A.M., 40 girls, ranging from new girls to experienced twelfth-graders, flocked into the large, airy practice room, clutching their bag lunches and looking excited. Many of them hadn't seen each other for three months. They were about to sing through most of the music that the director had chosen for services and concerts during the upcoming season.

The two head girls welcomed everyone and made sure that they wore name tags where they could be clearly seen. The librarian had already put all the music in the right order in neat piles on the music desks, so no time would be wasted in finding the next anthem. The senior girls took the new ones into their care and shared music with them. This thrilled the new girls a lot—at that age, they thought the big girls were wonderful! It also excited them to discover that when the older girls were sight-reading the new music they, too, seemed to be able to sing along with them. They already felt like part of the choir.

The director radiated energetic joy as he led the girls through each piece of music—pointing out interesting things to them and asking them why they thought he had chosen certain pieces for certain seasons. The older girls knew many of the answers, but occasionally a new girl put up her hand and ventured an answer, which delighted everyone.

Two hour-long practices were held in the morning, with an orange drink and donut holes in between, kindly supplied by some choir parents. At lunchtime the girls sat informally in groups on the grass, getting to know one another as they undid their bag lunches. Parents were presiding at a large trestle table from which yet more drinks were supplied as well as several plates of brownies, baked by the older girls.

After lunch the girls returned to the practice room for their third hour—they really enjoyed singing that day and got a lot of work done—after which a further treat was in store for them: the parents of one of the senior girls had offered the use of their pool for a swimming party to end the day. A fleet of cars, chauffeured by parents, was ready to take the excited girls to their hosts' home. The director drove three of the younger girls himself, but the car that everyone wanted to go in was a red and white convertible sports car driven by the head girl! This was immediately filled with older girls who waved at everyone as they quickly swept out of the church grounds to lead the way to the party.

The hosts had generously provided more snacks and drinks for the girls, and the director was glad, after his strenuous day, to sit down on the deck overlooking the pool. He found himself waited on hand and foot by both his hosts who were appreciative of the adventurous choir program which their daughter enjoyed so much. Sounds of happy screams and splashes reached his ears from the crowded pool as he regained his strength.

At 4:30 the party came to an end and contented girls, in twos and threes, thanked their hosts as they made their way to the cars of their parents who had come, punctually, to fetch them.

The director also thanked his hosts most warmly. "It's this sort of wonderfully active support that makes the running of our choir programs such a delight," he told them. They promptly invited him to stay for dinner, but he refused, gracefully as he had to drive to the airport to meet Bob. It had been a most successful day so far—the older girls had felt glad to be back in the choir again, and the new girls had most certainly felt the warmth of welcome from the other girls, the parents, and the director. Everyone eagerly looked forward to the start of the regular practice schedule next week.

Bob's plane was due in at 6:00 P.M. but his host arrived half an hour early, to be on the safe side.

He looked at the board announcing incoming flights and found that the flight had been delayed, so he bought himself a cup of coffee and went through the notes he had made of skills he wanted to pass on to Bob during the next few days. "There's enough material here to fill a book," he thought. "Perhaps I should write one to help all the other 'Bobs' who are starting their careers in church music, as well as others who need revitalizing."

He finished his coffee and took another look at the board: *Flight delayed two hours.* Dear, oh dear! he thought. Poor old Bob, he must be getting steamed up at the thought of being so late—he'll be tired and hungry when he lands. He'll certainly need cheering up when he eventually arrives.

The director made his way to a stationery store next to the cafe and bought himself a yellow notepad. "I may as well use the time profitably," he said to himself, "by making a start on writing this book!"

For the next two hours, as the busy life of the terminal swirled around him, he lost himself in sketching the first couple of chapters, fortified by several more cups of coffee.

Bob's flight finally landed. On his way to the gate, the director hurried into a novelty store to buy a rose to present to his guest. "I want him to feel really welcome," he thought, "and it's entirely up to me to dispel any sense of anxiety he may feel at being late (for it wasn't his fault!). How he feels five seconds after he sees me depends wholly on my own attitude to him—and so I shall make him feel thoroughly welcome!

WELCOME YOUR SINGERS, EVEN WHEN THEY ARE LATE!

Sure enough, five seconds after greeting his flustered, tired and disheveled guest, Bob began noticeably to relax as the director hugged him, pinned the rose onto his jacket, picked up his bags and led him to the terminal restaurant for a good meal.

"That must have been a tiring flight," commented the director as they relished their dinner. (Bob had ordered a juicy steak with french fries, but the director made do with a tuna salad—he was dieting.)

"I didn't know what to do," Bob answered. "I thought of you waiting for me and felt so helpless. Thanks for being so patient."

"That's the first secret in the art of training a choir which I'd planned to share with you," laughed the director, "but it's turned out to be a really practical demonstration instead."

"How do you mean?"

"When you were a student and you had a temporary job as a director, how did you feel when singers turned up late for your practices?"

"Oh, I made very sure that they knew I was displeased with them—they disrupted the other singers who had come on time and…uh-oh! I think you're trying to tell me something, aren't you?"

"Yes, I am! What am I trying to tell you?"

"That singers sometimes can't help being late?"

"Yes, indeed! You see," he said as he toyed with a lettuce leaf, "every member of our choirs will have made a special effort to be with us for the weekly practices—some have to travel several miles to get to church, some adults have to hire baby-sitters and some of the kids will have to stay up late when they get home to finish their homework, and so," he continued, cutting a tomato into thin slices, "if all our singers can look forward to receiving a really warm welcome from the director when they arrive, then the practice will get off to an excellent start."

"I've never thought of it like that," commented Bob as he put some more ketchup on his fries.

"I confess that I hadn't, either, until fairly recently when I experienced a marvelous welcome when I was touring South Africa."

"What happened?"

"Well, on one evening I'd been booked to conduct a rehearsal of the Port Elizabeth choral society. When I walked into the hall the atmosphere of welcome was so strong it was almost tangible. You must remember that South Africa didn't have too many visitors at that time. To have someone who'd come all the way from the U.S. to conduct them was a special event in their lives.

"The one hundred singers were all sitting ready; the accompanist had on her prettiest dress; about thirty directors, who'd driven long distances to observe the rehearsal, were in one corner of the hall, and in the other corner were tables loaded with food and drink for a party afterwards. Everyone was so welcoming that they really geared me up to do my very best for them, and we all had a wonderful time as a result.

"That taught me," he concluded as he chewed his final celery stick, "that if I want all my choir members to be geared up to do their very best for me, week after week, I must make them feel genuinely welcome when they arrive. This applies not only to those who arrive punctually but also..."

"Also to those who arrive late!" interrupted Bob with a laugh.

"Yes, indeed! But there are a couple of extra points you should watch."

"What are they?"

COURTESY TO THE CHOIR

"Adults who are late should always speak with you after the practice to tell you why they were late—this is a courtesy to you and to the choir. If they don't speak to you..."

"I should speak to them!"

"Yes. Courteously, of course, sympathizing with the problem they've experienced. But they need to know that you are on top of the situation, and that you care about them: you'll tend to have few people who are late through carelessness."

"And what's the other point?"

"Children who are late should come right up to you at the piano and whisper in your ear why they're late—this, again, is a courtesy to everyone, and it will show the rest of the choir that you do care about punctuality."

"Let me write that down," said Bob, rummaging in his suitcase. "I've brought a notebook with me specially for all the ideas I'll get this week." And he wrote:

Make every singer feel welcome at every practice—even latecomers!

PUNCTUALITY IS A COURTESY

"Of course," said the director as he handed the dessert menu to Bob, "the best way to ensure that everyone comes on time to your rehearsals is...is what?"

"Make the practices really worthwhile," answered Bob. "How do you do it?"

"We'll talk about that during the next few days. It's vitally important, for the way you conduct rehearsals determines if you stand or fall as a director of music!

"But there's another essential consideration that you have to observe for all rehearsals—what is it?" continued the director as he looked at his watch.

"Is it time to go?" asked Bob, somewhat startled by his host's action. "I was rather hoping for some dessert."

"No, I was giving you a hint—and, yes, there is time for dessert!"

"Oh!" said Bob, breaking into a sudden smile, "practices should always start and finish on time! I found that hard to do when I was a student," he frowned, "for so many singers came five or more minutes late."

"They came late because they'd conditioned you to accept their own schedule rather than your schedule. It's important that you always start rehearsals on time, even though there may be only a couple of people there to begin with. If you finish on time, then you can make a statement to the effect that, as you are being courteous to them by finishing punctually, they, in their turn should be courteous to their colleagues and to you by arriving punctually! Start as you mean to go on. You are in charge, not they!"

The director picked up the menu and added, "Someone once said that 'punctuality is the courtesy of kings.' Well, let punctuality also be the courtesy of directors.

"Now, what would you like after your steak?"

"I could manage a 'Death by chocolate,' I think. What will you have?"

"I'll make do with a coffee. Black!" he said with a sigh.

2
BEGINNING A NEW JOB

WHAT TO SAY TO YOUR CHOIR AT YOUR FIRST PRACTICE

"Well, I expect you're ready for a good night's sleep," said the director half an hour later as they drove out of the airport parking lot to begin their journey home.

"Yes, but let's use this driving time for more talk about choirs, please."

"Ask me as many questions as you like!"

"Well, when I was a student and I met my church choir for the very first time, I had no idea what to say to them."

"That's an excellent point," answered the director. "I can remember asking the very same question when I was a student. Let's see if we can make a simple list of things to do.

"One. Get to the practice half an hour early."

"Why should I do that?"

"To prepare the music, of course, and so that, when the singers arrive, you can meet them individually. Find out their names and learn a little about each one. Make sure that when you shake them warmly by the hand, you look into their eyes at the same time. This way you will quickly establish contact with everyone.

"Two. Ask your minister to arrive just before the practice is due to start so that he may introduce you formally. He'll know the right things to say in that situation.

"Three. Then you can say, in not more than one minute, how pleased you are to be there, how honored you are to follow your predecessor, and how happy you are at the prospect of working with all your singers, your assistant organist, and your minister."

"Why did you set a time limit?"

"Because your singers have come to sing, not to listen to a lot of speeches! And so," asked the director unexpectedly, "what should you do then?"

Bob thought for a moment and then said, "I should make my first choir practice really worthwhile."

"Right! That was my fourth point."

"But how do I go about leading an efficient rehearsal?"

"That's something you will learn this week, young man, if you keep your eyes and ears open! But I can tell you what you should have done before the practice."

"What's that?"

"Five. You should have talked with your assistant as to what needs a lot of rehearsing and what needs only a little polishing. Learn the music thoroughly so that you know exactly what you wish to achieve at that practice. A really good briefing by your assistant, who knows the singers and knows the music they will be rehearsing, is essential if you are to make your singers excited at the prospect of working with you for the next few years. Your first practice must be a winner, as far as you are concerned. So prepare yourself thoroughly beforehand."

"Wow! That was terrific; thank you!" exclaimed Bob.

AFTER THE FIRST PRACTICE

"And there's one more thing," added the director.

"What's that?"

"Tell me what you will do after the practice."

"I'll want to get home as quickly as possible, for that first rehearsal will have taken a lot out of me."

"Oh no you won't!" said the director with a smile as he safely negotiated the maze of roads that led out of the airport. "You'll stay in your practice room talking with the singers for as long as they wish to stay and visit with you. This first practice, as I've already said, is a vital one for you personally. If it goes really well, then the singers will look forward to working with you in the weeks and months ahead. Really go out of your way to show that you are a friendly person. If someone asks you to go with them to a local coffee bar, or wherever, the answer will be 'yes!' They will want to treat you, but make sure that you first offer to pay for them."

"Golly!" exclaimed Bob, "I hadn't realized that my first practice would be so important. I'd rather hoped to ease my way in gently."

"Not a bit of it! You should lead your first practice in such a way that your singers won't know what's hit them, because you'll make them sing better than they've ever done before. And you'll learn how to do that during your visit with me this week. That's a promise!"

TEACHING SIGHT-SINGING

They drove on in silence for a few minutes as they reached the main highway leading to the turnpike.

"One of the main reasons I've asked to see you at work," said Bob, "is because I've heard that you've perfected a system of teaching sight-singing so that all your choir members can read music."

"I wouldn't say that I've perfected my system—I'm always learning more. But you're quite right. I do teach my new children, and some adults, to read music, and it works! It makes the leading of practices so easy. All I have to do when presenting a new anthem to any of my choirs is to say, 'Here's the music—sing it!' and they do!

"I've written a book about it in which I explain every step. Anyone can do it—if," and the director grinned enigmatically at Bob, taking his eyes off the road for a moment, "if they have Five Wheels!"

"What do you mean by that?" asked Bob, hoping that the director had noticed a truck that wanted to pass them. "What have wheels got to do with sight-reading?"

"I'll give you a copy of the book and you'll find out!" he answered with a laugh. The director successfully avoided the truck and headed south for the turnpike.

"There are two essentials if you want to teach sight-singing success-fully," he added.

"I suppose one of them is setting aside a few minutes at every practice to learn how to do it," ventured Bob.

"No, no! A thousand times, no!" answered the director vehemently as he inadvertently swerved into the fast lane, narrowly missing a Mercedes that was doing seventy-five! "Whoops, sorry!" said the director as he steered his way back to the relative safety of the slow lane, "but I feel very strongly about this subject—we'd better save it until we're home.

"The first thing you have to alter, if you're going to have a choir which can sight-sing, is the way you lead your practices, and the other thing is to have a well thought-through scheme of teaching for all the new children. You'll see both of these in action starting on Monday when we begin practices.

"And also, of course," he added, "there's the Great Secret, which will enable you not only to teach sight-singing quickly, but it'll help you to train a choir to sing intelligently, sing with lovely tone, and it will help you always to fill your choirstalls with keen, punctual singers."

"What is the Great Secret?" asked Bob, as he got out his notebook to write down all the musical gems that were coming his way.

"I won't tell you—yet! But you'll see it in action on Monday, and then we'll talk about it!"

They approached the turnpike entrance and, taking a ticket from the machine, the director said "Okay, let's talk about a secret which I will share with you now.

"What will be your top priority when you start work in your new church?" he asked.

"Oh! there'll be lots of them: getting to know people, learning the repertoire, choosing music, leading efficient rehearsals, practicing the organ...the list is endless."

"Yes, all these things are vital and necessary, but there's one thing above all others that every new director has to do—in fact, you told me what it was when you called me last week!"

THE FIRST PRIORITY IS RECRUITING NEW SINGERS

"Oh yes! I've got to attract new singers into the choirs—the numbers are pretty low right now."

"Yes, a director's first priority is to attract new singers! How are you going to do that?"

"Well, I suppose I make an appeal in the parish newsletter and hope that that will bring people in," he responded rather helplessly.

"Is your pencil sharpened?" asked the director unexpectedly, "for here comes a list of ideas that really work.

START A NEW JOB WITH A BANG!

"When you start work at your church, make sure that everyone knows you have arrived! There'd be nothing worse than for you to have been at the church for a month without the parish noticing any difference!

"I learned that lesson many years ago from Fernando Germani, who was, at that time, the world's leading organ virtuoso. He said that before he gave his first recital in Rome, he made sure that the church would be packed to the doors. 'Ever since then,' he told me, 'I've always played to standing-room-only.'" The director continued, "I'd just been appointed organist of an English cathedral (the news came through when Germani was staying in my home) and so he suggested that I ask my dean to arrange a reception so that I could meet all the choir directors and clergy of the diocese. He did, and the bishop came too! And so I was able to start with a bang and announce the exciting musical plans I had for the cathedral and the diocese. I made sure that the press was there, too, and so the news spread through the whole county, with photographs.

"A new director, like a new minister or a new president, always starts off with a honeymoon period when everyone is being cooperative, waiting to see what great things the new man or woman has in mind for them. You need to take full advantage of that.

"So, ask your minister if you may be formally welcomed to the church during your first service. A short ceremony when he blesses you in front of the congregation is a wonderful way to start your new life.

"And then ask him to arrange a reception for you on your first Sunday, with refreshments. Then you can meet the congregation informally; get the press there and a photographer and, if possible, some distinguished outsider to introduce you and say nice things about you."

US AND THEM

The director paused while Bob wrote busily in his notebook. He continued, "And there are two long-term items which you should take care of."

"What are they?" asked Bob, looking up from his note-taking.

"One: you should show yourself as often as possible at congregational functions at your church."

"How do you mean?"

"There is, unfortunately, a built in us-and-them situation in all music directors' jobs; we have to concern ourselves with the choir, which is a clearly defined group within every parish structure. This can lead some church members, who are not involved with our music programs, to feel that the music director is not interested in what goes on in other parts of the church organization.

"If your church has Sunday forums, get yourself booked as one of the speakers at least once a year so that you can address the congregation. It would be a great opportunity for them to learn some new hymns and to experience what it's like to work with you!"

LEARN HOW TO ACCEPT THANKS

Acres of gas tanks on either side of the road made breathing unpleasant and conversation impossible for a few minutes. When the air cleared the director continued, "It is necessary for you to show yourself whenever it is appropriate. Don't be like one organ recitalist we had here who, after he'd given a recital, didn't come to the reception afterwards because he didn't like to be thanked! One of the things we have to learn is how to receive compliments without getting big-headed. Folks like saying thank-you after you've done something for them, be it opening a door or conducting a concert. You must allow them to do that, for it goes with the territory of being a public figure.

"It is vitally important to show that you really are interested in other facets of the church's life, by turning up at non-choir events so that you can be seen by as many people as possible who are involved with other programs. For it is they who, in large measure, pay your salary!"

"I've never thought of that," commented Bob. "Thank you for telling me. What's your second point?"

GET INVOLVED IN THE CHURCH
AND IN THE LOCAL COMMUNITY

"It's similar to the first. Get yourself involved in the local community as much as your musical duties allow. Be seen at concerts given by others; get to know leaders in other professions in your town as well as your musical colleagues. The danger of being a professional person is that one tends to mix only with those who have similar interests; attorneys mix with attorneys, doctors with other doctors and all the clergy of your area will most certainly know each other. It's so easy to become isolated.

"It's equally important for you, as the choirmaster, to circulate among your singers when you go on a coach outing. Your choristers, both young and old, will enjoy exchanging a few words with you during the journey, especially if you come bearing some cookies or soft drinks with you!

"And so," concluded the director, "when you do attend a concert, or some other function in your town, don't stay in your seat at the interval, but walk around the auditorium to get to know other folk in your community. Over time you will build up a fund of goodwill for yourself, for your program, and for your church."

He paused for a moment, and then added, "You might also think about writing a note of appreciation to the conductor of the concert, especially if he's a local person. That's a great way of introducing yourself to a new colleague."

CULTIVATING PERSONAL RELATIONSHIPS

He paused again while Bob turned another page in his notebook. "I learned a valuable lesson about cultivating personal relationships from one of my deans in England," continued the director.

"What was that?"

"Well, when this new dean arrived, he made time to talk with everyone he passed in the cathedral close. He didn't just give a cheery wave and walk past when he saw you, he actually stopped for a few minutes and asked how we were and what we were doing."

"That must have made a good impression," commented Bob.

"It certainly did, young man! We all thought that our new dean was a marvelous person. Why?" he asked suddenly.

"Because he showed that he was interested in other people."

"Absolutely right—well done!" answered the director with a broad grin. "If, when you begin your new job, you show that you are really interested in everyone you meet at your church..."

"By spending time with them and asking them about themselves," interrupted Bob.

"Yes, indeed—because people are interested first in themselves. If you show that you are interested in your choir families and members of the congregation, as well as your fellow staff members, you will create for yourself an enormous fund of goodwill at the very beginning of your ministry. This will help you in all sorts of practical ways as you begin to develop your program."

REFERENCES

The Turnpike made a gentle curve to the left, and the director remarked, "I suppose you must have asked a number of friends and professors to write to your new minister on your behalf when you applied for your new job."

"Oh yes!" said Bob gratefully. "They wrote directly to the minister without my seeing what they had to say. The minister felt that if I saw what my professors were writing about me, it would be so much less valuable than if only he saw what was written. He felt that my teachers could be more honest about me that way."

"He was quite right. A reference is so much more in your favor if your teacher can say that 90 percent of you is very good, but that there is a 10 percent area which needs attention. That way the minister really knows that he can put a lot of weight on the 90 percent. References that say the candidate is wholly wonderful can leave room for doubt, for no one is that perfect!" and he laughed.

"By the way," added the director, as the road became straighter, "I suppose that all those who wrote references for you must be pretty pleased that you've been hired?"

"Yes, I expect they are," responded Bob quietly.

"Why do you only expect they are pleased? Don't you know?"

"Well," said Bob uneasily, "I haven't got around to writing to them yet; there were so many more important things to do."

There was an uncomfortable silence after that remark. Eventually the director said, very quietly, "If I had taken the trouble to write a favorable reference for a pupil of mine, and if that pupil, as a result of my reference, was hired for the job, and if that pupil didn't get in touch with me as soon as possible to thank me for helping him to get the job he wanted, do you know what I would do?"

"No," came a small voice from the passenger seat.

"I would never write another reference for that person," said the director firmly. "For that pupil would have displayed to me a discourtesy which showed that he, or she, was not as fitted for that post as I had believed. Being a musician is all about communicating. Music is a vehicle for communication. If a musician failed to communicate with the people who helped him when he needed help most, then clearly, his advocates were mistaken about him, for he is not a natural communicator. To learn to say 'thank you' is one of the greatest lessons you can learn in this life, and every one of my pupils knows this." He paused for a moment, and then smiled kindly at Bob, "No one has told you that, have they?"

"No, they haven't."

"Well, what are you going to do about it?"

"I'll write to all of them as soon as I get home, to say 'thank you!' "

"Why wait that long? We aren't doing anything when we get home."

"Oh!" said Bob. "I should write to them tonight—I've brought my address book with me. Thank you!"

GET TO KNOW YOUR ASSISTANT

The director honked his horn at a car that suddenly cut in front of him. "Sorry about that!" he said. "Driving seems to bring out the worst in me!"

"Me, too!" responded Bob with a grin.

"But there's someone in your new church out of whom you should bring the best very quickly; someone we haven't mentioned yet. Who is it?"

Bob thought for a moment, and suggested, "The minister?"

"That's very true. We'll talk about him later. No," continued the director, "I was thinking of someone with whom you will work even more closely than your minister."

"Oh, you mean my assistant organist!"

"Yes, I most certainly do! Since you are fortunate enough to have an assistant, it's vitally important that you begin to get to know her during the first few days at your church."

"I've met her already. She's a delightful person."

"Good! What am I suggesting that you do?"

"I don't think you're suggesting anything," answered Bob with a smile. "You're telling me, pretty strongly, that I should spend time with her. I'll ask her and her husband out to dinner as soon as I get back."

"Good!" said the director again. "But you need to do even more than that. Asking her to dinner is a great idea. You should also set up weekly meetings with her in your office when you can ask her all about your new job and the people with whom you will be working. Really listen to what she says, for her input will be of the greatest help to you."

They drove on in silence while Bob filled another page in his new notebook. "If you can quickly get her on your side, through sympathetic listening and words of appreciation, your early days in your new job will be so much easier for you, and they'll be more fruitful."

"What's 'sympathetic listening'?" asked Bob.

"Giving your whole attention to what she is saying, and asking intelligent questions, just as you are doing with me right now!" answered the director with a laugh.

ATTRACTING NEW ADULT SINGERS

He paused again as he passed several cars which were doing only fifty, and then said, "But let's get back to the important welcoming reception at your church, for you need to recruit new singers into your choirs, and this is a great opportunity to do that. *(Coffee Hour:)*

"You should be prepared to say a few words after you've been introduced. Start with a funny story and remember to thank the leaders of the church for hiring you. Tell the congregation how much you look forward to working with them and getting to know them. Say a few words of genuine appreciation for what your predecessor did and also mention your assistant. Then you should announce specific plans for the next few months, such as a concert, or a carol service or whatever. Then say that you need so many extra singers and instrumentalists to help you put this on and when rehearsals will begin. *Betsie though act to follow...*

"Let your plans be both short-term and long-term." *even song*

"How do you mean?" asked Bob, who continued writing energetically in his notebook.

"You could say, 'In two months we're going to do this, but by this time next year we shall do that!' But you're more likely to get new adults into your choir program if they know that their commitment will be for a limited period—say eight rehearsals to put on a performance of Faure's *Requiem,* after which their commitment ceases.

"Once they're in your choir it's up to you to make the rehearsals so worthwhile that they'll want to become permanent members, and some will!"

3
RECRUITING CHILDREN

They drove on in silence for a while, and then Bob asked, "What about attracting children into the choir program?"

"That's more difficult, but it's also more rewarding in the long run."

"Why?"

"Because if you can start training children in the right way, you've made converts for life, and there's a strong likelihood that you'll get their parents to come to church as well. This job is as much pastoral as it is musical."

"How do I go about that?"

"Well, there are lots of things you can do, and should do. Some of these ideas will work for you right now, and others will work after you've been there for a year or so. Here goes:

ADVERTISE: VACANCIES NOW BEING FILLED

"Write an article in the parish magazine to the effect that *Vacancies are now being filled... call the director without obligation.* Do not say, 'We desperately need singers and there are lots of vacancies.' You must always look at advertising from the customer's point of view, not yours. And so if you say, 'Vacancies are being filled right now,' that has the effect of making potential singers think, 'I must apply immediately before they all get filled up.' Whereas, if you say, 'We desperately need singers'— this has the effect of saying, 'Our choir program is in a bad way, so it's not worth joining.'

"You need to repeat this message of 'vacancies are now being filled' in the church weekly service bulletin—and you might want to ask your minister if you could make a brief verbal announcement during one of the services.

NEWCOMERS' PROGRAMS

"Many churches have newcomers' programs. Ask your minister if you may write to the new families to 'sell' the choir to them. By the way, you need to work very closely with your clergy in this matter, for the leaders of other church programs will also be contacting the new families. You must avoid any hint of rivalry between the programs.

APPROACH THE CHURCH SCHOOL LEADER

"Meet with your church school leader to see if it is possible to have some of the same children in both your programs, rather than have you-can't-belong-to-both-so-choose-mine situation, which is unhealthy for good staff relationships.

"I confess that, in my church, I am very blessed, for our church school leader had all three of her own children in the choir, and so she's very much in favor of kids joining my program. Every year she gives me the names of her third-graders who are most likely to want to join the choir. Many of them do, but you'll find very few church school leaders so accommodating!

EDUCATE YOUR MINISTER

"Talk with your minister about the educational value of your program. If he can see that belonging to a really well-run choir program is a Christian educational experience, he might well be disposed to help you in your relations with his church school. Our associate minister told me only last week that the reason he is ordained is because he sang in a church choir when he was a boy. 'It was a far greater influence on my Christian upbringing than any church school program,' he said. I was thrilled!

PERSONAL RELATIONSHIPS

"It's the director's vocation not only to make harmony through music, but also to foster harmony in personal relationships within his church. This sometimes takes a lot of work and isn't easy. It all comes down to the sort of person you are; if you are easily threatened, then you will have a bad time and you will cause others to have a bad time. If, on the other hand, you can have the attitude that 'all things work together for good for those that love God' and are able to talk problems through face-to-face with those with whom you are experiencing problems, then you will be a peacemaker, and bless-ed will you be!"

"Golly!" exclaimed Bob, "I'd no idea that being a director involved so many things other than music."

RECRUITING CHILDREN

"Yes it does, young man!" said the director with a smile as the car sped along the turnpike homewards. "But let's get on with recruitment ideas:

"Printed publicity about your choir program, once you've got it going, could be displayed on the church notice board and in shops. Make it short, with attractive photographs. There's sure to be someone in your congregation who knows about how to prepare such a leaflet—such as a newspaper reporter or professional artist. Find out who they are and work together on producing something really eye-catching.

CHOIR MAGAZINE

"There's a church choir in Chicago which publishes its own magazine. It's most attractively produced. I used to do this when I was director of music of an English cathedral. We even won a national prize! I found it a useful tool for stimulating support among the congregation and for getting the choir better known in the town and beyond. It was also a great vehicle for recruiting new singers."

"That's a fine idea!" responded Bob, enthusiastically.

SINGERS RECRUIT OTHER SINGERS

"The best people to recruit new members to your choir are those who are already singing with you, and also their parents. Parents really appreciate what you are doing for their children. Ask your choir parents to approach their friends who have kids to tell them how much the choir means to them and their families. If they really enjoy being involved in your program they will want their friends to join in, too. Some choir children will have younger brothers and sisters. Get them to bring them along one Sunday to meet you. I've got one child coming to see me tomorrow, and I'll show you how I audition really creatively."

"Audition?" echoed Bob with amazement. "I'll need every kid I can get—I won't be able to afford the luxury of weeding out some kids in favor of others."

"I knew you'd misunderstand me," laughed the director, "that's why I said it! I also need every kid I can get—even those who seem unpromising. It's my job to turn every child who comes through my practice-room door into an educated, practical musician, and the process begins when we first set eyes on each other. You'll see that happen tomorrow, I promise you!

WRITING LETTERS

"Now, are you good at writing letters?" he continued as the car made its way steadily southwards.

"Writing letters? What's that got to do with being a director?"

"It's got everything to do with being a director! Our job is not only to be creators of harmony but also vehicles of communication. Music is all to do with communication—communicating spiritual truths that words cannot. Benjamin Britten talked about the holy triangle of composer, performer and listener. All three have to be linked. Unless you are communicating when you are making music you're not doing your job. Your choir has to communicate the message of its music to the congregation every Sunday. In order to do that it first has to understand the message of the anthem it is singing. But we'll go into that, too, during the next few days.

"I asked if you were good at writing letters because you'll find that much of your time will be spent sitting at your desk communicating with your singers and their families through letters as well as phone calls. Letter-writing comes into this situation right at the beginning of the recruiting process.

"When you've got the names of possible families to contact do not call them to ask if Willie wants to join the choir, for the answer is almost certain to be 'no.'"

"What should I do, then?" Bob asked, fascinated by this new world which was opening up to him. He'd never learned these things in his student years at music school.

"You write to the parents, saying that Willie's name has been given to you by the minister, or some other authority figure, as a possible candidate for the choir. Then you go on to say a brief word about the program, how exciting it is and educational, and that you will be performing so-and-so during the coming year. Finish the letter by inviting the parents to bring Willie to church next Sunday when you can meet after the service to discuss the situation, without obligation. Keep the letter short; if it's long, it'll be thrown in the trash.

"By the way," he added, "make the letter as personalized as possible. Certainly write it on your word processor, but if you write *Dear Mr. & Mrs. Smith* in your own hand, as well as signing it, the chances of it being read will increase."

"Then what happens?" asked Bob as the director drove on to the turnpike exit.

FOLLOW UP FAST!

"Well, you don't wait until next Sunday to see if they turn up! I learned something recently when I led a week's workshop for choral directors. One of those present had been an insurance salesman and he told me the technique that he had been trained to use when he wrote to prospective customers. He said:

"'We always called the customer the very next day to ask if they'd received the letter. If I waited for two days the effect was weaker—three days and it was weaker still.'"

The director paid his toll and negotiated several rather dangerous curves that led onto the highway. He continued, "Then this former salesman told us, 'Whatever the customer said in answer to my question I always said *Fine!'*

"'Did you get my letter?'

"'Yes, and tore it up!' *Fine!*

"'No, what letter?' *Fine!*

"'Saying *Fine* kept the contact going between us—the longer I kept the conversation going, the better chance I had of making a sale.'

"And so," continued the director, "the same applies to us. Keep the contact going in order to 'sell' what you want, which is...what?"

"That Willie should join the choir," answered Bob happily.

"No, it isn't!" answered the director rather strongly, taking his eyes off the road for a moment to give Bob a direct look, even though they were coming onto the main highway. Fortunately there wasn't much traffic at that time of night.

"Whoops!" thought Bob, "this man holds strong views—I must try harder!" He thought for a moment and then said, "Oh! Your object is to get the parents to come to church next Sunday and bring Willie with them."

"That's better," responded the director encouragingly. "And so ask questions about Willie—parents like nothing better than to talk about their children—and show genuine interest in the things he's doing. Express the hope that you can all meet for 'a few minutes next Sunday, when we can discuss this further, without obligation.'

"You'll see tomorrow how I go on from there and make Willie really enthusiastic about wanting to join us!" he added, with a laugh.

4
MORE RECRUITING METHODS

They were making good time on their journey homewards as the traffic lights, every few miles, were kind to them. "Once you've established yourself in your new church," said the director, just beating a light that was about to turn red, "there's another thing you can do to attract new children that is very effective."

"What's?"

"You can send a short cassette, or even a video of your choir to parents, with a brochure showing photos of some of the exciting things you've been doing recently. All this will cost money, but it's money well spent. There's nothing like making a recording to raise the enthusiasm of a choir. Carols sell best. We've even made a CD of anthems sung 'live' at services during the last few years. The occasional cough in the congregation seems to add to the effect of our music, for it shows us as we really are—and our best singing is pretty good. You might see if someone can set up a good recording system for you so that you can tape your music on a regular basis."

"My word! you've given me a lot to think about." said Bob as he closed his notebook.

"Why don't you make a brief summary of what we've been talking about? You'll find it a help when you get back home and you want to remember what we've said."

"Thanks," said Bob, opening his notebook again and turning to a clean page. Silence reigned during the next ten minutes as Bob read his notes again and wrote:

RECRUITING
1 Regular publicity in local press, parish magazine & service leaflet.
2 Verbal announcement in services.
3 Meet with minister and church school leader.
4 Get names of newcomers.
5 Write to new parents and follow up!
6 Design publicity brochure.
7 Investigate recording choir—cassettes/video.
8 Encourage children to bring their friends.

TELL YOUR CHOIR ONLY ONCE

Bob closed his book for the second time and leaned back in his seat. He'd had a tiring day.

"Read out what you've just written," commanded the director unexpectedly.

"Does this man never stop?" thought Bob as he struggled to sit up. He opened his book for the second time and read out the eight secrets of recruiting.

"Good—but you've missed two of the most important secrets."

What are they? asked Bob incredulously, for he thought he'd reread his notes pretty thoroughly!

"Why should I tell you a second time?" answered the director rather firmly. "You've written them down already."

Bob sat up straighter at this mild rebuke and began to thumb through his notes yet again. While he was doing it the director added, "I did that to you on purpose, Bob. Sorry! I just wanted to illustrate one of the lessons that many directors never learn: give instructions to your choir only once. Most choirs condition their directors to say things two or even three times before the message gets home—it wastes so much valuable time.

"But of course," the director continued, "that gives the choirmaster a special responsibility."

Bob wondered if he dare ask what that responsibility might be, when it suddenly struck him that he knew what it was. "That means," he said, "that what the choirmaster says has to be worth listening to!"

"Right! We choirmasters tend to talk far too much. A tape recording of one of our practices can be a painful, but a most useful lesson to most of us!" And he turned to Bob with a grin to show that what he had said was meant to be helpful. It was!

As they drove along in silence for the next couple of miles Bob spotted the two major points he'd missed earlier. How could I have been so blind? he thought, as the car sped on its way homewards.

VISIT CHOIR PARENTS IN THEIR HOMES

"Well, we're nearly home," said the director as he turned off the highway into a pleasant residential area. "There's just time to discuss how you will spend the evenings of the first few weeks at your new job."

"Apart from taking choir practices and practicing the organ, I'll look forward to some time to myself getting my apartment in order," answered Bob.

"Oh no you won't!" said the director, as he steered the car round a seemingly endless number of small roads lined with houses. "Your second priority is as important as the first; not only do you have to attract new singers into your choirs, you also have to get to know the present members, for you'll need their cooperation if you are to achieve anything worthwhile in your early months there."

"I'll get to know them at practices, won't I?"

"Yes, but only slightly. You'll only see one side of them there—their singing side. You will have in your care whole persons, not just 'singing units.' Your singers have families and they have many other interests apart from church and choir. And so what am I recommending that you do?"

LISTEN, LEARN AND SAY THANK YOU

"You're not recommending anything," said Bob with a smile, "you're telling me that I should visit all my singers in their homes so that I can get to know them better..."

"And so that they can get to know you, too!" interrupted the director. "You'll find that there'll be no shortage of conversational topics once you go through their front doors. The parents will talk about their children— all you'll have to say is 'yes' and 'how interesting!' And the adults singers will talk about the good old days of the choir and how glad they are that you have come to lead them.

"They'll also talk about your predecessor. It's vitally important, when this happens, that you show courtesy to his memory and appreciation for what he achieved. Our predecessors have, in their time, earned great respect and affection from all the good folk with whom you will be working. It's up to you to make this work for you rather than against you."

"How do I do that?"

"By discovering what they did well and doing it even better!"

"That's asking rather a lot, isn't it?"

"That's one of the reasons that you were chosen for the post instead of someone else. Your church certainly didn't hire you to do less well than your predecessor! By allowing yourself to learn from his example you will find your own abilities increasing. If you ever stop learning, that's the time to retire!"

The car turned one more corner and the director's house came into view.

"Make sure you take a notebook when you visit with choir families. Afterwards, jot down what they have told you—you'll find it very helpful in formulating your own plans."

"Do I just drop by and hope they're in?" asked Bob as the car turned into a short driveway.

"No, you ask each family, individually, if it will be convenient for you to pop in for an hour some evening so that you can say "hello." By the way, make sure that your first visit is to the singer who's been in the choir the longest. Your assistant organist will be able to advise you here. If you can get this singer on your side, the word will spread and you'll be on a home run.

"You'll find that most folk will ask you to have a meal with them. They'll make it a special occasion—so put on nice clothes as a courtesy to them, and don't forget to take a small present with you—a box of candy, a bottle or some flowers. You'll get so much food from your choir families during your first couple of months that even you may have to think about going on diet!" and he laughed as he got out of the car, collected Bob's cases from the trunk and led his guest into his own home.

He opened the front door and welcomed Bob to his home. "There's one essential thing you should do after you've visited your singers' homes," he added.

"What's that?" asked Bob, looking at some of the photographs which covered the walls of his host's home.

"Remember to write a courteous letter of thanks the following day. If you don't write that letter, all the good that your visit had done will be void."

Bob took his eyes off the pictures and looked at his host gratefully. "I needed to hear that," he said, "for I'm not very good at saying thank you. Thank you!" And they both laughed.

That night, before he went to sleep, Bob wrote six letters of thanks to his professors and friends who had helped him get his new job. After it was done he felt good about it. "They will be happy to hear from me," he thought as he stuck stamps on to the envelopes, "and I certainly feel much happier in my relationships with them—for they have been important people in my life, and I hope they'll go on helping me." He added to his growing list the techniques he had learned by writing in his notebook: *Visit with choir members and their families. Listen, learn and remember to say thank you!*

"Wow," he thought as he turned out the light, "What a great day that was. I wonder what's in store for me tomorrow!"

♪ SUNDAY ♪

5
AUDITIONS

The following morning, after breakfast, Bob drove with the director to church, posting his six letters in a mailbox that they passed on the way. The director said a heartfelt, "Well done!" when he saw the fruit of Bob's labor the previous night. "It's the last Sunday of our summer season," added the director as he drove the half dozen miles to town alongside green fields and tall trees that lined both sides of the road. "So we're having a volunteer choir—members of all our choirs and some other singers who want to join in the celebration of homecoming. There'll be a parish picnic afterwards on the church lawn; the food's always good there—so I'll forget about my diet just this once!"

"I suppose you'll just be singing hymns," said Bob, "for you won't have time to teach them a new anthem."

"Nonsense!" responded the director with a snort, "As you know full well, they can all read music: kids, teens and adults. I've chosen an anthem we haven't sung for two years. They'll pick it up in next to no time—you'll see."

And see he did! Bob was amazed that, in the 45-minute preservice practice, the director was able to rehearse not only the new anthem, which everyone sang well, but also a psalm, four hymns, and a descant.

After the rehearsal was over, Bob accompanied the director to the organ loft and asked, "How is it that they all read music so well? I suppose you must weed out a lot of potential singers when you audition them."

"Nonsense!" exclaimed the director again as he prepared to play the prelude. "I told you yesterday what my policy is. Don't you remember, or are you still jet-lagged?"

"Oh yes! You said that you needed every kid that you could get, but that you turned them all into musicians. How do you do that?"

"You'll see after the service when I audition a new boy. His mother's bringing him to this service, and we'll meet afterwards. Now," he added as he pulled out some stops, "let's get on with what we're here for—worshipping God!" and he began to play.

HOW TO "AUDITION" A NEW SINGER SUCCESSFULLY

The service was exhilarating. Everyone sang their hearts out, and the minister set the tone for the coming season with a thought-provoking homily. Afterwards, the director and Bob went down the organ loft steps to find a woman standing there, accompanied by an eight-year-old, fair-haired boy.

"Mrs. McArthur?" asked the director, introducing himself and Bob to her. "Welcome to our church! And is this Shelton?" he added, shaking his hand, also. They chatted for a few minutes and then walked through the churchyard. They were greeted by the sounds of bells being rung on the carillon in the tower. Once they reached the spacious choir room, they found the choir librarian putting music away assisted by a couple of teenagers.

"Deane, I wonder if you'd like to show Mrs. McArthur around for a few minutes while Shelton and I get to know one another?"

"Certainly," said the librarian, who knew that the director needed to have the boy to himself without his Mom looking on. Bob also took the hint and hid himself behind some notice boards where he could hear but not be seen.

TWELVE COMMANDMENTS FOR A SUCCESSFUL AUDITION

1 "Well now, Shelton," said the director as he led the boy towards the grand piano at the end of the room, "that's a smart badge you're wearing on your blazer. What is it?" He sat down on the piano stool so that the boy would be less intimidated by him.

"Oh, it means that I'm on the school tennis team."

"You play tennis, do you? That must be exciting."

"Yes, it is. We're playing a match against another junior school next Saturday."

"How often do you do that?"

"About once a month."

"Do you win?"

"Sometimes." He paused and the director waited for him to continue. "I'm starting piano lessons this term," he added.

"That's terrific! You're pretty busy then?"

"Yes! I sing in the school choir, too."

2 "Well, sing this note for me," and he played middle G and modeled an 'Ah' vowel for the boy. What came out wasn't very good, but at least it was on pitch.

3 "Yes, Shelton! When you sing, should your mouth be open or closed?" "Open." "Yes! Put two fingers in your mouth, like this," and the director again showed the boy what he wanted. "Now that's an 'Ah' mouth! Sing that note again with a super mouth."

4 "Did that sound better?" "Yes!" "Okay, now sing the same note while I count four, like this," and the director sang the note for four counts, coming off on the fifth as he pointed rhythmically to the fingers of his left hand, coming off when he reached the thumb. The boy did it, but stopped too soon.

5 "Was that wholly right?" "No." "What did you do wrong?" "I stopped too soon." "Yes! If a note is four counts long, on which beat

should you finish, the fourth or the fifth?" There was a pause while the boy thought. "The fifth." "Yes. Let's do it again." He did, and it was right. "Great! Do it once more." the director enthused. The boy did it again and the director beamed him a smile of congratulations.

6   "That was the right length—well done! How was your mouth?" "Oh, it was shut." "Let's try three fingers in your mouth this time for a really good 'Ah.'" The boy grinned and tried it, then sang the note as the director counted on his fingers so that he could see exactly when to start and when to stop. "Was that right?" "Yes!" "Yes, it was indeed. Well done! Do it again, but this time count on your own fingers." He did and earned a warm nod of approval from his mentor.

7   The director turned round on his swivel chair and drew a trumpet on the chalkboard behind him. "What instrument is that?" he asked. "A trumpet." "Yes. And do you know that if this part of the trumpet wasn't there (pointing to the bell), the trumpet would sound all squeaky, like this," and he squoke. The boy smiled. "And so," continued the choirmaster, "if singers are to make a really good sound, they need to get their lips into a trumpet shape, like this," and he pushed his lips forward a little. "Can you do that?" After a few attempts the boy succeeded.

"Great!" smiled the director, showing evident pleasure at Shelton's progress. "Now let's sing that note again with a trumpet-shaped mouth." Shelton sang the same note. "Does that sound better?" "Yes, it does!" "That's why I asked you to sing with a trumpet-shaped mouth—not because I said so but..." "But because I can make a better sound," said Shelton, obviously pleased that he'd learned something practical.

8   And for the next couple of minutes the director led the boy in singing G and a few notes higher for five, six, and up to ten beats in length, always counting on his fingers so that the boy would succeed. Occasionally Shelton forgot to open his mouth as much as he should, or sustained a note too long or too short, but each time the director followed the pattern of saying what he had done right and then asking him, not telling him, what he needed to correct. (e.g. "You're making a great sound, Shelton; your mouth's super, but did you sustain that note for its full five beats?")

9   "Do you know 'My Country, 'Tis of Thee'?" asked the director, opening a hymnal. "Yes, we sing it at school," answered Shelton, becoming more talkative, now that he was getting to know this man. "Oh, good! Then let's sing a stanza," and he played the opening chord lightly on the piano.

"By the way, Shelton," said the director, noticing that the boy's stance left a lot to be desired, "show me how you think you ought to stand when you're holding a music book." He immediately stood straighter and, with the director's help, held the book a little away from his chest. "Great! Here we go, then," and the boy sang while the director played a very light accompaniment underneath, for he wanted to see how much Shelton could sing without his help.

The performance wasn't good: the boy's mouth was shut again, the enunciation was barely discernible, and Shelton breathed almost every other measure. Despite this the director said "Good!" a couple of times as the verse was being sung.

10 "Well, now then," said the director when it was over, "Do you know how many beats there are on the last note?" The boy looked at the last note and said, after a pause, "Three!" "Yes, well done. And so if there are three beats on the word *ring*, on which beat will you stop, the third or the fourth?" "The fourth!" "Good—then do it." And he did, unaccompanied, as the director counted the beats on his fingers again.

"Well done. Can you do this?" The director trilled an R for him and the boy copied him with a smile. "Super! Now can you do it on the word *ring*? "Rrrrrrring!" "That's great! On what other word can you trill an R in that last line?" The boy looked for a moment and said, "Frrrrreedom!" "Terrific! Let's sing that last line again—'let freedom ring.'" And he did, but forgot to trill the R on *ring*.

From behind the notice board, Bob realized that the director again told Shelton what he'd done well, asked him what he hadn't done right, and then got him to do it correctly. He also saw how the director enabled Shelton to put a T on *let* by asking him the right question. "What letter aren't you pronouncing on the word *leTT*?" He hardly ever tells him a thing, he thought with surprise, but always gets the boy to tell him. What a great way to teach!

11 "Well, now then," said the director, taking the hymnal from a rather exhausted but exhilarated Shelton, "you don't know if you want to join the choir yet, because you haven't heard them, have you?"

"No." replied Shelton, slightly surprised.

"And the choir doesn't know about you, does it, because it hasn't heard you?"

"No!" said Shelton again, even more surprised.

"Well how would it be if you came along to a few of our practices so that you could see if you like the choir, and..." he paused, waiting for Shelton to complete the sentence.

"And the choir could see if it likes me!"

"Right!" smiled the director, encouragingly. "I'm sure they will for you did jolly well today, didn't you?"

"Yes, I enjoyed it."

"Great! Well, let's go and find your Mom," and he stood up and led the way out of the practice room. They found Mrs. McArthur talking with the librarian on the lawn.

12 "Well," said the director breezily, "you've got a singer in the family. Tell your mother what you've been doing, Shelton."

"I sang *rrrring* for three beats, coming off on the fourth!"

"Did you really!" said his mother, entering into the spirit of the game. "What else did you do?"

"I sang *Ah* with a trumpet-shaped mouth!"

"My goodness!"

"Yes, Mrs. McArthur," chimed in the director, "young Shelton did very well. But he doesn't know if he wants to join the choir yet because he hasn't seen them. And you all need to discover if our practice schedule will fit in with your family's schedule. We wondered if you'd like Shelton to come along to a few practices to see what he thinks of us, and we can see what we think of him," he added with a smile. "After that you can decide together if he'd like to join us. What do you think?"

"That sounds like a good idea," responded Mrs. McArthur. "Would you like to do that, Shelton?"

"Yes, I would!" responded Shelton, eagerly.

"Okay," said the director, "our first practice for new boys is tomorrow at 3:30 and it lasts forty-five minutes. Could you manage that?"

"Oh yes, we could," said Mrs. McArthur as she shook the director's hand and said good-bye to the librarian, "We'll see you tomorrow."

"Keep up that tennis practice, Shelton," said the director as they turned to go, "I want to hear that you've won next week's match!"

6
MORE AUDITIONS

The director went into the practice room again to collect Bob who'd been watching the scene through a window.

"Come on, Bob, let's see if there's any food left at the parish picnic. I'm starving." And they made their way through a swirling mass of parishioners past tables with brightly colored signs which proclaimed some of the many programs that the church was offering, including a choir table from which two choir parents were doing a brisk trade in selling the choir's latest CD. They came to some longer tables on which an appreciable amount of food was still available. Homemade salads of mouth-watering variety crowded one table and a galaxy of desserts another. Brightly colored balloons decorated the trees, music poured forth from a battery of loudspeakers, and hamburgers were being cooked on a nearby grill. The two of them filled their plates as the director introduced Bob to the minister and to many other friends who were standing nearby including the music secretary, Rena Elvin, whose son, Jay, was head choirboy. "I couldn't do without Mrs. Elvin," said the director, "She looks after every facet of our music program as well as keeping me in order!"

"Let's find a quiet table where we can talk about what you just did with that boy," said Bob. "I've never seen anything like it—you really put him through it!"

THE PURPOSE OF THE AUDITION PROCESS

"Yes, I did, but did he enjoy it?" asked the director as they sat at a small table under the shade of a large tree.

"Oh, certainly! He was clearly thrilled at what he was achieving with you."

"That's the whole point of the exercise," said the director, looking at Bob straight in the face. (Uh-oh! He feels strongly about this, thought Bob, I must pay attention.) "What I was doing was enabling that boy to do things musically with me that he'd never done before; to reach a standard of singing he'd never thought possible in the shortest possible time and to discover that the whole process is really fun! The message he was receiving throughout was *being with this man is a Good Thing, therefore I want to come again!*

IMMEDIATELY SET THE STANDARD

"And I was giving him another, equally important message. I wonder if you spotted what it was?"

Bob thought for a moment, and said, "There were so many things: you got him to stand well, to hold his book well, to open his mouth well, to think..."

"Yes, but what standard of accuracy was I aiming at all the time?"

"Oh, everything had to be right!"

"Yes indeed, you've got it! He had to discover that I was satisfied with nothing less than 100 percent accuracy. Everything I challenged him to do he had to achieve. He didn't know that he could do it, but I most certainly did. If I'd let him get away with 'that's nearly right, so it'll do,' the opportunity to excel wouldn't have been there. That lad is excited at the prospect of joining us because he knows that, with my help, he will be able to scale heights that he never dreamed were possible. My whole object in doing what I did was to make him want to come again next time. Did I achieve it?"

"You surely did," answered Bob admiringly. "I can hardly wait to get back to my new church to try it on the girls and boys there. They won't know what's hit them!"

"Great!" said the director, "That's my object in having you here with me—to have you go off at the end of the week with a host of practical ideas to try on your own people—for you will have seen that they really do work!"

AUDITIONS FOR YOUNGER CHILDREN?

"Will your audition technique work with even younger children? There are several first-graders in the choir program in my church, and I know that the minister is keen to start a choir for them."

"Yes, of course it will—but you'll have to amend it to fit their potential abilities."

"How do you mean?"

"Well, clearly you're not going to get them singing 'My Country, 'Tis of Thee' or sustaining a note for ten beats. But you can get them to sing for four counts, and to match a variety of pitches while you count the beats for them. Your experience will tell you just how far you can go."

"I suppose the important thing is to challenge them just a little beyond what they think they can do, so that they feel good about the effort they make to achieve what you ask of them," observed Bob.

"That's exactly it!" exclaimed the director, slapping the table in his enthusiasm and disturbing a wasp that was trying to share the remains of his hamburger. "When children of any age come to join one of your choirs—and the same applies to adults—you must establish immediately that your organization has standards, and therefore it's worth giving their valuable time and energy to it. No one wants to join something which has no standards, no sense of direction or purpose; so aim high and expect your singers to give of their best immediately!

"Their best may not necessarily be very good to start with, but that's what being a member of your choir is all about. If you lead them in the ways that I shall show you this week, your standards will rise continuously.

ADAPT ALL THESE IDEAS TO YOUR OWN SITUATION

"But let me give you a helpful word:

"Don't take what you see here and apply it literally to your choirs. Instead, take the ideas you see in action here and adapt them so that they suit your choirs, in your situation, modified by your own gifts and abilities.

"You've told me, for example, that you have some first-grade children in your choir, and that you want to attract even younger children. That's fine! So, see what I am doing here for third-graders and then work out your own schemes to fit what you will do with your younger children. I'll give you the principals on which I work—but you must transform them into wholly practical procedures that will enable you to build up your own choir programs where you are."

TONE-IMPAIRED CHILDREN

"Thanks," said Bob. "Obviously I've got to do a lot of thinking when I get home. But, to get back to your audition procedure: what about kids who can't match pitch? You can't expect them to sing 'My Country, 'Tis of Thee,' can you?"

"Indeed you can't. But the same rule applies to them as to everyone else: find out where they are musically, and then stretch them a little further. Then they will know that being with you enables them to sing better than they've ever done before. Your experience will enable you to spot quickly if a singer can or cannot attempt 'My Country, 'Tis of Thee', or any of the other musical hurdles I asked Shelton to jump over.

"And so, when you have a singer who can't match pitch, spend time in trying to get him or her to sing just one note correctly—it may take one minute or five; but, all the time, you can be asking him or her to sing with a beautiful mouth, to stand well, to sing whatever-note-it-is for the correct number of beats. If the child can't sing the note that you are playing, it's up to you to play the note that the child is singing, and go on from there!

"You then have to decide if the choir is the appropriate organization for this child to join; he or she may be happier and more fulfilled in some other church program, but it's certainly worth inviting the child to try the choir for a few weeks to see how it goes—I'm often amazed at how quickly a seemingly tone-disadvantaged child can match pitch, given a lot of individual help from me."

He picked up their empty plates and put them in one of the trash cans that were scattered at strategic intervals around the large lawn. "Let's go and have some ice cream—we'll have to stand in line, I fear, for it's delicious and everyone wants some."

7
AND STILL MORE AUDITIONS

Sure enough, there was a line of at least thirty people on the other side of the lawn waiting for their helping of tasty homemade ice cream. A team of young people was sweating under a colored awning scooping out the frozen delights at great speed from enormous tubs, but even their youthful energy couldn't keep pace with the demand. It didn't matter, for everyone was in holiday mood and the chatter of friends nearly drowned out the sound of music which was coming from the loudspeakers nearby.

The director introduced Bob to still more of his friends and the time flew by as they inched toward their goal.

They eventually reached the head of the line and Bob asked, "What flavors do you have left?"

"There's a bit of chocolate, some raspberry and plenty of vanilla," said a blue-eyed girl who wore an enormous chef's hat.

"Can I have a scoop of all three, please?"

"And the same for me, please Jenny," said the director. "Bob, I'd like you to meet Jenny, one of our head girls. She's terrific!"

"Hi, Bob," said Jenny, and she handed him his bowl, which overflowed alarmingly. She turned to the director and said, "I thought you were on a diet!"

"Not today. Sunday's a feast day! Bob's coming to our practices this week, and so he'll see you again." They made way to allow Jenny to serve her next customer. "We've got a great group of girls this year—you'll love them," said the director as they wandered off to another quiet corner of the lawn, relishing the sweet delights in their hands.

SINGALONGS

"When do you begin your rehearsals with the girls?" asked Bob as they sat down on a convenient bench.

"We had three yesterday!" And he told Bob all about the Singalong Day which had been such a success.

Bob put down his ice cream and wrote: *Hold a singalong for children before the season begins. Invite new singers to join in. Provide food and fun.*

"Do you have a singalong practice for your adults, too?" he asked, as he dug into his ice cream again.

"Yes. Our adult choir met last Thursday evening for an informal run-through of upcoming anthems—we invited potential new members to sing with us. A couple of adults acted as hosts, welcoming everyone as they came in and putting name tags on them, so that we all knew who everyone was. And then, at the end of the practice we had a wine and cheese party. It makes a great start to the season."

Bob added to what he had just written: *It works for adults, too!*

The director continued, "Our adult choir also organizes two or three lunch parties in members' homes during the season. They all bring food and drink—spouses come too, and also the clergy. It's a great way to bond us all together and it's so good to visit each others' homes." And Bob made yet another addition to his notes.

MOTIVATION BEHIND THE AUDITION PROCESS

(Compare the following points with the equivalent stages in Shelton's audition)

Bob then asked, "Would you go through the stages of Shelton's audition with me, please, to make sure that I picked up everything you did?"

"Certainly, but let's keep it short for it's time to go home.

1 Take an interest in the boy's or girl's interests. You can't expect them to be interested in you unless you first show that you are interested in them.

2 Work easily toward getting the child to sing one note, so that there's no threat.

3 Work toward getting that note sung well, by asking the right questions. Resist the temptation to tell the child what to do. There's no fun in that for him or her. They will enjoy doing it right if they've found out for themselves how to do it right.

4 Introduce singing sustained notes for exact numbers of beats. Most children's choirs can't do this! Ours can, because they do it immediately, and it's so simple!

5 When a child's done something right, immediately get him to do it again. The first time he's had a battle to win, the second time he has a victory to celebrate.

6 Show genuine pleasure when the child tries hard as well as when he gets it right.

7 It's so easy to get a child to sing with a 'trumpet mouth' from the very start, if this is required of them.

8   Once the basic matters of mouth and beats have been established, extend the range of notes and the numbers of beats upwards to stretch the child. Don't go beyond what you know he or she can achieve. This must be a wholly successful experience for both of you.

9   Choose a song that the child knows well ('My Country, 'Tis of Thee' readily springs to mind) and make encouraging noises while he sings one verse, however bad it may be.

10   Then get the child to sing just one short phrase really well, introducing one thing at a time and, if possible, getting the child to tell you what is required.

11   The child now realizes that being with you is challenging, fulfilling and fun. But this is the time NOT to say 'You must join the choir' for that could make him feel trapped. This is, on the contrary, the time to push the child, very gently, away from you (like stroking a cat) so that he or she will push gently towards you!

12   Repeat this gentle pushing away with the parents, while, at the same time, demonstrating just how clever their child is. Leave the parents and the child plenty of room for an 'out.' Be like a car salesman who says, 'Drive it for yourself to see what you think of it.' If there's no pressure to buy, then there's equally no pressure to resist on their part. You know you have a good product to sell—let the product sell itself.

THE IMPORTANCE OF FOLLOW UP

13   "And finally, there are two more things," added the director, as they made their way to his car. "Tonight I shall call Mrs. McArthur to say how much I enjoyed meeting her and Shelton, and that I look forward to seeing them tomorrow.

14   "And two days later I shall write her a letter telling her how well Shelton did at practice the previous day, and that I look forward to seeing him again next time.

"That way I shall be 99 percent sure that Shelton will join the choir, and also involve his parents as new and active members of our congregation. One of my choir parents told me that the reason his son joined us was because I both wrote and called him. He told me that that was the first time he'd really experienced a genuinely warm welcome at any church. He and his whole family became wholly dedicated to everything we do here. In fact," he added, "he took all the photographs of the choirs which are on the choir room walls, and framed them at his own expense. This all happened because I called him and also wrote him a letter after I'd auditioned his son.

"That's why I feel so strongly about the importance of auditions and follow-up," he ended triumphantly as he unlocked the car doors. "They really work!"

"Golly!" said Bob faintly as he slid into his seat. He'd learned more about choirtraining in one day with this man than in a month at music school. What would be in store for him next?

8
FOUR IMMEDIATELY PRACTICAL TIPS

That evening, after the director had called Mrs. McArthur to tell her how much he'd enjoyed meeting her and Shelton, he took Bob out to a nearby eatery for a cholesterol-filled meal.

"This is a fun place," said Bob as he took another handful of popcorn from the overflowing basket on their table.

"Yes, I thought it would give us the right environment in which to talk shop again," responded the director, as he dug into the popcorn. It was still a feast-day, so the diet could be put on hold.

"The first few secrets I shared with you were pretty long, but I've learned a whole host of other secrets which we can cover quickly. The same holds true for the Great Secret, which we'll discuss tomorrow."

"Yes, I want to know about this Great Secret," said Bob as the waitress took their orders for tacos and chili.

"It's the most important thing I've learned about choirtraining—and I didn't know it for years! You'll be able to put it into operation immediately when you start with your new choirs. How I envy you! But, that's for tomorrow!"

"I can hardly wait!"

TIME SAVER IN REHEARSALS

"For right now, here's a tip to save time during practices. I learned it from Dr. Gerre Hancock., director of music at St. Thomas' Church in New York City."

"Let me get out my notebook....Okay, shoot!"

"When you're rehearsing an anthem, instead of telling your choir to 'go back to page three, second system, first measure, fourth beat,' Dr. Hancock says simply: '3, 2, 1, 4.'"

"Isn't that simple!"

"Wow, yes!"

RETHINK YOUR CHILDREN'S SEATING

"Here's another one:

"In your experience, which kids sing best for you in rehearsals, those sitting nearest to you or those sitting furthest away?"

"Oh, that's easy. Those sitting nearest to me."

"Right! And do they tend to be the most experienced children?"

"Yes, they do."

"Who needs your help more, the experienced singers or the less experienced?"

"The less experienced—that's obvious."

"In that case, what obvious steps will you take to alter the situation to help those who need it most?"

"Of course! I should move the younger children nearer to me and the older children further away. Why didn't I think of that before?"

"You didn't think of it because it's so very obvious—and it's a simple secret that many directors need to know.

"What you might do," continued the director, "is to mix up your children, by putting an experienced child next to an inexperienced one. That way the new kid can learn from the older one.

"Let me put that down," said Bob, turning another page in his notebook.

SHARE COPIES OF MUSIC

"Dr. George Guest, the former director of music at St. John's College in Cambridge, England, used to get his older choristers to share copies with new singers. That's an excellent way to help the younger ones learn to read music during a practice, for the older child can point to the music as it's being sung to keep the younger one's attention in the right place. It's also a very good way of saving money," added the director.

"How's that?"

"Well, if you've got your children sharing copies, how many copies do you have to buy?"

"Oh, only half as many as there are children," laughed Bob.

PHOTOCOPYING

"But there's an even better way to save money when buying music," continued Bob.

"What's that?"

"You just buy one copy and photocopy the rest for your choir. We used to do that a lot in my first church," he added somewhat smugly.

The director looked at Bob with a looked of horror and pained surprise. "Don't you know that was illegal?" he asked.

"Yes, but everybody does it, don't they?"

"No, they don't!" answered the director forcefully. "And for three very good reasons. One: composers earn their living largely through the number of copies of their works which are sold. As a composer I strongly resent folk who sing my music but don't pay me for the work which I put in to creating it. Two: publishers are in the business of making sheet music available to the public. If all choirmasters were to photocopy music as you've suggested the publishers would quickly go out of business and the music industry would grind to a halt."

"Oh, I hadn't thought of it like that," responded a somewhat chastened Bob.

"And the third reason," continued the director relentlessly, "is that, if you are caught photocopying music, the financial penalties could ruin you. Fines can reach many thousands of dollars for even photocopying one page. It's just not worth the financial risk, so don't do it!"

They sat in silence for a few minutes while Bob digested this information and rethought his whole approach to photocopying. "I could make a practical start when brides come to me with photocopies of music they want soloists to sing at their weddings," he said.

"That's a very good idea," smiled the director.

"Yes, I could refuse to accept the photocopy and ask them to buy a printed one for me and also one for themselves."

"You'd have to do it tactfully," warned the director. "You might say, 'I daren't play from a photocopy or even accompany your soloist singing from a photocopy, because a friend of mine was caught doing that recently and he was fined several thousand dollars. It's not worth the risk.'"

"Wow, what a great idea!" responded Bob, busily writing in his notebook.

NO, NO!

"There's time for one more quick tip before our meal comes.

"What is the most destructive word that you can say to children? It's very short and it's said over and over again."

Bob thought for a moment and then said a firm, "No!"

"Exactly right! Do you know that, by the time a child is twelve, he's had the word *no* said to him some 100,000 times—by parents, teachers and friends. Just think what that does to stifle initiative and his questing spirit! A *no* means 'You're not right now, and you're not likely to be even if you try a second time, so you may as well shut up!'

"I use another word starting with N which actively encourages the child to try again."

"What is it?" asked Bob with his pencil poised.

"Let me ask you a question!"

Here we go again, thought Bob. This man never let's you sit back; he's forever prodding you to make an effort. I suppose that's why he is such a good director! Out loud he said, "Okay, ask!"

"Before I had my house painted last year it was one of two colors; it was either green or brown. Which do you think it was?"

"Green?"

"Nearly! Try again!"

"Brown!"

"Absolutely right. How clever of you!"

Despite the juvenile standard of the game they were playing, Bob was surprised to feel a sense of pride. After a little encouragement, he'd given the right answer. If it works for me, then it'll certainly work for children, he thought. He wrote the word *Nearly* in big letters in his notebook as the waitress approached their table carrying a tray laden with good things.

For the next ten minutes they were busily engaged in getting large helpings of taco and chili inside them, washed down by appropriate liquid. When they'd nearly finished, the director looked up and said, "The whole point of getting you here is so that I can share some of the many secrets about training choirs which I've picked up over the years—points I wish I had known when I was starting in this profession.

9

Two Secrets to Help Fill Your Choirstalls

WORK!

"However, there's one vital secret I did learn while I was still a student. It has helped me always to have full choirstalls and enthusiastic singers at practices. Do you want to know what it is?

"I certainly do," responded Bob enthusiastically, pushing his almost empty plate to one side and getting out his notebook. "I'm all ears!"

"Well, I had a traumatic experience when I was a second-year student at Cambridge. I was in a class of twelve students which was led by Dr. Hubert Middleton, the organist at Trinity College. He was a pretty fierce lecturer. Every week he would give us an hour's work to do in class while he would call each of us to his table, one at a time, to mark the work we'd done for him during the previous week.

"One week he'd set us to write a string quartet in the style of Mozart; I was pleased with what I'd created and so, when my turn came to go up to his table and sit alongside him, I expected him to smile at me and say, 'That's good!'

"He didn't!" added the director with a wry grin.

"What did he say?" asked Bob with his mouth open.

"He turned over a few pages and snorted—*snorted!*—and said, 'Would you expect a young lady cellist from Girton College, five miles outside the city, to come into Cambridge, on a wet Monday night, on the bus, carrying her heavy cello, to play THAT?!'

"And I stammered, 'N-no, Dr. Middleton!' He threw the music back at me and said, 'In that case, write her a decent cello part to make her journey worthwhile!'

"Well," concluded the director, "I can't tell you the effect that had on me; I was pretty stunned. I took the very simple part I'd written for her and, during the week, filled it with double stopping and running sixteenths—it looked more like Berlioz by the time I'd finished it—but I'd got the message.

"The message is…is what?" he asked, looking Bob straight in the face.

"The message is that you're not going to get folk coming to your church practice room on a wet Monday night unless you're going to make it worth their while."

"And what, practically speaking, does that mean?"

"It means that, as far as children are concerned, the musical games I work out for them…"

"Rubbish!" interrupted the director in a loud voice and banging the table with both hands so that some other diners turned their heads to see what all the noise was about. "You haven't been listening to me. There's a four-letter word which you must offer all your singers—and it's not *game*—its second letter is a vowel, and its last letter is *K*. What is it?"

There was a pause as the student reviewed several possibilities, all of which were unacceptable, until he, too, suddenly slapped the table and shouted, "WORK!"

"Right! You've got it at last," smiled the director as the waitress, drawn by the noise, hurried over to their table to ask if there was anything they wanted.

"Yes!" beamed the director recklessly, "let's have two double chocolate chocolate chip ice creams with nuts, a cherry on top, and some Tia Maria poured over them, followed by coffee. Will that be okay, Bob?"

"Yes, it will!" agreed Bob, for they clearly had something to celebrate. He'd finally learned the secret of how to attract singers to practices—not by playing games but by making them work!

F—F—F!

"Let me press this message home," said the director, quelling his conscience following his willful order for dessert. He'd have to diet for an extra week to take off all the weight he was putting on at this meal.

"There was a wonderful woman in England, some years ago, who had a gift for training animals. She had a weekly TV program on which she demonstrated how easy it was to train dogs to be obedient."

"Oh, yes!" Bob interrupted, "Barbara Woodhouse—I've seen some of her reruns. She was marvelous!"

"Right! Every week was the same: some inoffensive owner would be dragged by their ill-disciplined pet to Mrs. Woodhouse who would immediately take charge.

"She'd hold the dog's lead, look the animal straight in the eyes and say, 'Rover! SI-TTT!!' And Rover, who'd never been talked to like that before, immediately sa-ttt! She and the dog would look at each other for five seconds, and then Barbara gave the dog a friendly pat and said 'Well done, Rover!' and Rover would wag his tail and feel pleased with himself.

"Well, she had three words that summed up her successful technique."

"What were they?" asked Bob, opening his notebook again.

"You tell me!"

Here we go one more time! thought Bob.

"They all start with F and two of them have four letters." Several more possibilities immediately crossed Bob's mind, but he dismissed them as he waited for more input.

"When she said, 'Rover! SI-TTT!', she was being…"

"FIRM!"

"Right. Now, notice that she only asked Rover to do what she knew Rover could do, even though Rover didn't know it at the time. Therefore she was…"

"FAIR!"

"Right again! And the important result of all this was that Rover found the whole experience…"

"FUN!"

"Yes, he did.

"Now, the important message you need to take right into your innermost being," continued the director, leaning forward and looking Bob straight in the eyes, "is the order in which those three words come."

I feel a bit like Rover, thought Bob. I hope he doesn't get me to si-ttt up and beg!

"Notice that the work came first, and the fun came as a result of work well done.

"So many leaders of children's choirs seem to run their rehearsals by saying, 'Now, kiddies, we're going to start today with a lovely game.' And the kids play with bells and drums and this and that, and finally the director says, 'Now we've got to stop having fun because there's some music we have to learn for Sunday!' which immediately brings cries of 'Oh dear' from the kids to whom work has been presented as the unpalatable part of a practice."

Bob winced slightly as he remembered that he'd been brought up to lead children's rehearsals rather like that. The director was absolutely right!

"Now, as for my children, and my adults, too, they know full well that when they walk through the practice room door they are going to work, and work very hard. But they also know that the result of that work will be a heightened sense of self-worth brought about through exciting achievement, new techniques learned, and singing thoroughly worthwhile music—which they've worked out for themselves by reading it at sight. And they feel so good about this process that they're present every time, punctual and keen.

"I've found this to be true all my life, thanks to Dr. Middleton. Singers have always arrived punctually for me, and some have even been willing to give up sporting activities in order to be at my practices. It's so thrilling!" And the director sat back, beaming at Bob as the waitress staggered towards them bearing enormous helpings of ice cream and steaming cups of coffee.

"What a great end to a great day," said Bob. "Thank you!"

As he covered his mouth with chocolate for the third time within twenty-four hours, he thought, If it works for dogs, it should work for kids, and adults, too! and he grinned.

10
WEDDING MUSIC

On their way home the director said, "After you leave us on Friday I shall have to hurry back to see a couple who are getting married here in a few months' time."

"Oh!" said Bob, getting out his notebook again, "that's something we didn't discuss much at music school. What do you do when you meet with a bridal couple?"

MEET EARLY

"The first thing is to meet with them well in advance of the date of their wedding. You never know when someone will ask you to provide a choir or some instrumentalists. You need to book your musicians early."

"What's the next thing?"

"You should meet with the couple either in your practice room or in the church, for they will want to discuss what you should play as the bride enters the church and as the happy couple leave.

CASSETTE TAPE

"I commend to you a time-saving device here," said the director as he drove his car through a maze of streets.

"What's that?"

"Make a cassette tape of all the music which you think appropriate for weddings. You can then send it to the couple in advance of your meeting, and they can choose what they want. Some couples know exactly what they want, but others have no idea at all. Your tape would be very helpful both to them, for choosing appropriate music, and to you, for saving time."

"That's a great idea," said Bob as he scribbled in the darkened car.

"And, talking of appropriate music," continued the director, "you will need to decide, in consultation with your minister, just what sort of music is appropriate for weddings in your church."

"What do you mean by that?"

"Some couples ask for unusual tunes, perhaps a selection from the latest Broadway musical or something from the pops' chart. If you and your minister decide on the parameters of suitability, you will be able to guide your wedding couple more easily into acceptable choices.

"But whenever possible you should seriously consider accommodating the choices that couples suggest, for it is their special day."

"What about prelude music?"

"This, again, should be included in your cassette tape. Basically you need to play fairly soft, cheerful music that is tuneful. Wedding guests do like to talk before the service, and loud prelude music could quickly become oppressive."

SOLOISTS

"What should I do if the couple asks me for a soloist?"

"That's a good question. You need to get to know what soloists are available in your area—singers and trumpeters especially. Make a list of such musicians, with their addresses, phone numbers and also the fees they require. Ask them what solos they like to perform so that you can quickly ask the right soloist for the right occasion.

"You should beware," added the director, "when couples want a relation to sing a song at the ceremony. Frequently, the soloist can be quite good, but sometimes they are not. You must meet with this soloist well in advance, for you may need more than one rehearsal and you should charge an extra fee for this.

"And, speaking of trumpeters," added the director, "if you want to use brass players for your Christmas and Easter services, you need to book them a year in advance."

"Why is that?"

"Because they are in such great demand for those seasons. Trumpeters tend to align themselves with one particular church for a number of years. If your church doesn't have its own brass players for these services, you need to begin to search for your own instrumentalists straight away."

"How do I do that?"

"By calling a few of the leading brass players in the area and asking them if they know of any colleagues who might like to play for you. Brass players know each other and so they are your best bet for finding other players. They also charge quite high fees for their services on those days, so make sure that they are included in your music budget."

FEES

"I'll need to rehearse with the soloist, won't I, not only for Christmas and Easter services but also for weddings?"

"Yes, you will. And you need to charge an extra fee for this when soloists rehearse with you for weddings."

"What fee should I ask for playing for a wedding?"

"This will be a matter of church policy. You should discuss this with your minister after having been in touch with your local American Guild of Organists chapter, and also comparable churches in your area.

"You will need to focus on three things here:

"One. The fee for playing for the wedding, and for a rehearsal with a soloist.

"Two. The fee for attending the wedding rehearsal, if necessary.

"Three. Reviewing the fee every two or three years.

"By the way," added the director, "sometimes a bridal couple would like a guest organist to play for them instead of you. There are two matters which you need to attend to when this situation arises."

"What are they?"

"One. Check on the guest organist's competence. If he or she cannot play well enough, you should not allow them to play your organ. This will have to be done tactfully, and your minister, again, is the person to advise you best how this should be handled.

"Two. If this guest organist does play, you should receive your normal fee, for it is your organ. Most churches I know have no problem with this policy.

"It's very helpful," continued the director, "when churches issue a leaflet to couples giving them full details of everything they should know about preparing for their wedding. And this includes music policy and fees, too."

WEDDING REHEARSAL

"Some ministers like their organist to be present for wedding rehearsals. We used to do this here but, recently, we've abandoned this practice."

"Why?"

"Because I know exactly what is required to time correctly the procession, so that I stop playing within a few seconds of the bride reaching the altar. The organist needs to be able to edit processional music on the spot so that the bride doesn't finish her procession in silence, or be left hanging around for a minute or more while the organist completes the processional music. That's where the music of Purcell comes in so handy—you can skip whole sections and repeat others so that the processional music turns out to be exactly the right length.

"You may want to attend rehearsals for weddings in your early days at your new church to get a feel of how things are done. Ask your minister if he would be kind enough to rehearse the two processions first so that you need not stay for more than half an hour or so. There's nothing more frustrating for an organist than hanging around for a long rehearsal and being asked to play for only five minutes at the end."

"Is there anything else I need to know?"

"Yes! Not all brides arrive punctually. You need to add to your list of fees an extra fee for lateness! If a bride turns up fifteen minutes late for her wedding or for her rehearsal (and some arrive even later than that!), your whole schedule could be thrown off. Some churches ask for a deposit against unpunctuality. This is something you should discuss with your minister.

BRIDES' MOTHERS

"You should be careful when talking with brides' mothers!"

"What do you mean?"

"Some mothers tend to take over their daughters' wedding arrangements entirely. This is not right, for it is the bride's day not her mother's. When this occurs, as it most surely will sometime, you need to stress, gently but firmly, that you want to hear what the bride wants for her wedding. Her mother had her own day when she was married and you are sure that she would want to allow her daughter the same freedom to choose that she had."

The director's home came into view as he added, "You can tell when a bride's mother wants to take over the situation, for she will call you several times about the arrangements she is making. You need to exercise a lot of self-control on these occasions and show courtesy to the mother even though you don't feel like it."

"It doesn't get as bad as that, does it?" asked Bob as they got out of the car and made their way into the house.

"Not often. Learn to speak slowly with lots of pauses. This will give you time to think as well as showing the mother that she does need to listen to what you are saying."

The director closed the front door and said, "We've had a busy day."

"Thank you for sharing so much with me. I'm having a great time!"

"There's much more to come tomorrow. Sleep well, young man."

"I shall!"

Learn to speak slowly with lots of pauses.

♪ MONDAY ♪

11
OFFICE PROCEDURE
AND PAPERWORK

The next morning the director drove Bob to church and told him he'd have to look after himself until lunch time because there was a lot of office work to be done. "There's always a pile of letters to be answered," he said, "and somehow I never get them cleared before the next batch arrives."

"Oh, I'll spend most of my time practicing when I start my new job," said Bob confidently. "There's lots of new organ music I want to learn and…"

"My dear young man!" exclaimed the director. "I'm afraid you're in for a big shock. Unless you make a habit of practicing before breakfast every day you'll have no time to touch the organ. Much of this job has to do with administration: sitting at a desk answering the phone, answering letters, making calls, planning next month's choir outing, planning rehearsals for services and concerts, contacting soloists, meeting couples who are about to be married, attending staff meetings, and following up on matters which arise. And last, but not least, giving your whole attention to people who drop by your office who want you to do something for them.

INTERRUPTIONS!

"I read of a professor who was frustrated because he found he couldn't get on with his job on account of all the people who constantly interrupted him. His frustration vanished when, one day, he realized that his main job was not to lecture students, but to minister to everyone who came to see him.

"I've tried putting that thought to work in my situation," he added wistfully as they drove into the church parking lot. "It helps some, but I still find myself wondering how I can deal more efficiently with my own paperwork."

The director led the way into the music building and up the stairs to his office. He opened the door. There were papers everywhere. "You see what I mean?" he said as he removed a pile of anthems from a chair so that Bob could sit down.

OFFICE PROCEDURE

"My goodness!" exclaimed Bob, uncertain what he should say. "This'll keep you busy all morning."

"Yes, it will. It's always like this after vacations. I seem to get more mail than almost any other member of staff."

"How do you deal with it, then?"

"The only way to stay on top of paperwork is to get to the office an hour or more before anyone else. That way you're sure of not being interrupted by phone calls. Once you start doing that, as a matter of course, you'll find that your desk will tend to stay fairly clear."

Bob looked at the filing cabinets by the director's desk. "Tell me about your filing system."

"I've had to work out my own," answered the director as he opened the top drawer of a filing cabinet. "Since I do a number of outside engagements, lectures, and concerts, I file all of this material here. As soon as someone asks me to give a lecture or lead a workshop, I open a file and put in it all the correspondence that develops about that engagement."

He showed Bob his current collection of files. Each file was clearly labeled with date and place, and put in chronological order in the drawer.

"I see that you've got files for as far ahead as three years!" Bob exclaimed.

"Yes, you'll find that this will happen to you, too, if you wish to pursue a career as a recitalist as well as being director of music of your church."

FEES AND EXPENSES

"How do you decide what fees to charge?"

"You need to test the market. When you are beginning your career you can ask those who invite you what fee they will offer. Discuss this with your local American Guild of Organists (AGO) dean who should be able to advise you. Once you've decided on a fee, you should consider raising it every year or so, to keep pace with inflation, and also to keep pace with your rising popularity."

"What about expenses?"

"A professional engagement always means that travel expenses and hospitality will be met over and above your fee.

"It's also very important to keep a close record of these for tax purposes. I make a photocopy of every check I receive and attach it, and all receipts for the expenses I've incurred, such as turnpike dues and car parking fees, to the letter of engagement so that my accountant has full records when tax time comes round."

PERSONAL PUBLICITY BROCHURE

The director closed the drawer and said, "When you've decided if you want to pursue a subsidiary career as a recitalist, you'll need your own publicity brochure."

"How do I go about designing one of those?"

"No problem! You'll receive so many brochures from other soloists who want to play for you that you'll be able to decide just what is right for you."

"To whom should I send them?"

"Here again, there's no problem. You'll receive an increasing flood of music brochures from churches all round the country. Keep them and make a note of the names and addresses of the directors of music and also the types of concerts they sponsor. Send your brochure to them! Once you've given some successful recitals, your name will begin to get known.

"You should also consider entering the annual organ playing competition arranged by the AGO. That's a sure way to hit the headlines, if you're any good!"

CALENDAR

The director went over to his desk and said, "By the way, it's very important that you have only one calendar. Make sure it's a large one that's difficult to lose," he added, holding up his own calendar, which was a foot high!

"Why is that?"

"Because if you have two calendars, you're almost bound to make double bookings when you forget to transfer an engagement from one calendar to the other."

"But it's so useful to have a calendar that you can carry in your pocket."

"Why?"

"Because, when you're invited to lead a workshop or give a recital, you can look in your calendar and tell your potential host if you're available."

"Yes, but when that happens you have no record of the details of the engagement. When folk ask me to lecture I always ask them to put it in writing so that I have something to refer to. I need to know not only the date and place of the engagement, but also what they want me to do. You can't put all that in a pocket calendar."

"Oh, I see what you mean," said Bob. "I'll have to get a bigger one."

KEEP RECORDS OF MEETINGS

The director returned to his filing cabinet and opened a second drawer. It, too, was filled with folders, all neatly labeled.

"What's in that drawer?" asked Bob.

"This is where I keep the minutes of all the meetings I attend."

"What sort of meetings?"

"Choir support committee, church council meetings, concerts' committee, diocesan committees, and so on. If you're going to be a useful member of your church and diocese, you need to keep a record of what you discussed. It's simple to do once you make a start on it."

The director opened the third drawer in which were a number of large notebooks.

"What do you have here?"

"These are notebooks which I take to the various meetings I attend. One book for each committee. I write in them matters that I wish to raise, and then, during the meeting, I make a note of things I have to follow up on. Having all this material in one book for every committee, enables me to keep my own record of what was decided as well as enabling me to check that I really have followed through on matters that I said I would attend to."

The director closed the drawer and went back to his desk.

"But there's a fourth drawer," observed Bob. "What's in that?"

"Oh, yes!" said the director returning to the cabinet and opening the bottom drawer. "In this I keep some of my personal papers such as bank statements, mortgage repayment forms and so on."

CONCERT PROGRAMS AND SERVICE LEAFLETS

He turned to his second filing cabinet and showed Bob that, in one drawer, he kept copies of programs of concerts given at the church. "They're a very useful reference point when we're planning a new season." Bob saw on each program the director's notes of the number of people who attended; what special arrangements had been made for certain concerts, such as organizing platforms and risers; and also special lighting for orchestral players.

In the second drawer the director kept copies of service leaflets, filed neatly into seasons. "We need to see what we did last Easter and the Easter before when we're planning next year's Easter services," he explained. "It also reminds me of the music we sang and the preludes that were played." Bob noticed that the director had also made notes on these papers, such as 'Choose a longer hymn for the processional next year,' and 'Remember to give prayer books to all choir members for this service.'

SPRING CLEAN ANNUALLY

He closed the drawer and returned once more to his desk. "You'll find that papers pile up alarmingly over the course of a year. It is a good idea, at the end of the season, to set aside a day for clearing out papers that you don't need. If you don't do this regularly you'll find that the system you began so well will quickly grind to a halt."

"Wow!" exclaimed Bob yet again, "that will be very helpful."

FOLLOW UP, AGAIN!

They sat down in two swivel chairs and the director said, "We were talking about your first priority at your new church..."

"Visiting with my choir members in their homes," interrupted Bob.

"Yes. How will you follow up every visit?"

Bob thought for a moment, and said, "You told me to make notes about each family, so that I could remember them all and..."

"Yes," interrupted the director as he switched on his word processor, "but there's an essential courtesy to your hosts that you must fulfill in order to foster good personal relationships with your choir families. If you don't follow through, instead of opening up a way of cooperation between you, your visit will have thrown up a barrier. I mentioned it to you yesterday. What is it?"

There was silence as Bob thought furiously, but no answer came.

"Well," said the director as he sat down and clicked his mouse, "my first letters this morning are going to the two sets of parents who organized the food and the chauffeuring for the girls' singalong on Saturday, and the third will be to..."

"To the hosts at the swim party!" Bob smiled. "Now I know what you're getting at. I should have remembered that saying "thank you" in writing was so important."

12
CHOOSING MUSIC

"You might like to take this copy of our choirs' program for the year," said the director, handing Bob a fifty-page book. "We can talk about it over lunch."

Bob took the hint and left the director to deal with the piles of paper that cluttered his office. He spent an hour playing the glorious organ in church and then wandered around the town seeing the sights. When he dropped into a coffee shop for a quick cup he remembered the book the director had given him. He took it out of his pocket and opened it. He was amazed!

The professionally produced choirbook covered everything that anyone could possibly want to know about the music programs at church. It included:

- The names and addresses of the music staff.
- Names and addresses of every choir member.
- How the choirs were organized, especially the children.
- On which days the different grades of boys and girls rehearsed.
- The season's schedule of practices and services for every choir.
- Several pages of detailed choir schedules for special occasions, such as dress rehearsals for concerts and even the bus' departure time for when a choir is going to sing in the big city in six months' time! He noticed that last week's Girls' Singalong Day was included, complete with schedule and how to find the house where the swim party was held.

- There were ten pages detailing all the music every choir would sing for the entire season, Sunday by Sunday.
- Who's who on the church staff.
- How to prepare choir suppers (choir suppers?).
- The agenda for choir support committee meetings for the entire year.
- And if that weren't enough, the last ten pages were devoted to the alumni association.

"There must be over two hundred names here," thought Bob, "complete with addresses all over the country. I've never seen anything like it," he mused as he pushed his cup of cold coffee away and stood up. He'd have to hurry if he was going to be on time to meet the director for lunch. "I'd love to direct a program like this. What I'm learning this week would fill a book twice this size!" He put the choirbook in his pocket and began to run.

"Sorry I'm late," said Bob breathlessly as he arrived at the restaurant, "I was reading your choirbook and completely lost track of the time."

"That's okay," said the director kindly, "I've only just got here myself." They were shown to a quiet table at the far end of the room and sat down.

"I've been looking at your choirbook," said Bob. "I'm amazed that you plan in such detail so far ahead."

"It's purely self-defense," answered the director. "When I first came here, in the middle of a season, I had no idea what music we were going to sing the following week, and this went on for several months. And of course the repertoire of this particular church was unfamiliar to me. It felt like living on the edge of a precipice and I swore that I'd never go through that experience again.

"And so," he continued, "before my first season ended I began to plan the following season's music little by little, and I found it was surprisingly easy."

"How did you do it? I've found it an awful chore to choose music even for a couple of months ahead."

"To do it for a whole season is much easier than planning for just two months."

"Why?"

"Because you can repeat music if you plan your program for nine months. For example," he said, as he handed Bob the menu, "if we're singing a new anthem in October we could easily sing it again in February, and perhaps once more in May, if the words are suitable."

"What have the words got to do with it? I just pick out the anthems I like best or compositions I think the choir can sing!"

"My dear young man!" exclaimed the director. He paused as the waiter came for their order—a pizza for Bob and a salad for the director.

"Look, let me show you the way I do it." And the choirmaster took Bob's notebook, found a blank page and began writing.

"First, I made out a page with space for all the music needed for one month, like this:

MONTH
Sunday(date)   Theme
9:00 A.M.   Choir
            Anthem
11:00 A.M. Choir
            Canticle
            Anthem

Sunday(date)   Theme...(etc.)

"What do you mean by theme?" asked Bob.

"What are the subjects of the lessons, prayers, and psalms for that particular day. It's easy to find this information if you're working in a liturgical church which has these laid out for several years ahead. If you don't, then you'll have to ask your minister what themes he has chosen for sermons, etc., and hope that he's planning as far forward as you are!

"For my church, I look through all the set readings for each Sunday and make a concise precis of them, which I write down on the 'theme' space."

"This must take a long time."

"No, only a couple of hours at most.

"For example," he said, taking Bob's copy of the choirbook that was on the table, "look at the last Sunday of this month; my summary of the set lessons is: *Heaven opened, angels ascending on Son of Man. Jesus is the great High Priest.*

"Well, I go through the entire year like that, and then I walk round my choir library, from one end to the other, choosing anthems that I would like to do, balancing new ones with well-known ones, and seeing where they would fit into the themes that I'd noted.

"When I came across Edgar Bainton's 'And I saw a new heaven,' I knew it was exactly the right anthem for that particular Sunday, and wrote it down. We've got a pretty large music library at church, including several collections of excellent anthems, which are very useful.

"After about six hours' work I've filled in most of the available spaces with appropriate music, and I've only to fill in the remainder either with repeats or new music. And so, the entry for that particular Sunday looks like this," concluded the director as he finished writing and pushed Bob's notebook over to him.

MONTH *September*
Sunday(date) *29* Theme *Heaven opened. Angels ascending on Son of Man. Jesus is Gt. High Priest.*
9:00 A.M.   Choir *Adult*
            Anthem *And I saw a new heaven—Bainton*
11:00 A.M. Choir *Men & Boys*
            Canticle *Glory to God in the highest—Near*
            Anthem *Ecce Sacerdos (Behold, a great High Priest)—Bruckner*

"That's terrific!" said Bob. "It must make life so much easier for you, knowing what you have to rehearse next week, next month or even in six months' time!"

"Yes. *Easier* is one appropriate word; another way of describing it is 'more efficient.' The two go together. Organizing music this way helps not only me, but also the librarian who puts music in everyone's cubby for at least one month in advance. It also helps the assistant organist to prepare ahead and allows me to budget more responsibly. I can use all of the music in our library during the course of three or four years and therefore plan on buying some new music each year within the music budget.

"Now that we've invested in a computer it will be even easier to choose music, for we're putting our music library onto a database, cross-referenced by: title, composer, scoring, difficulty, subject, season, when last sung, and number of copies.

"It's taking a lot of time but, when it's finished, it'll increase our efficiency beyond measure," smiled the director.

"What about choosing hymns?" asked Bob.

"You'll need to talk to your minister about this. Some denominations publish helpful lists of hymns for all seasons. But I strongly urge you to keep a record of all the hymns that are sung in your church each year. This will help you not only in your choice of hymns for the following year, but also your choice of anthems."

"I'm beginning to see why you have to spend so long at your desk," commented Bob as the food arrived.

"There's more to come," said the director, "much more!"

"What are you referring to?" asked Bob with a grin, "more food or more paperwork?"

"Both!" laughed the director as he toyed with his salad—today was a back-to-the-diet day!

13
SCHEDULING CHILDREN'S CHOIRS

"This afternoon you'll see four choir practices, and you'll also see the Great Secret in operation. You probably won't even notice it until I point it out to you, but, if you put it into operation with your choirs, you'll be assured of full choirstalls all your life and enthusiastic and well-instructed singers!"

"In your choirbook you mention choir organization. Tell me how you organize your children's choirs," said Bob.

ORGANIZING CHILDREN'S CHOIRS

"There is a cardinal rule you need to follow if you are to run successful children's programs," answered the director.

"Every child must know, from the moment he or she enters your program, that they are part of a well-thought-through situation in which they can experience progress."

"What do you mean by that?"

HOW NOT TO DO IT!

"The easiest way to answer that is to tell you what I don't mean! I was recently asked to conduct a children's choir composed of boys and girls from the age of six through thirteen. There were about twenty of them, and they were hopeless!"

"Why were they hopeless?"

"Because the director mixed children of widely differing ages and abilities in the one choir; consequently, when the older children were singing, the little children were lost, because the music was too difficult for them. The experience was teaching the little ones that, in order to be a member of a choir, all you have to do is show up and let the others do the singing for you! They didn't even have to pay attention or make any effort! Once you start a child thinking that way, you're never going to get him or her out of it. I struggled with those children for an hour in a so-called demonstration practice, but found their attitudes so ingrained that I could do very little with them."

"A similar problem afflicted the older boys. Girls develop physically, in their early teens, more quickly than boys. This means, in practice, that they will sing more strongly. We had four or five teenage girls who were leading the singing better than the boys. The boys, clearly, were losing heart, and it was evident to me that those boys wouldn't remain in that choir while their singing was overshadowed by the girls.

"The middle-age children were ineffective because they hadn't been well-taught when they first joined the choir. It was too late to start; they'd already been conditioned to give minimum effort and concentration. It was a sorry affair."

HOW TO RECTIFY A FAULTY SITUATION

"What would you have done to alter that situation?" asked Bob.

"That's an excellent question!" answered the director, putting down his fork.

"Basically, I would have divided the choir into four smaller groups: younger children, middle-age children, older boys, and older girls. I would have held separate practices for each group. Forty-five minutes for the first group, forty-five minutes or more for the middle range, and one hour each for the older children.

"I would have started the younger children from the very beginning, giving them little challenges that they could achieve, similar to the challenges I gave Shelton McArthur when I was auditioning him yester-day, rather than big ones they couldn't achieve. At every practice those kids would have been given a lot of individual help, and they would have realized that they were progressing, week by week. This would have made every practice an exciting adventure for them as well as for their choirmaster.

"I would have had to find out what the middle-age children actually knew about choir work. I am sure that they had all been taught by rote... excuse me," he interrupted himself, "while I wash out my mouth. That four-letter word, *ROTE,* is for me the height of obscenity, but we'll talk about that later this afternoon," and he paused to take a long drink from the glass of iced water in front of him.

"Where were we?" he continued.

"You were finding out what the middle-age children knew."

"Oh, yes! Once I'd found out where they were musically, I would then adjust my teaching to their level with a strong emphasis on teaching sight-singing, giving a lot of attention to individuals so that everyone knew that they were progressing at every practice.

"And then I'd have given a lot of time to restore the self-respect of the older boys—even if there were only two or three of them. I would have structured my practices so that they knew I was on their side and that they were important to the success of the whole choir. I'd have made them sing better than they'd ever sung before by knowing in myself that they could do it and would do it. I'd have set high standards immediately so that they, also, would be challenged and made to realize that it was thoroughly worth their while coming to an hour's practice with me.

"You've got to love your children enough to bring out the best in them. It's called 'tough love,' I believe. It means, in practice, that you have to push them hard, rather like a fitness instructor. It's sometimes painful to get fit and to keep fit. It isn't always easy to pursue excellence—it can hurt—but, afterwards, the singers, and their parents thank you for it.

"And, finally, I'd have encouraged the older girls in their leadership—giving them even more responsibility in singing—by rehearsing music that they already knew, as well as new music, to a much higher stan-dard. They would sing better than they'd ever done before, and therefore be encouraged.

"And after I'd made a start on that," concluded the director as he contin-ued eating his salad, "I'd have worked out a program whereby children from a lower group could earn their way to the next group up through a system of carefully thought-out teaching on my part and achievable goals on their part. You'll see that in action with some of my children this afternoon."

PRACTICE SCHEDULE FOR DIFFERENT ABILITIES OF SINGERS

"But that would mean," said Bob, finding the page in the choir book which gave details of the various rehearsal schedules for the many grades of boys and girls, "that when a boy or girl is promoted from one grade to the next, they have to come at a different time."

"It sometimes means that their rehearsals are also held on different days," laughed the director.

"Surely that would play havoc with their families' schedules?" asked Bob.

"Well," answered the director, "this was the plan I inherited from my distinguished predecessor. I would never have dared to introduce it myself, but, surprisingly, I find that it works wonderfully well."

"Why?"

"Because when boys and girls earn the right, through hard work on their training cards, to be promoted to the next rank up, not only do they join a new peer group, which they love, but their promotion can also be seen in that they have to alter their schedule. They really feel that they have been promoted: a big factor in their feeling of esteem.

"Look," he continued, leaning forward and showing Bob the right page in the choir book, "See what happens when a boy, for example, joins our choir. (The girls' schedule is simpler, for their rehearsals are all held on Tuesdays.) A new boy attends twice a week, on Mondays and Wednesdays for forty-five minutes. When he has earned the right to become a member of our choir he becomes a novice. Novices rehearse forty-five minutes after the probationers, and so, coming forty-five minutes later on Mondays and Wednesdays is seen as a promotion."

The director turned a page in the choir book. "But when he earns his next promotion, to become a junior singing boy, he really is beginning to make a useful contribution to the choir. It is important that he now rehearses once a week with all the boys. They have their rehearsals on Thursdays for seventy-five minutes."

"That's a big step up in time commitment," remarked Bob.

"Yes, it is," agreed the director. "But you will have noticed that he will also have, once a week, a practice with his new peer group, the junior singing boys. They rehearse for forty-five minutes after the novices, on Wednesdays."

"Let me get this clear," said Bob, who was a little confused. "Probationers and novices rehearse on Mondays and Wednesdays."

"Right!"

"But junior singing boys rehearse on Wednesdays and Thursdays."

"Right again!"

"Does the schedule alter when the children are promoted next time?"

"Yes—and the time after that, when they become choristers!"

"Look," said the director, pointing to the pages in the choir book, "It's written very plainly here."

Bob looked where the director was pointing, and, after a minute or so, it all became clear to him.

MONDAYS
Probationers—45 minutes
Novices—45 minutes
Junior and senior choristers—75 minutes
WEDNESDAYS
Probationers—45 minutes
Novices—45 minutes
Junior singing boys—45 minutes
Senior singing boys—60 minutes
THURSDAYS
Junior singing boys, senior singing boys, and choristers—75 minutes
Choir supper, after which junior singing boys go home
Senior singing boys, choristers, and men—75 minutes

COMMITMENT TO THE SCHEDULE

"That's a very full schedule!" commented Bob. "You must find it difficult to get all the singers there every week."

"No, I don't," answered the director, "because this schedule is made clear to them and their parents before they make the commitment to join us. You see," he continued, returning the choir book to Bob, "all the children, and the adults, too, come regularly because I make it thoroughly worth their while to attend every rehearsal.

"Incidentally," added the director, "when girls and boys are promoted I find that their singing, in their new peer group, improves by leaps and bounds. It's a very exciting situation for them to be with slightly older children to whom they've looked up. They have qualified to join this new peer group and this gives them a challenge and the incentive to try even harder."

"I wish my choirs could be like that," said Bob, wistfully.

"That's what you are here to discover, and to put into operation when you return," answered the director with a smile.

MATCH YOUR NEEDS WITH YOUR OPPORTUNITIES

"But I couldn't possibly arrange a schedule like that for my children," said Bob with a worried frown.

"My friend," answered the director patiently as he finished the last of his salad, "don't you remember what I told you on Sunday morning?"

"Oh, yes!" answered Bob with a look of relief. "You told me to take the ideas which I see in action here and alter them so that they will fit comfortably into the situation in my church."

"Quite right! Every church is different as every organ is different. Find out what your opportunities and needs are, and then work out your own program to match your needs with your opportunities."

14
A TRAINING PLAN
FOR CHILDREN'S CHOIRS

RULE #1

"All those extra practices would have added a lot of time to your schedule," observed Bob, who was busily writing in his notebook.

"You've hit on one of the basic fundamentals of choirtraining," answered the director. "You can't run a successful choir program unless you are willing to spend a lot of time with your singers. It's like gardening."

"How do you mean?"

"Successful gardeners, those whose grass is a delight to look at and whose flower beds are filled with color the summer through, are those who spend time, every day, tending their garden. They do a little often. They weed this small area one day, cut the grass the next day, sow seeds in another part of their garden the following day, and so on. They are always busy.

"And so directors, in their turn, need to weed a little (to correct basic faults that spring up), to polish a little (working on vocal production and getting perhaps just one page of an anthem sung really well, aiming at quality rather than quantity), and they need to supply their choirs with new music from time to time to keep up their interest.

"Which leads me to the second cardinal rule for directors..."

"Give me a moment to write the first cardinal rule," asked Bob, as he wrote, *Create a plan that will enable every child to experience progress at every practice from the very first day!*

RULE #2

The director waited a moment and then continued.

"The second cardinal rule is: give your choirs music that is really worthwhile to sing.

"I'm appalled at the amount of rubbish that is being churned out today by many choirs! Not only is the music often trite and illiterate, but the theology of the words is narrow and equally platitudinous. So many songs seem to give the message, 'I love buttercups and so does Jesus. Alleluia!' Why should kids have to put up with that sort of garbage?" He banged the table several times in his frustration; heads of nearby customers turned to see what was the matter.

Oh dear! thought Bob. We went through this sort of thing yesterday.

Sure enough, the waiter came over and asked what they wanted. "A coffee each, please," answered the director with a hastily assumed smile. "The salad was delicious—how was your pizza, Bob?" "Fine, thank you," answered Bob, eager to follow the director's lead in pacifying the staff and customers.

"Fortunately there are some publishers today who are enabling enlightened composers' music to be made available," continued the director as the waiter hurried off. "I think the word is beginning to spread. Whenever I lead workshops I ask directors if they are satisfied with the diet of rubbish that they're being offered, and the answer is always a resounding No!"

While they were waiting for their coffee Bob wrote down the second cardinal rule: *Give choirs worthwhile music to sing!*

A SUCCESSFUL GRADED TRAINING PROGRAM

"But what do you teach your children?" asked Bob as the waiter brought the coffee for them with their check. "It's all very well telling me to organize the children into small groups, but what do you actually give them to do?"

"That's another good question," said the director. "I can show you exactly what I do with new children, for I've got it all written down." He rummaged in his pocket and brought out a leaflet, which he then passed over the table to Bob.

FIRST CHURCH, HOMETOWN
(609) 555-1110

TRAINING FOR ADMISSION TO THE CHOIR
FROM PROBATIONER TO NOVICE

Name _____

Date training begun _____

PUNCTUALITY and EFFORT at rehearsals and services:
You need to arrive a few minutes early for every practice so that we may start ON TIME. Collect your hymnal and test card from your cubby. When you do well you will be given a bonus dot. You need to win plenty of dots to show that you are trying hard.

TRAINING FOR ADMISSION TO THE CHOIR	DATE EACH TEST IS PASSED
1. BREATHING A: Show that you can breathe like a singer: Shoulders DOWN, chest UP, tummy expanding when breathing IN, and contracting to squeeze the air OUT. Stand well on both feet and keep relaxed.	

2. BREATHING B: Hiss out to the count of TEN, showing that you can do all the things listed in #1. Then hiss out to the count of TWELVE, and FIFTEEN.	
3. BREATHING C: SING, with a steady tone (because you can breathe well) THREE NOTES on the vowel *Oo* to the count of 15. The notes are G, B and D. Discover how to push your lips into a "TRUMPET" shape to help you make a lovely sound.	
4. READING: Show that you can READ EASILY, by reading the words of ONE VERSE from THREE different hymns. In order to be able to concentrate on the music you will have to sing at church, your reading of words must be fluent.	

5. SINGING DOWNWARD SCALES to *Ah*:
Sing with a clear voice, and be able to sing the higher notes as easily as the lower ones. Sustain the last note for FOUR COUNTS.
    1. D major
    2. E-flat major
    3. E major
    4. F major	

6. SINGING WITH YOUR HEAD VOICE: Learn how easy it is to sing really high notes. Using the SIREN method, be able to sing at least a high A, and to hold it for the count of six.	
7. KNOWING the names of FIVE NOTES, and SINGING THEM: Understand where the note "G" is, and from that note be able to work out where the notes F, A, C and E are. You will be asked to name TEN notes from a piece of music (F, G, A, C, and E), and sing each note with the help of the piano. When you name and sing all ten notes correctly AT ONE ATTEMPT you will have passed this test. You may make as many attempts as you need.	
8. CLAP RHYTHM: Learn how to clap quarter notes, halves and whole notes, and then clap the rhythm of FOUR four-measure sections of hymn tunes. Each must be right first time. (Possible hymn tunes: *Puer nobis nascitur, O quanta*	

qualia, Lobet den Herren, Old 100th, Ellers. You may make as many attempts as you need.)

1

2

3

4

9. SPEAK THE WORDS OF A HYMN IN CORRECT RHYTHM:

You will be shown how to match rhythm with words. Then you will be asked to speak the words of ONE line of FOUR different hymns in correct rhythm. Each must be right first time, but you can have as many tries as you need. (Use the hymns as listed in test #8)

1

2

3

4

10. SING ONE VERSE OF A HYMN ABSOLUTELY RIGHT!

Practice, with the director, a verse of a hymn. You will have to work out how the notes sound and how the words fit in with them—but you will be helped in this until you can sing the verse absolutely right!

Things to get right:

1. Stand well and hold your book proudly.
2. The tune must be right.
3. The words must be sung clearly—you can do this by opening your mouth well and using your lips.
4. Make a pleasant sound on every note.
5. Breathe at the right places.
6. Hold the long notes for their correct length.
7. Sing in tune.

This test may take you several weeks—but you will get better every time you try.

11. FOLLOWING MUSIC WITH YOUR FINGER:

Show that you can follow notes with your finger—pointing to the note that is being sung at exactly the moment when it is being sung, or played. One-beat notes one 'jab', two-beat notes two 'jabs' and four-beat notes four 'jabs.' You will be shown how to do this.

In order to pass this test you must point to the notes of THREE different hymn-tunes as they are played to you. You must get each test right at the FIRST try—but you can have as many tries as you need.

1.

2.

3.

12. READING MUSIC: (SIGHT-SINGING)

At every practice you will be shown how you can begin to sight-read music. That means that you will be able to sing the tune of a hymn without it having been played to you!

To pass this test you must sing three short melodies of four measures to *Lah* with only the first note and the key chord having been played for you. Each test must be right first time, but you can have as many tries as you need. *(Old 124th, Wareham, Psalm 42, Puer nobis, Deo gracias, St. Flavian)*

1.

2.

3.

13. SAY THE NEW LORD'S PRAYER, from memory:

Our Father in heaven,
hallowed be your name,
your kingdom come,
your will be done,
on earth as in heaven.
Give us today our daily bread.
Forgive us our sins as we forgive those who sin
    against us.
Save us from the time of trial and deliver us from evil.
For the kingdom, the power, and the glory are yours,
now and forever. Amen

14. SERVICE LEAFLET, with HYMNAL and PRAYER BOOK:

You need to show that you can find your way through our Service Leaflet (which we are given every Sunday). With the help of the director go through a Sunday Service and "find the next thing": hymns, prayers, anthems, etc....

Once you can do this well, you should be nearly ready to join the choir!

15. SIT WELL THROUGH SERVICE
You will sit with some adults near the choir who will look after you. You must show that you can pay attention well, and sit still for quite long periods. The Head Boy/Girl will be watching you!
 	
After every service take this card to the Head Boy/Girl and ask them to mark it for you. A CHECK shows that you have done well!
 	
Checks: 1   2   3   4   5   6   7
      8   9 10 11 12 13 14 15
  16 17 18 19 20 21 22 23	

16. SPECIAL TRAINING You may need some special help with one or two things to enable you to become a really excellent member of our choir.	
17. SITTING WITH THE CHOIR for FOUR Sundays: 1 2 3 4 When you have passed tests 1 through 16 you will be given a cassock and allowed to sit in the choirstalls! If you show that you can try hard when sitting in the choirstalls for four weeks, you will be admitted into full membership of our choir and given a COTTA to wear over your cassock. When this happens to you make sure that your parents are there to watch the ceremony!	
DATE I WAS ADMITTED TO THE CHOIR:	

"Wow!" exclaimed Bob, after he'd read it through, "This is amazing. You've covered everything that a boy or girl should know when they join a choir—from how to sing well, to how to behave, and also how to find their way around the order of service."

"Yes," answered the director, pleased that the training card had made such an impact on Bob, "this gives me plenty of material to choose from when I have to work with the new children. I do ten minutes of this and then ten minutes of that to give them variety and to make the practices as varied, interesting and useful as possible.

"I sometimes pass children for tests during practices," added the director.

"How do you mean?"

"Well, when a child is due to pass her hymn-singing test, if she sings a verse of a hymn really well during the course of an ordinary practice I tell her that she has just passed that test."

"That must encourage her and the other children to try even harder during practices," observed Bob.

"Yes, it does!

"But let me warn you again, don't replicate this training program for your own choir. What should you do instead?"

"I should see what the needs and opportunities are for my children and for my schedule, and amend the training scheme to fit my own situation."

"Right! Well done!" grinned the director rummaging in his pocket again. He put some loose change on the table and took the check to the counter where a young man was sitting at the cash register. "May I have a receipt, please?" he asked.

"What's that for?" remarked Bob.

"Oh, your visit to me will be counted as a tax deduction. Didn't you know that?"

"No!"

"Any expenses which you incur with respect to your profession should be noted on your tax return. It's to your advantage that you keep every receipt, duly marked as to what it was for. Have a word with your church finance person when you return home; you'll find him or her a great help in giving you a list of tax benefits that you can claim."

They left the restaurant and went into the busy street filled with afternoon shoppers. "Let's walk back to church; we can talk as we go."

15
MORE TRAINING FOR CHILDREN'S CHOIRS

WILL A GRADED TRAINING PROGRAM WORK IN ALL CIRCUMSTANCES?

"There are some questions I'd like to ask about your training card," said Bob as they walked along the sun-filled street, busy with shoppers.

"Fire away."

"In some churches I know, when a child says she wants to join the choir one Sunday she finds herself fully robed and sitting in the choirstalls the following Sunday. What do you think of that?"

"I don't think, I know! People value only those things which cost them something! If it costs you nothing to join the choir, then 'nothing' is what it is worth to you. Directors who follow that policy tend to find that children drop out from their program very easily.

"I make sure that my children have to work for the privilege of joining my choir—and they enjoy every moment! When the time comes for them to be admitted into membership it means a great deal to them. They are thrilled, and so are their parents who bring their cameras to record the moment when little Mary or Willie is formally made a member of our choir. This really works!"

HOW LONG DOES TRAINING TAKE?

"That leads me on to my next question," continued Bob. "How long does it take a child to qualify to join your choir?"

"It takes as long as it takes," answered the director, as they stood at the curbside waiting for the traffic lights to change. "Some children take only a couple of months to get through all the training successfully, whereas others take twice as long, or even longer. I had one boy, a few years ago, who took the whole nine-month season to pass his tests; but, my goodness, on the day he completed them he turned cartwheels all round my practice room! He was thrilled, and so was I! The important thing for you and the children to realize is that each child goes at his or her own pace. They know that they are progressing because they can see their training cards gradually filling with check marks as they pass each test."

The light turned green and they crossed the road. "What's your next question?"

"What do you do once a child becomes a member? Is their training over?"

"My goodness, no!" laughed the director. "Being a member of my choirs is a continuing educational experience for children, for teens and, for that matter, for adults. All my practices are opportunities for learning. The teaching for teens and adults is informal and arises from the music we are singing at any one time. But the teaching for children, for several years, continues to be codified. I've compiled training cards for the next few grades of singers so that they, too, will have plenty to occupy them when they come to practices."

"May I see them?" asked Bob.

"I suggest that it may be more helpful if you didn't," answered the director unexpectedly. "What you need to do when you arrive at your church is to work out your own plan for training in your own situation.

"For example," he continued as they turned a corner into Church Street, "work out in your own mind what skills you expect of a new boy or girl when they first join the choir. For me, it is being able to sing simple hymns. Then decide what you would expect children to have achieved, say, six months later. The next steps could be what you expect of a child who's been singing with you for a year, two years and three years. If you work out your own plan of training you will find that they really work for you, because you believe in them. If you believe in them, your children will also believe in them and want to fulfill the goals that you set them."

USE OF VESTMENTS IN A TRAINING PLAN

They turned into the church grounds and made their way to the music building.

"What I will tell you," said the director as he opened the door and led the way to the robing room, "is the names of the grades I have for the children, and what we do in the way of robes to recognize the different grades.

"*Probationer*—knows nothing; comes to church in 'Sunday best,' for we insist on smart clothes here. It's all to do with self-respect and respect for the choir.

"*Novice*—knows just enough to be able to sit in the choirstalls and sing simple hymns.

"*Junior singing boy/girl*—able to sing simple anthems.

"*Senior singing boy/girl*—able to sing all the music we perform after detailed rehearsal.

"And then comes a big jump to *Chorister*.

"*Junior chorister*—gives a lead in all we do.

"*Senior chorister*—gives a strong lead. Senior choristers can read anything at first sight, have well developed voices and can 'carry' the choir. Often they can match the expertise of even professional adult singers!"

"How old are the children in these grades?"

"Well, for me, I start children at the age of eight—third grade. I'm aware that many churches have choirs of much younger children, and that's fine—this system will work for them just as well.

"And these," continued the director pulling aside a curtain and revealing a row of neatly hung vestments, "these are the robes the children wear.

"A *novice* is given a cassock when he passes all his tests and sits with the choir for four Sundays. Once he has done that successfully he is admitted formally and given a cotta.

A *junior singer* is given a medallion with a pale blue ribbon round her neck.

A *senior singer* wears a dark blue ribbon.

A *junior chorister* wears a green ribbon, and a *senior chorister* wears a red ribbon.

Head choristers wear wide purple ribbons. They look very splendid," concluded the director.

THE ROYAL SCHOOL OF CHURCH MUSIC

"Where do the medallions come from?" asked Bob.

"We get them from the Royal School of Church Music in America."

"That's sounds pretty awe-inspiring!"

"On the contrary, it's a wonderfully supportive and helpful body made up of skilled choir directors from all over the country and beyond, who run both large and small choir programs, but who have lots of experience and share it with people like you and me.

"This organization covers the entire world and assists churches of every denomination. I strongly urge you to get in touch with them as soon as you get back home." (See Appendix B for the address of the RSCM/A.)

The director replaced the colorful robes and ribbons and drew the curtain back over them. From outside came the sound of some children playing. "I'm taking the new boys for their first practice in ten minutes," he said, looking at his watch, "Monday is mostly boys and tomorrow is girls. Come and see what we do."

"I've got one more question, please."

"What is it?" asked the director as he led the way again, down the corridor into the airy practice room.

"You mentioned a formal ceremony when a boy or girl is admitted into the choir. Can you show me what you do on those occasions?"

"Yes, but not right now. We'll talk about that a little later, I've got to get things ready for this most important practice."

"Why is it 'most important'?"

The director halted in his tracks and turned to look Bob squarely in the face. "If your next practice is not the most important thing in your whole life, you'd better give up being a director! If this practice is not most important thing to you, it's certainly not going to be the most important event in the lives of your singers, is it?

"I'm reminded of a curate who was asked by his minister if he expected to convert people through every sermon he preached. 'No,' he answered. 'Then you won't!' said his minister. It's the same with you; your singers will take your valuation of the practice that you are conducting. If you really care about what you are doing, so will they, and they'll come back for more next time.

"But now," he said as he opened the outside door to call the boys in, "I have four solid hours of choir practice, when you will see the Great Secret in action as well as the two basic practical essentials which will enable your singers to read music well. You do remember what they are, don't you?" he asked as he left Bob to fetch the boys.

Golly, what were they? thought Bob frantically as he thumbed through his notes. He's told me so much in such a short time that it's not easy to remember it all. But after a couple of minutes Bob found the place where he'd written down the two essentials—how could he have forgotten them?

16
LEADING PRACTICES FOR NEW CHILDREN

(3:30—4:15)

The next four hours passed in a whirl for Bob as he watched the director take four separate and distinct groups of young people, starting with four new boys, then six novices, eight choristers and finally, no fewer than twenty-two teenagers from ninth through twelfth grade.

Although every group was different he noticed several things they had in common:

1 All practices started and finished punctually, and almost every singer was there on time. Those who knew they would be late had told the director beforehand. The same was true with those who were absent.

2 The director gave every singer an enthusiastic welcome and managed to exchange a few words with everyone as they came in.

3 They were all pleased to be there.

4 They all tried hard for the full length of their rehearsal.

5 The time was spent entirely in productive work—not a moment was wasted.

6 He seemed to teach, not by telling the singers facts, but by asking them questions. I wonder why? thought Bob, for it would be so much quicker to tell them rather than to waste time while they thought of the right answer.

7 A lot of progress was made in each group.

8 Everyone enjoyed the experience.

9 For some reason, the more experienced singers kept putting up their hands during the rehearsal—he couldn't think why, because the director seemed to take no notice.

10 The director spent only a part of each rehearsal behind the piano, which he played softly and rather staccato; much of the rest of the time he walked between the singers, who were all standing at music desks, and he looked them straight in the face while they were singing.

How does he arouse so much enthusiasm? wondered Bob as he sat in a corner taking notes.

He realized, first, how the director quickly got the attention of the four new boys. He gathered them around the grand piano so that they were all facing him and gave each one his training card. He made the writing of each boy's name on his card a special moment, explaining just what they had to do in order to qualify for membership of the choir. He also explained that, whenever a boy sang a small solo well at a practice, or passed a test, he would be given a 'dot.' "And at the end of the practice we'll see who's earned the most dots," he added with a smile. He then started them singing.

This part of the practice is very like the audition that Shelton had yesterday, thought Bob. He's getting these four boys to sing single notes for four or more beats, and at the same time he's showing them how to stand well, how to breathe, how to open their mouths in a "trumpet" shape. There's no letup at all; everyone has to concentrate hard in order to keep up with the rapid pace he's set. But he's teaching only one thing at a time, so that the boys don't get confused. He insists that everything he asks them to do they do correctly!

CHALKBOARD

Bob saw, with interest, that the director wrote on the chalkboard, as the practice proceeded, a list of things that the new boys should remember. He got them to tell him each one, such as, "How should you stand when you're singing? Should you stand tall or should you droop?" "Stand tall!" came the answer. The director promptly wrote their answer on the chalkboard. 1) *Stand tall.*

Other helpful words included, 2) *Breathing.* 3) *Mouth—trumpet.* 4) *Concentration,* and so on. When a boy was not fulfilling one of these points, the director would ask him, "Shelton, which of these did you forget?" The boy would looked at the list and say, "Number 2!" "Right! Let's do it again," and invariably Shelton would remember to do it right, because it was he who had reminded himself to do it, and not the director.

BEGINNING TO TEACH SIGHT-READING

He then noticed how the director began to teach the rudiments of reading music: how many lines there are on a stave, what the G-clef means, and even to distinguish between singing G and A when he wrote them on the chalkboard, strategically placed directly behind the piano. Note by note he steadily worked up to writing the scale of D on the board. While the boys were singing it, he pointed to the notes of the scale, so that the boys could begin associating the written notes with the notes they were singing.

"He seems to work at one thing for ten minutes and then do something entirely different," noted Bob as the director introduced the clapping of rhythm, which the boys thoroughly enjoyed. Each boy was able to pass at least one test during those forty-five minutes, which made everyone feel very good—especially the director, who showed his delight at what they had achieved during their first rehearsal.

"My goodness, how the time flew by!" thought Bob, as the director asked the boys, at the end of the practice, what they had learned. Hands shot quickly into the air and a stream of answers poured forth. They'd clearly remembered nearly everything he'd taught them.

He read out the dots that they had earned: two boys had four dots, another had five, but Shelton had earned six, and so he came out on top that day. Shelton almost lit up with pleasure as the director complimented him and the other boys in doing so well.

The director then asked them if they'd enjoyed themselves. "Yes!" they said with happy faces. "Good! I'll see you again on Wednesday when we can pass some more tests," and he got up and led the boys out to their waiting parents with whom he exchanged a few encouraging words about their sons' progress.

"How was that, Bob?" he asked as he came back into the practice room, followed by six boys who were just a little older than the first group.

"Great!" answered Bob. "But I've got a whole list of questions I need to ask you."

"You can ask them tonight when we've finished here. We'll both need reviving with a good meal," and he began his second practice.

17

LEADING PRACTICES FOR MORE EXPERIENCED CHILDREN

THE GREAT SECRET IN ACTION! (4:15-5:00)

At that point the door opened again and they were joined by a lady. "Bob," said the director, "I'd like you to meet the associate director of music, Nancy Willis. Nancy's come to help me with the novice boys."

"Hi, Nancy! How can two of you take a practice with only six boys?"

"Oh, I take boys out two at a time, and give them instruction for ten minutes based on their training cards, while the director continues his practice with the remaining boys. You'll see how smoothly it goes!" And with that she sat near Bob while the director prepared to start the practice with all six boys.

The boys collected their own training cards and music from their cubbies and went to their places in two desks on either side of the piano. They were chattering quietly among themselves as the director wrote on the chalkboard: *Hymnal,* "O Come, Ye Servants," *Tye.*

As soon as the director began writing the boys quickly found the music they needed. The director waited for a minute until everyone had the right music, and then he said, unexpectedly, "Sing me a B-flat!" (above middle C). The boys immediately stood up very straight and sang *Oo* to a variety of notes which made a most peculiar chord! The director let the chord linger for a few moments and then he played B-flat in sub-octaves on the piano. (Why sub-octaves?) "Who was right?" he asked, and three boys put their hands in the air. "Well done! And who was nearly right?" Three more hands were raised. "Good! You were pretty close today. Let's all sing that note to *Oo* while I count to fifteen." And they did.

While they were singing the director got up from the piano and walked round in front of the boys, looking each one straight in the face, smiling and encouraging them. He made sure that they were breathing deeply, and he asked one boy, who raised his shoulders when he took a breath, if he was breathing correctly. "No!" responded the boy. "Then show me how you should do it: put your hands on your tummy—get rid of all the air by pretending that you're blowing out the candles on your birthday cake—now fill up really low like a balloon—that's right. Now let's all sing that note again while I count to fifteen." And they did.

"Next note for sixteen!" he commanded, and, as he was away from the piano, the boys had to pitch the next note a half-step higher without his help—which they did. And so it went on until they reached E-flat, for the count of twenty. All the time the director was checking the boys' breathing and stance, and making sure that their necks were relaxed. "Roll your heads from side to side as you sing, to make sure that you're relaxed," and they did.

"Scale to *Aw*!" he said, as he returned to the piano and led the tonality into the key of E major. The boys sang a one-octave scale descending and ascending, all in one breath, sustaining the last note for four counts. Again he checked a boy who seemed to stick his chin out when singing. "Keep that chin in, Micah, and think of the sound as going straight out of the top of your head!" He gradually led them up to the scale of A major, to *Ah*, sung with very easy head tone.

He's hardly playing the piano at all, noted Bob. But why should he, for the boys don't need it!

And then the director commanded, "Sirens!" and all the boys released a great whoop starting around the B-flat on which they began their warm-ups and sailing right up to notes well over top C and down again: "Oooo-waaaa-oooo!"

"I've never heard anything like that!" thought Bob.

"Okay, William, you have a go," he said, turning to the first boy on his left. William promptly sang his siren, whereupon the director immediately played the top note that the boy had reached so easily and said, "Sing me a scale down!" which the boy did.

Whatever note is that? thought Bob.

The director accompanied William lightly on the piano and, as he was approaching the end of his octave, the director said, "Two octaves—change to *Ee*," and the boy, reaching the halfway mark changed his vowel to *Ee* and ended with a fine chest sound.

"Now, what note do you think that was?" asked the director, as he turned to the chalkboard and quickly drew five lines and a G-clef. "It was E-flat above top C, William—well done!" and he wrote the note for everyone to see.

He did the same for every boy, giving each lad his opportunity to sing a siren and then sing a two-octave scale starting on the highest note he had just reached. Some boys were able to sing higher than William, but a couple were able to reach only high C. The director showed that he was pleased with them all, for they'd all been trying very hard. Bob turned yet another page in his rapidly filling notebook: *Be pleased with effort, not just achievement.*

"Now, Mrs. Willis will take her first two boys—off you go." Two boys quietly left the practice room, clutching their music and their training cards, as Mrs. Willis led the way to another room down the corridor. During the next ten minutes sounds of singing filtered into the main practice room as she worked with the two boys on the next tests they had to pass. Meanwhile the director continued his practice with the remaining four boys.

He can give even more individual attention to them now that there are fewer boys, thought Bob. What a great way to lead a teaching practice!

"Hymn 324," commanded the director, and the boys speedily opened their hymnals. When they'd all found the hymn the director said, "Sing me the first note." There was a slight pause and several boys began singing a fairly low note. As before, the director waited a moment and then played the right note, in sub-octaves. Several boys immediately smiled. Clearly they'd got it right!

The director played the key chord and the first note, leaned away from the keyboard, and said, "Okay, sing the tune to *Oo*—quarter notes go at this speed." He began tapping a steady beat on the piano top. "One, two, ready, breathe!" and off they went, without any accompaniment. The result was not wholly accurate, but Bob instantly recognized the tune *Picardy,* set to the words, "Let all mortal flesh keep silence."

Text: *Liturgy of St. James;* tr. Gerard Moultrie, 1829–1885
Tune: *Picardy,* French folk tune, 17th cent.

After the first few measures the director stopped them and said, "Was that wholly right?" "No!" "What was wrong?" "Someone didn't count two beats on the two-beat note." "Right! Let's clap the rhythm of the whole tune," and he began tapping a steady beat on the piano lid with a pencil. "One, two, ready, GO!" and the boys began clapping the rhythm, which almost everyone did correctly.

"Yes! That was nearly right. But how many beats on the last note, Ashton?" "Four!" "Right! How many did you clap?" "Two!" "Okay—clap those last three measures for me again, Ashton," and he did—and he was right.

"Okay. Let's see if we can sing the first three measures to *Oo* absolutely right. Follow the notes with your finger!"

At the other end of the practice room Bob was beginning to squirm. Why doesn't he play it for them? It would be so much quicker if he did— then they'd sing it right and he could go on to more interesting music, for there's an anthem to learn and time's getting on!

The director played the tonic chord and the first note and started them off again, without any help from the piano. "One, two, ready, breathe!" and he tapped a steady quarter beat as they sang. It was right.

"Well done. Now, Danny, you sing me the next three measures. How can you sing your first note correctly?" "It's the same as the last two notes we've just sung." "Right! Sing it for me." And Danny sang a note, but it was too low.

I wish he would play it for him instead of wasting time like this, thought Bob.

"Can anyone sing Danny's note for him?" William immediately sang the *A* and everyone else followed him. "Good! Okay, Danny, off you go!" and he tapped the quarter beat for him. Danny began, but sang *A, B-flat, C, D* instead of *A, A, B-flat, C.*

"Hey, Danny!" the director interrupted, "Was that right?" "I think it was nearly right." "What should you have been doing with your finger when you were singing?" "Oh, it should have been pointing to the notes." "Right. So, try it again." Danny tried it again, and this time he sang the first four notes correctly, but then went on to sing the first note of the second system incorrectly.

"You got those first four notes right!" beamed the director, "Well done. You've earned a dot!" Danny smiled. "But was the first note of the next line right?" "No." "Is that first note up or down from the last note of the top line?" Almost everyone looked, except William who had turned round and was looking out of the window. The director waited for five seconds in silence until William realized that he'd let his attention wander. He turned to look at his hymnal again. "Thank you, William," said the director, "we need you here!" and he smiled.

POSITIVE REINFORCEMENT OF GOOD BEHAVIOR

"Now, who can answer my question?" Three hands shot up. William hadn't heard the question so his hand remained down. "Yes, Ashton?" "It goes down from the last note on the top line!" "Yes, well done! That answer deserves a dot," and he placed a merit dot in the register opposite Ashton's name. William realized that he could have earned a dot if he'd been paying attention. I must try harder, he thought.

"Let's all sing the last measure on the top line and then go as far as the first note on the second line. Who can sing me the first note?" William did. "Well done, William, that deserves a dot." Hooray! thought William, trying hard pays!

"All fingers pointing to the notes? One, two, ready, breathe!" and the boys sang the five notes correctly. Ashton, however continued singing the next three notes to finish off the phrase. "That was very good, Ashton. Let's all do that." And they sang the three measures to *Oo* correctly.

"Now let's sing up as far as there from the beginning. Who can sing me the first note?"

Dear, oh dear! thought Bob again. Clearly the boys are really interested in what the director is doing with them—he's presenting little problems for them to solve all the time and mixing solo attempts with all the boys singing together. There's no denying that they are really tuned into his wavelength, but he's spent ten minutes on this hymn already and they've only sung as far as measure six! They haven't begun to sing the words. His agenda for use of time is very different from mine. If I were taking the practice I'd play the whole tune through to them in single notes, very firmly, and then, perhaps get them to sing it to *Oo*, following it with their fingers, if they can. That way they'd get it right in a couple of minutes. What's he aiming for?

The practice continued in the same manner—it took thirty minutes to get to the point when the boys sang the words of the first verse, for the director made sure that everyone really understood, and was able to solve, every musical problem that presented itself.

(Music directors: You will be able to spot the musical difficulties in the previous musical example. Take a moment to see how many you can find, and then check them off from the list that follows.)

SPECIFIC PROBLEMS TO SOLVE

1   How many beats on the whole-note in measure 6? Not four but three, because one beat must be taken out of the four-beat note for a breath. This needs explaining to the children, and then they must do it! Next they need to be asked if there are any other examples. There are! but only two more examples, not three. Why?

2   Having sorted that out, you need to tackle the number of beats there will be on the second note of measure 3...and have them find similar examples.

3   And having solved that, the children will need to tell you how many measures they should sing in one breath—and then they should do it!

4   Why are measures 7-11 easy? Someone needs to tell you.

5   How are the singers going to pitch the jump of a fourth in measure 13? You should write, on your chalkboard, the notes A and D, and then get them to discover how many notes are between A and D (and thus you can tell them why that interval is called a "fourth"). Get them to sing up from A to D, while you point to the notes on the board. Having done that twice (for repetition helps to get the right answer more firmly in their heads), ask them to point to A and D to see if they can remember what those notes sound like.

6   Are there any more rising fourths in this tune? Sing them—having given the singers only the first note.

7   How are they going to pitch the falling fourth that immediately follows the rising fourth? (Don't despise the simplicity of this question—not

all children will immediately see that they've just sung the A!) Once they have spotted the answer—they need to do it. This is something that many choirmasters fail to do.

8   What about the intervals of a third in the last two lines? The children need to be able to pitch falling thirds to "cuck-oo." Once they can do this, they can pitch rising thirds to "oo-cuck"!

9   Do the boys know why there are three beats on a dotted half? (NOT because a dot adds a beat, but because a dot adds half the length of the note to the note. This needs explaining carefully with lots of examples.)

Now we tackle the words.

10   Slurs need explaining. The theory is simple—getting children to sing one syllable on two notes is another matter. They can do it if you pattern it for them—but how much better it is if they can actually work it out for themselves! Someone in a group is usually able to do this, if you ask the right questions. Once he or she has solved the problem of the first slur, get all the children to copy. Then ask someone where the next slur is, and get the next child to sing that one, and so on. Special merit for the child who can sing *scend* on the four-note slur, especially as "oo-cucks" are involved!

11   Having previously decided that two beat notes at ends of phrases have to be sung for one beat, plus a one-beat breath (you might find it helpful to rewrite these passages on the board, as they should be sung— i.e. changing the last half note into a quarter note, plus a quarter note rest), the children must be able to tell you on which beat the c of *silence* is sung in measure 3. They should be able to work this out, if you have taught them that a four-beat note finishes on the fifth beat. (One-two-three-four-*off*). You can spend a lot of constructive, competitive time getting children to sing last words of phrases with the final consonant on the fourth beat of the measure.

But let's return to our narrative:

At the other end of the practice-room, during the remainder of the practice Bob noted :

The practice continued in the same manner—with the director constructively drawing attention to the written notes of a second hymn, but he spent less time on that so that he could begin to look at the first page of "O Come, Ye Servants of the Lord" by Tye.

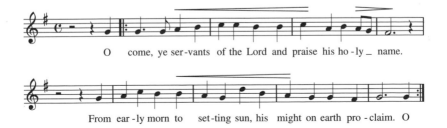

The director spent five minutes getting the boys to clap the dotted-quarter/eighth rhythm correctly in the first phrase and correctly sing the "cuck-oo" interval in the second phrase.

1   He asked the boys to look at the first note, and attempt to pitch it.

2   He then played the right note and the key-chord, and asked them to attempt to sight-sing a few measures to *Lah,* with little or no help from the keyboard. When he did play, he played only the harmonic basis of the melody (the ATB parts) and left out the melody, so that the boys would have to work it out for themselves.

3   Occasionally, if the music was particularly difficult for them, he would ask them to clap the rhythm while he played the melody for them. He would also illustrate points on the chalkboard behind him—showing them, for example, how to clap eighth notes and dotted-quarter/eighth which were new to them.

4   And every ten minutes the two boys who'd been working with Mrs. Willis came back into the room, wreathed in smiles, for clearly they'd achieved a lot with her and enjoyed every minute of it, and it would be the turn of the next two boys to go out.

5   When the final two boys had returned from their time with Mrs. Willis, the director brought the practice to an end with all the boys singing the first verse of "Let All Mortal Flesh" that they had been rehearsing. They sang it well.

MERIT DOTS

"Right," said the director, "Let's all close our music and put it in a neat pile in front of us." The boys obeyed with alacrity and then stood very still, looking at the director expectantly.

"Now you can tell me how many dots Mrs. Willis gave each of you." Most had earned two or three dots, but one diminutive boy, Chuck, had been given five. "Five!" said the director, "what have you been doing so well?" "I passed three tests," answered Chuck with barely-concealed pride; his head only just appeared over the top of the choir desk. "Yes," said Nancy from the other end of the practice room, "all the boys did well today, but Chuck did especially well."

The director then read out, from his register, the number of dots each boy earned at that practice; two had five dots, two more had six, one had seven, and Chuck, who led the group, had eight. "Well done, all of you!" beamed the director, looking each boy straight in the face. "That was a very good practice; I'm proud of you. When do I see you next?" "Wednesday!" they shouted and they trooped off chatting happily. They put their music and test cards in their cubbies and went outside to meet their waiting parents, accompanied by Nancy.

Whew! thought Bob, that was a fine practice! But what was the Great Secret?

18
LEADING PRACTICES FOR MOST EXPERIENCED CHILDREN

(5:00-6:15 PLUS 10 MORE MINUTES)

"I don't know about you, Bob, but I'm pretty exhausted already," said the director as he opened a thermos of tea that he carried around with him, "and we aren't even halfway through the evening yet!"

"Those were thrilling practices," enthused Bob, standing up and stretching himself. "Those boys really concentrated so hard all the time and they achieved so much!"

"Wait until you see the girls tomorrow—they try even harder! But, you ain't seen nuthin yet," he added as he finished his drink of tea and went over to the chalkboard. "We're now going to jump up three ranks in the boys' choir, going from Novice to Chorister, missing out the Junior and Senior Singing Boys who have their practices on Wednesday. You're about to see the fruit of all that careful teaching that Nancy and I give to the young boys. This next practice is for our most experienced trebles who have been in the choir for three or four years, so make sure that your pencil is sharpened!"

He then added more anthems to the list of music that was already on the board for the previous practice, including Parry's "I Was Glad," a Magnificat and Nunc Dimittis by Howells and another setting by Stanford, a Handel coronation anthem, Latin motets by Palestrina and Lassus, a Jubilate by Britten and anthems by Mozart and Gerald Near.

He'll never get through all that in seventy-five minutes, thought Bob. There's enough music there to keep some choirs fully occupied for several months!

Eight older boys came into the room, dumped their school bags and sports equipment on the floor, and, carrying a heavy load of music from their cubbies, made their way to the movable choirdesks. They arranged them in an open square around the grand piano. They were much taller than the other boys, and Bob noticed, with interest, that the desks were not only easily movable, but also their height could be adjusted, which is what the boys were doing at that moment.

The director exchanged a few words with each boy, but clearly this was a different scene. There was an atmosphere of responsibility about all the boys that clearly augured well for the long practice about to follow. He handed his register to the head boy, who took charge of it and marked who was present. As the practice got under way, the head boy occasionally put a dot opposite someone's name when they'd sung a small solo correctly, without any prompting from the director.

The practice began in exactly the same way as the previous practice. The boys found all their music, as listed on the board, and then the director said, "Sing me a B-flat!" They all did—and the note was right, even though it hadn't been played on the piano. The boys sang it to *Oo* as the director walked round the desks looking each boy in the face. The singing was continuous and each boy breathed when he needed to.

The director returned to the piano, and said to the boys on his left, "Carry on with that note," and to the boys on the middle stall he said, "Sing me D," and to the boys on his right, "Sing F." The chord of B-flat major filled the room. "Change to *Aw*...all go up a half-step!" (B major). "...and again...and again...and again," ending on D major with an A at the top, sung clearly with easily produced head tone, and without accompaniment.

"Right! Scale to *Ah*," and he led the boys into the scale of F major, which they sang descending and ascending, sustaining the final top note for four counts. Bob silently observed, He hardly plays the piano at all. He just gives them the keychord and away they go! What a superb sound they make!

The director led them into F-sharp major. "Firsts starting, then seconds," he commanded. Half the boys began the scale followed, two notes later, by the other half, so that the room was filled with the sound of a scale sung in thirds.

Warmup scale in thirds

He led them into G major. "In threes!" and he pointed to the boys on his left who began the scale, followed two notes later by the boys in the middle and finally by the boys on his right—producing a scale sung in triads. The singers who began first reached the final note before the others, but they sustained it until the remaining boys had caught up with them.

A-flat major came next, led by the boys in the middle, and finally A major, led by the boys on the director's right.

"Okay! All together—two octaves!" and he led into the scale of B-flat major. At the halfway point the boys automatically changed to *Ee* and altered their production from head voice to chest voice, reversing the process as they came up again. It was a thrilling sound.

"Hymn 324!"

He doesn't waste words, thought Bob. He could have said, "Now, let's all sing a couple of verses of hymn 324," but he didn't. This is an efficient practice!

PRACTICE

Bob noted that the practice followed a pattern very similar to that for the novice boys, except that the standard of singing here was of a professional quality. Almost all the music was new to the boys but they read it as though they had known it for weeks! The director never gave a first note—for the boys volunteered the singing of what they thought the first note was without being asked. The director then checked it on the piano for accuracy and, more often than not, the note they sang was right. This was always greeted by triumphant smiles by director and boys alike.

These guys really think all the time! Whenever he plays the piano it is always very lightly, not playing the tune, and very often playing with chords detached so that the boys can clearly hear themselves in the gaps between notes.

Every boy was given an opportunity, in turn, to sing a few measure by himself when the music got more difficult. Some succeeded the first time, others were nearly right. Each boy was allowed two attempts, and then the next boy was given his turn. There was a delightful atmosphere of friendly rivalry between the boys. No one lost face when he didn't quite make it, but the boys who did sing accurately were honored by their colleagues with grins when they got it right, and the head boy noted their little triumphs with a dot opposite their name in the register.

Halfway through the practice the director let the tension relax by asking the boys what was happening at school and at home. There were a couple of minutes of lively conversation as he learned about some of the main activities that the boys were engaged in: Joel was in a school play, Greg was playing in an orchestra, Charlie's grandparents were coming to stay for several weeks, and Alex's father had just returned from a business trip to Paris.

My word! thought Bob, there's a lot going on in their lives. I'd never have thought of asking them about their activities, but he's showing a genuine interest.

The director then brought the conversation to a halt by telling the boys that they needed to rehearse the remaining music—and so the spirit of concentration resumed, all the better for having had a break.

At the end of the practice, which the director finished on a good note—with the boys singing the last couple of pages of a new anthem for the second time so that they felt more secure, he got them to put their music in neat piles in front of them and then asked the head boy to read out the number of dots each chorister had earned. This time the dots were between six and eleven, with the deputy head boy beating the head boy by one!

"Who am I seeing tonight?" he asked. "Oh yes, Jay and Joe.

"All standing straight!" he commanded suddenly, and the boys stood instantly to attention. He looked at each desk critically and then said to the boys on his left (who were standing straightest), "You can go...and you...and you," and the boys happily collected their music and put it in their cubbies, leaving Jay and Joe who brought their music to the piano, standing one on the left and the other on the right.

The director then spent the next ten minutes giving Jay and Joe an advanced singing lesson, using an anthem they'd just sung to enable them to concentrate on beauty of tone, exact intonation, clarity of diction, purity of vowels, and creating a lovely sense of phrasing as they sang four measures to a breath. Each boy in turn was given opportunities to excel and, again, there was friendly rivalry between the two evenly matched singers; one was able to sing with clearer vowels while the other sang with creative consonants; thus, each learned from the other. The atmosphere was much more informal than in the full practice, and the boys clearly benefited from those brief minutes with their director and each other. "Great!" he said when they'd finished, "You really are super leaders—have another three dots each!" and the boys went off, exhausted but happy.

19

LEADING PRACTICES FOR TEENAGERS

(6:30-7:30)

The director remained sitting on his swivel stool behind the piano, mopped his brow and took a long drink of tea from his thermos. He looked across at Bob, who came to join him.

"Those boys are terrific," said Bob, "they could hold their own with almost any professional adult."

"They do," answered the director, "every Sunday. We couldn't pay professional sopranos for what these boys do for us. They're getting a practical music education here that will last them a lifetime. They become leaders in the high school choirs and, when they graduate, they fill similar roles in their college choirs. Their only complaint is that the college choirs aren't as good as this one. It's rather embarrassing, really, for it keeps on happening!"

While they were talking, the room was filling up with high schoolers, some of whom were taller than the director.

"Who are these?" asked Bob.

"These are teen members of our men and boys choir who have all been through the ranks and so they, too, are first-rate sight-singers.

"But there are some girls, too!"

"Yes! My predecessor added six senior girls to the choir some years ago, as a gesture of equality. I'm very glad he did, for they add so much to the singing, without taking away from the boys' prime responsibility for leading the treble line.

"We audition the girls from the girls' choir. There's keen competition to get into this choir because the repertoire is much more varied, and, of course, they are singing with young men of their own age, which makes membership even more attractive for them!"

"Do they still sing in the girls' choir?"

"Oh yes! These girls put in more hours a week than anyone else—they're marvelous. Wait till you hear them; but we must begin."

Bob took the hint and went back to his seat at the far end of the room as the director mingled with the teens and had a few words with most of them before the church clock struck the half hour.

Bob noted that the director didn't begin with traditional warmups but by asking them to sing a simple hymn-tune to various vowels—Oo, Aw, Ee and Ah—and to sing it unaccompanied and softly. The sound they produced varied, because the singers were so mixed. The five senior high girls made a lovely sound, but the teen men varied. There were four or five altos, some of whom were clearly experienced. But others, who were younger and who had only just made the transition from the boys' choir, were feeling their way and singing particularly softly. There was a lone sixteen-year-old tenor, who also sang softly and just a little flat, and there were about eight basses who were a particularly assorted bunch! The youngest looked only fourteen-years-old and made hardly any sound, but the fifteen- and sixteen-year-old basses tended to sing too loudly, especially notes which were in the higher part of their range. The three eighteen-year-old basses sang really well and made a good sound.

HOW TO ACHIEVE BLEND AND BALANCE—QUICKLY!

How's he going to turn this disparate group into a musical, well-balanced choir? wondered Bob.

"Hey, people!" said the director in a friendly tone, "That was a pretty awful row! Sing me the first chord to a soft Oo and listen to it!" They did, and within five seconds the individual singers altered their tone to produce a really cohesive sound.

That's amazing! thought Bob, All he did was to get them to listen to themselves and they did the rest! I must ask him about that, for they turned themselves, almost instantly, from a bunch of individual singers into a real choir!

"That's much better," said the director. "Now let's sing the whole tune like that," and off they went again—but the tone immediately reverted to its original unbalanced sound, with a number of singers pushing their voices too hard. "Hey! You're not listening to yourselves," said the director kindly but firmly. "Sing the first chord again, softly," and they did. "Now the next chord," and they did; and then the director led them, slowly at first but gradually increasing the pace, chord by chord, until they were able to sing in rhythm and also listen to themselves at the same time.

He then asked the choir to sing the words of the first verse and followed the same procedure—getting them to listen to the first syllable, and then the second, and so on until they were able to sing the notes, sing the words, and listen to themselves and to each other all at the same time.

MUSICAL PROBLEMS FOR YOUNG TEENS

Having established the tone he wanted from them, the director began rehearsing anthems.

Because everyone could read music, there was little or no note-teaching. The only time this was needed was when some of the younger basses, who were still finding out how to control their new voices, sometimes found it difficult to pitch an interval, especially when singing in harmony with the other voices.

Clearly this is a physical problem rather than a musical one, observed Bob silently. They've got a set of new equipment which they're learning how to use. It's rather like learning to drive a car after having ridden a bicycle. But he's dealing with them very gently and with good humor, while, all the same time, being very firm about what he wants and expects from them. They respect him for this, for he shows that he's aware of their problems and is helping them to overcome them.

The lone tenor was in a category by himself, for there was no possibility of him singing strongly enough to balance with the rest of the singers. But, every so often, the director would say "Well done!" to him, and point out where he needed to sing a little sharper, so that, after fifteen minutes, he was making a really useful contribution to the singing.

MODUS OPERANDI

Bob noticed several other important things:

The singers were standing, not in groups of voices, with all the sopranos, all the altos and all the basses together, but most singers seemed to be next to someone who was singing another part. That must make it very difficult for them, thought Bob I wonder why he does it—I must ask him tonight!

His method of rehearsing an anthem, generally, was to sing it straight through, at a steady pace, so that the singers could get most of the notes right immediately. Then he would go back and rehearse passages which had caused problems, occasionally having all the basses singing their line or even asking individuals to try their skill on their own. If the difficulty persisted, he'd get everyone to sing the bass line at their own pitch, thus involving all the singers.

He would then rehearse a couple of pages of the anthem in detail, marking breathing (they all had pencils) and aiming at expressive phrasing, clear diction and balance.

He was very insistent that everyone sing absolutely together. To do this he would give the chord on the piano, stand up, look at every singer, give two beats and then bring them in. Again, Bob was puzzled. Why does he take so long before they start singing? It must take five seconds to look at them all, and this adds up during a practice, for he does it over and over again!

ABSENTEES AND LATECOMERS

Bob also noticed how he dealt with latecomers. The director had already written on the chalkboard, alongside the list of the music they would be singing, a short notice:

> *Apologies for absence:*
> *Ted & Chris*
> *(their band is playing in the city)*
> *Late arrivals:*
> *Justin (wrestling match)*
> *Molly (school play audition)*

When Justin and Molly slipped into the practice, fifteen minutes late, the director acknowledged their presence with a friendly nod and, at the first available opportunity, asked, "How did it go?" "I was beaten!" said Justin. "Hard luck!" But Molly said, "I was chosen for the lead!" "Well done!"

He's saying, in effect, "It's good to see you here, thanks for letting me know you'd be late," realized Bob.

But another teen arrived twenty minutes late, and his name was not on the board. He, too, slipped into the practice and was given a friendly nod by the director. When there was a gap in the singing, the director asked him, "Hi, Arthur, what happened?" "My Mom's car broke down." "I'm sorry. Did she get it fixed?" "Yes, thanks." And Bob thought, He's saying, "It's good to see you, too, but we need to clear up, for everyone's sake, why you are late." In other words, attendance and punctuality at this practice are important for him and for the whole choir. He doesn't let anything slip past him. He's got standards, and the kids know what they are. That's why they're here!

Bob also noticed that the director spent a lot of time, as in the other practices, walking among the choir while they were singing. He even walked into the back rows of singers to listen to them close at hand.

At the end of the hour the director said another appreciative, "Well done and thanks!" and walked among them, chatting, as the singers put their music away. They hadn't got through all the music that the director had intended, but at least they'd prepared the music for next Sunday and begun to look at the music for the Sunday following.

UNEXPLAINED ABSENCES

Jenny came up to the director as he was putting his music away and said, "Where was Sheila tonight?" "I don't know," responded the director, "I haven't heard from her. Will you call her when you get home, please, and find out if there's anything wrong, for we missed her."

As Jenny went out, Bob came over to him and asked, "Why did you ask Jenny to call Sheila instead of doing it yourself?"

"Quite right, Bob, I should. But tonight I'm looking after you full-time, and so I can't. It's important to follow up unexplained absences immediately, for it shows your concern for the singers who are away, and it also impresses on them the importance you attach to regular attendance. But by asking Jenny to call I'm really involving her in the organizational process of the choir. That's good for her and also for Sheila, who will be pleased that the senior girl cares enough about her to call her. Always try to bring good from an otherwise potentially flawed situation."

WORKING WITH INDIVIDUALS, AGAIN

Bob had noticed, near the end of the practice, that a choirman had come into the practice room. The director introduced him to Bob. "Bob, this is Jack Keen, one of the superb tenors in our men and boys' choir, who comes every week to give two of our teens, in rotation, a short singing lesson." Bob watched as Mr. Keen took over the director's stool behind the piano and began to work with two sixteen-year-old basses. He concentrated, mainly, on problems of vocal production to complement the director's input which had dealt more on interpretation, so that the young singers were given a really well-rounded music educational experience that evening.

"Jack's marvelous," said the director to Bob as they made their way out of the practice room. "He comes every week out of the goodness of his heart—for he loves all those kids and they love him. He really knows what they need musically and he's worth his weight in gold!

"Well," he continued as they got into his car, "I don't know about you, but I'm ready for a good meal!"

"So am I," said Bob, "and a good talk, so lead on!"

20
QUESTIONS AND ANSWERS

The director drove his car out of the church parking lot and turned towards home. "I thought we'd eat at my place tonight, Bob, so we can spend the whole time talking. I'm ready to collapse into a chair after all those rehearsals."

"Great! What will you be cooking?"

"Oh, there are some microwave meals in my fridge that will only take a few minutes, with ice cream to follow."

Bob sat in silence for a while as the car pursued its leisurely way through the town. Packaged foods were not high on his list of favorite things. He turned to the director and said, "Would you like me to cook us a meal? I really enjoy it, and it's about time I began to repay you for your hospitality."

The director brightened. "That sounds marvelous, Bob. There's almost nothing I enjoy more than watching guests use my super kitchen, thank you!"

"Would you like stir-fry chicken?"

"Would I!"

"Have you got any chicken at home?"

"No."

"Sesame oil?"

"No."

"Bean sprouts and water chestnuts?"

"No."

"Well perhaps we could stop at a supermarket and stock up."

"Okay. We pass one on our way home. But let's start now on your questions."

WHY ASK QUESTIONS?

"First question: Why did you ask the kids so many questions? Surely it would be much quicker to tell them what they should know, rather than spend time until they hit on the right answer."

"You're quite right, it would have been quicker to tell them, for example, that a black note is a quarter note, and the white one is a half note, rather than ask them to guess; but..." and the director turned to look at Bob, "but would it have been better?"

"How do you mean?"

"What am I aiming for with my children?"

"You're aiming to get them to sing songs really beautifully."

"No, I'm not! You've missed the whole point of what I was doing tonight!"

A CHOIR OF THINKING MUSICIANS, NOT PARROTS

The director turned away from Bob. "What I'm aiming for is to have a choir made up of thinking musicians who can read music as well as sing their songs beautifully."

"Oh, I see now," said Bob, mightily relieved that he was no longer under the director's concentrated gaze which, at such close quarters, was rather intimidating.

"That's why you're here, I hope," continued the director, as the supermarket came into view. "There are thousands of choirs in this country that sing music beautifully, but very few of them are made up of creative, thinking musicians."

"What do you mean?" asked Bob again.

"The singers in most children's choirs sing beautifully because their directors tell them to 'sing it like this.' Now, teaching by giving a role model is a fine way of leading a choir, but if that is all you do, then you are, in effect, training a choir of parrots who just repeat back to you what you sing for them. The kids can sing beautifully when the director is there to lead them, but when they leave the choir, unable to read music or to think creatively, they are musically helpless. And what's more, they don't own the music they are singing. They can't sing without having someone stand in front of them to say 'sing it like this,' because that's what they're used to. They've never been taught to think, they've only been taught to copy. It's so sad!" and he thumped the steering wheel in his frustration at so many opportunities lost by so many singers.

SINGERS WHO THINK CREATIVELY

The director drove into the parking lot, found a convenient space near the store and got out of the car, still talking.

"What I'm aiming for is to train my children to think, and the only way you can train them to think is…is what?" he asked as he found an empty cart outside the store and wheeled it through the automatic doors.

"The only way to train anybody to do anything," answered Bob, walking in the director's wake, "is to get them to do it from the word *go!*"

"Right!" smiled the director as he led the way to the meat counter. "The quickest way to bore people is to tell them what you think they ought to know. That immediately puts them into a passive, receiving mode. But the best way to get people, both adults and children, to be mentally alert is…is what?"

"Is constantly to challenge them to be part of the creative process of a practice," answered Bob looking at the rows of chicken parts that lay before him.

"My word, that's a well thought-out answer!" said the director admiringly. "Why?"

"Because every time we talk you constantly challenge me to think," answered Bob who'd selected a package of four boneless chicken breasts. "You expect me to think creatively, and so I find myself doing it better all the time. You do exactly the same at all your practices. I confess that I had thought, tonight, that the pace of learning was rather slow, especially among some of the younger children. You sometimes spent five minutes just getting one phrase right."

MEETING SUNDAY'S DEADLINE

"I'm glad you noticed that," answered the director as they made their way through the store, gradually filling their cart with provisions. "Many choirmasters aim at a 'quick fix' when teaching hymns or songs. What they want is to have their younger children sing the music right as soon as possible. Why is that a short-sighted aim?"

Bob paused, considering which rice to choose as well as how to answer the director's question intelligently. "Brown rice, I think," he said, "but I can't put into words why it's better to take longer to learn a song rather than a shorter time. It would seem to me that all choral directors have a time constraint built into their program. They've always got next Sunday's deadline to meet. It would seem better to learn the music quickly rather than your way."

"You've hit on the key issues here," said the director as they made their way to the checkout counter. "Next Sunday's deadline must always be met, but who's going to meet it, the younger children or those who have been in the choir for two or three years?"

"This is my treat," said Bob squeezing his way past the director and getting out his wallet. "I suppose the young kids like to join in all the music that the rest of the children will be singing on Sunday, so it would be good if they could."

"Yes," answered the director, squeezing past Bob to start bagging the food, "but you can't have both; you can't have all the young children singing all the music that the older children sing (assuming they perform pretty frequently) and at the same time, teach them how to read music really well—so well that, when they've been in the choir for a couple of years, you have no note-teaching to do. This is where you have to make a choice."

SHORT-TERM OR LONG-TERM GOAL?

He finished bagging, thanked the assistant who bade them to have a good evening, and led the way out of the store to the car.

"That's where many directors make the wrong choice."

"How do you mean?" asked Bob, yet again, as he wheeled the cart to the parking lot.

"Well, they will never experience the enormous thrill of handing a piece of music to a choir of, say, eleven-year-olds and hear them sing it right at first sight. Or," he added as he opened his trunk, "handing an SATB anthem to a group of senior girls, such as I have here, and finding that they ask if they can sing it in three parts straight away."

"How do you mean?" asked Bob predictably, as they got into the car.

"Well this happened to me only last season," answered the director as he began to drive the short distance to his home. "I gave my girls Stainer's 'God So Loved the World' to sing, and they asked if a third of them could sing the soprano line, a third sing alto and a third of them sing the tenor part an octave higher. They immediately sang the whole anthem absolutely right in three parts, and all I did was to play the bass part, softly, on the piano. I was so thrilled that I got them to sing it like that the following Sunday. They, and the congregation, loved it! And please remember," he continued, "that all these children are local children—they are not hand-picked, but they're the kind of children that go to make up any church choir. The only reason they're special is because I teach them how to be special.

"When children first join your choir, unless you spend time teaching them to read music—which involves keeping them mentally alert through asking constant questions—you'll never experience that sort of thrill I had when the girls sang that anthem in three parts. My older kids do this to me time after time—they're so wonderful that, sometimes, I can hardly stand it," and he laughed as he drove into his short driveway.

21
TWELVE PRACTICAL SUGGESTIONS

TEACHING CHILDREN TO READ MUSIC

"How do you teach your children to read music?" asked Bob as he helped the director unload the car.

"Teaching children to read music is a gift from you to them beyond price," said the director as he unlocked his front door with one hand while balancing an overflowing food bag with the other.

"Alas, so few choir directors enable their children to read really well—so well, in fact, that they can hold their own with many professional adults. That is what we do for them here. I've written a book about it, showing the whole process, stage by simple stage.

"Why don't you unpack the food and start cooking while I go upstairs to get a copy?" And he left Bob in the kitchen surrounded by brown paper bags and everything that he needed to begin cooking a delicious dinner.

A couple of minutes later the director bounded down the stairs holding his book, *Five Wheels to Successful Sight-Singing.* "You'll find everything you need to know in this book about how to teach your singers to read music really well." He opened the book and wrote, *To Bob—may this become as true for you as it is for me,* and signed it.

"Gosh, thanks!" said Bob. "I can't touch it now—my hands are covered in grease—but I'll take it to bed with me tonight and read it."

HANDS UP!

"Speaking of hands," continued Bob as he placed the chicken breasts into a large wok, "why did your children keep on putting up their hands during their practices today? Clearly they weren't asking questions or wanting to leave the room."

"That's another very useful tool to encourage children to think and to take responsibility for their singing. Did you notice when they put up their hands?"

"Yes. They did it when they'd made a mistake. That's a pretty awful thing to ask them to do, isn't it?"

"Why?" asked the director looking Bob straight in the face.

Bob noticed the direct look but continued his argument. "To have to confess in front of their peers that they're dumb seems to be a pretty humiliating situation."

"My dear young man," said the director raising his eyebrows, "you've completely misunderstood the idea of the exercise.

"Look," he said, as he sat on a high kitchen stool watching Bob add spices to the sizzling chicken parts, "don't you realize that the singers who put up their hands were, on the contrary, showing how intelligent they were? They were saying, in effect, 'I made a mistake but I know what the mistake was and so you needn't stop the practice to correct it.'"

"Oh!" exclaimed Bob as he turned his eyes from the nicely browning meat to look at the director, "that puts it in an entirely different light. If a singer makes a mistake and doesn't realize that he's made it, you have to stop and correct him. But if he knows what the mistake was he's unlikely to do it again. How very simple!" And he began to chop up some tomatoes and green peppers to add to the chicken.

"Everything I tell you is simple! Most basic principles are simple, but it often takes a lifetime of experience to realize just how important they are. What could be simpler than the design of the hang glider, and yet no one thought of it until a few years ago.

"Kids, and adults too, really appreciate the opportunity to put up their hands when they've made a mistake or sung something less than perfectly," continued the director, "for it is a direct means of one-on-one communication during a practice between singer and choirmaster. However small or large the choir is, the singer knows that he can send a sort of telegraphic message to the conductor saying, 'Here I am, I know that you spotted my mistake—so did I, and it's okay!'"

"That means," said Bob, "that the conductor has to be very wide awake during practices to spot mistakes. He's really got to listen to what his choir is doing."

LISTEN!

"And about listening," continued Bob as he put the finishing touches to the meal he was preparing, "I noticed that you began the teens' practice by getting them to listen to each other while they were singing the first chord of a hymn."

"Yes, that's one of the most important tools a choirmaster has—to get his or her singers to listen to themselves. Most choir members don't do that and so the actual sound the choir makes is not cohesive, it's just a collection of individual voices that tend not to blend.

"It's the easiest thing in the world to get a choir to make an overall beautiful sound," said the director as he opened a drawer to get knives and forks. "It comes under the heading of achieving just one thing at a time, which is one of my strongest beliefs."

"No one can think of more than one thing at a time and really succeed," he continued as he opened a bottle of wine. "And so instead of telling my choir to blend while they are busy singing an anthem—when their thoughts must be about singing the right notes, singing together, singing in tune, producing their voices well, breathing in the right places and all the other things that a singer has to do—I just ask them to sing one note, the first note of a piece of music, and to listen to the sound they are actually making."

He began pouring a cool, amber liquid into two tall glasses. "I've found, time and time again, not only with my own choirs but also when

I've conducted other choirs, that within five seconds the individual singers realize just what sound they are making and how it relates to those around them. They sing more softly and that immediately leads to a more gracious tone production and an awareness that each singer is part of a greater whole.

"I've learned only one thing from all the books on choirtraining that I've read."

"What's that?"

"'Soft singing cures a host of faults.' That was written by Walter Vale, who was a leading English choirmaster many years ago. I've proved that to be true time and time again. If a choir is singing flat, I get them to sing softly. If they are sharp, I do the same. If they are making a nasty noise I get them to sing the passage softly, and their tone improves immediately. If the choir is overexcited and restless, getting them to sing softly calms them down. It's the musical equivalent of an aspirin."

BLEND

"Wow!" exclaimed Bob as he began to fill two plates with delicious steaming chicken. "I noticed that it really worked with your teens. Some had pleasant voices but others had voices which were potentially rough, for they were still young and unformed."

"Yes," said the director as he arranged two high stools on either side of his counter for himself and his guest. "And you'll have noticed that although they did blend well once they'd listened to themselves singing the first chord, when they began to sing the hymn they immediately reverted to their old ways. What did I do to correct that?"

"You got them to sustain the first chord again and listen to it," said Bob as he brought two plates overflowing with good things to the counter top, "and then once that was right they sang the next chord, listened to it, and then moved on to the third chord, and so on."

The two musicians sat down and lifted their glasses to each other in a toast. "Yes," said the director. "Listening to oneself is a habit that has to be cultivated. If singers can be led to do this at the beginning of a practice and achieve a good blend, then the whole rehearsal will tend to go well."

"And it did," said Bob with a smile. "But why did they find it so easy to hear each other?"

GROUPING SINGERS

"That's easy," said the director through a mouthful of food. "This is delicious—you're a superb chef!"

"And you're a superb choirmaster!" laughed Bob. "Why was it easy for those teens to hear each other?" he repeated.

"Did you notice how I grouped the voices?"

"Oh yes! You had a bass standing next to a soprano who was next to an alto who was next to the tenor. No one stood next to a singer who sang the same voice part."

"That's nearly right. I had a couple of the newest basses standing next to a more experienced bass to help them. But otherwise I mixed up all the voice parts."

"That must have made it difficult for them to sing correctly," observed Bob. "I don't know many church choirs who could manage to do that."

"You're quite right. It does make it more difficult for singers if they have to sustain their own part when the singers either side of them are singing a different part. Your average church choir wouldn't be able to attempt such a grouping without a long-term education process in the art of reading music."

"But your teens achieved it very well."

"Yes, they did—because I'd trained them when they were in third grade to sight-sing and to stand on their own feet musically. When I first came here I did put all the basses together and the altos and the sopranos. But a couple of years ago I asked them to try standing in individual voice groups, as an experiment. At the end of the practice I asked them how they felt about it. I remember the senior girl, Megan, saying, 'We had to work much harder—but we enjoyed it!' Because they had to work harder that meant that they enjoyed the experience more, their journey to church that night was more worthwhile and their singing improved. That's how it's been ever since. Kids, and adults too, enjoy rising to a challenge. That's the whole ethos of the way I run practices. I challenge the singers at every moment to do better than they think they can and, more often than not, they rise to that challenge and come through triumphantly."

He smiled at his empty plate. "I must have some more—tonight's a feast night and the diet can wait!"

Bob got up for a second helping, too. "But what can you do with your average church choir to mix up the voices?" he asked as he replenished his host's plate.

"You can take the principle I used with our newest teen singers. Those who would find it difficult to sing on their own should stand next to a more competent singer. Those who can sustain a part on their own should be encouraged to do so. It's very difficult for one soprano, stuck in the middle of a lot of other sopranos, really to hear herself. It's much easier if she can hear different voice parts around her and hear the overall effect of the anthem."

They resumed their seats and the director refilled their glasses. "In practice, I would suggest that you divide the group in half—with a complete quartet of voices on either side of the aisle: half the basses, tenors, altos, and sopranos grouped together on one side, and half on the other side."

"There'd be some grumbling at that, wouldn't there?"

"That's very perceptive of you!" said the director with a smile. "Yes, there's nothing so conservative as a long-time singer. There's always someone who will say, 'I've sat in this seat for forty years and I'm not going to change now!'"

"How do you get around that situation?"

"You say, 'I'd like to try an experiment, just for one week.' That way the singers know that they can return to their old ways if it doesn't work and so there'll be less opposition."

"That's a crafty move!"

"Yes, but it's also very practical. You need to get your way in matters musical but only with their cooperation. If you don't have their willing cooperation you can't do a thing. It's up to you to discover how best to encourage them to cooperate, and the phrase 'experiment for a limited period' is one way of achieving this. Then get one side of the choir really to listen to the other side. Have them singing separately for a chord or a few measures. That will help them to comprehend the bigger picture of what singing in a choir is all about.

"Once the choir has experienced the new way of grouping," the director continued as he took another mouthful of spicy chicken, "you should find, if you have done your preparation well, that most singers would be happy to continue in the new format. Their singing, both individually and corporately, should have improved. If there is no improvement then, clearly, you should revert to your former seating, for the whole object of the exercise is to raise the standards of your choir."

They ate in silence for a while, savoring the delicious cuisine that Bob had created.

WHY WAIT BEFORE CONDUCTING?

"Creative silence!" said the director unexpectedly.

"What?" asked Bob, his mouth full of food.

"Do you know that silence can be creative—especially just before you begin conducting? That's one of the lessons that I have learned here only quite recently—I can't think why no one told me about it before."

"Please explain."

"Did you notice during the teens practice that, before I conducted them in an unaccompanied anthem, I waited a few seconds before beginning?"

"Oh yes! I remember now. I wondered why you took so long. You gave the chord, looked every singer in the eye and then began. Why did you do that?"

"I did it so that everyone would be wholly focused on the singing, and that takes time. This message was driven home to me after I'd been conducting a warmup rehearsal with my chamber choir a few years ago. The husband of one of my sopranos—a forthright chap who always spoke his mind directly—came up to me just before the concert and said, 'If you waited five more seconds before you started conducting you'd find that everyone would be completely concentrated and ready to begin.'

"I tried it at the concert and found that he was absolutely right! It was just like getting your camera into focus before taking a picture; you have to take time to ensure that it's one hundred percent right, and then you can begin. The choir noticed the difference immediately and I've done it with all my choirs ever since."

"And there's another group of people you have to prepare before your choir starts to sing," added the director enigmatically.

"Who's that?"

"The audience!"

"But I've got my back turned to them! How can I control them?"

"You do it by concentrating entirely upon your choir; raising your arms to begin conducting and waiting for about three seconds before you bring them in. You will hear the audience grow still for you, and you'll know that everyone is ready to hear what you are about to offer them.

"I attended a concert in New York recently," continued the director, "where I heard a superb choir sing a concert in a beautiful church. But the young conductor didn't wait for those three crucial seconds before beginning each piece of music. The audience wasn't ready, there was some coughing and rustling of programs, and so the beginning of each piece was spoiled, even though the choir sang superbly, because the audience was not focused. Try it next time you conduct a concert and you'll see what I mean."

EYE CONTACT

"I'd never thought of doing that," said Bob as he chased the last portion of chicken around the plate with his fork. "I've just assumed that the singers and the audience were ready when I've given the chord."

"Well, they're not," said the director, pushing his empty plate away with a satisfied sigh. "Singers don't come with automatic focus built in. Many conductors are not aware how crucial it is to make eye contact with all their singers before they begin conducting, as well as during the singing of an anthem."

"Tell me exactly what you do."

"I ensure that the singers are ready to begin before the chord is given."

"How?"

"It's vital that every singer really listens to the note, otherwise they won't start in tune. And so you should look at the choir with an embracing glance..."

"What's an embracing glance?" interrupted Bob.

"It's a deliberate looking at the whole choir, from one side to the other, which sends the message 'you and I are now in contact;' it only takes a couple of seconds, but it's like turning on the ignition switch of your car. It means that the power is now on and we're about to go."

"Terrific!" commented Bob, opening his notebook and beginning to write furiously. "I'll have to try that."

BREATHE FOR YOUR CHOIR

"And talking about breathing," said the director, leaning on the counter, "that's another vital part of conducting."

"I thought it was the singers who needed to breathe, not the conductor."

"Wrong! The singers need the conductor to show them when to breathe, and the most important breath of a whole song comes immediately before they begin to sing!"

"Why is that?"

"Because the singers have to begin absolutely together, and the only way they can do that is if they breathe together exactly one beat before they begin. And it's the conductor who directs them in this."

"How's that?"

HOW TO BEGIN CONDUCTING A SONG

"Let me go back to the question you asked me a couple of minutes ago: you wanted to know exactly what I do to begin a piece of music.

1 "I make sure that all the singers are ready, music held well and everyone looking at me, by giving them an embracing glance.

2 "The note is given (if the song is unaccompanied), and I give them a longer embracing glance—for fully five seconds, creating in my own mind the mood of the song, its tempo and especially how the opening phrase should sound. I reflect all this by the expression on my face. If it's a calm song I look calm, if it's an energetic song I look energetic. I focus the essential essence of the song into my whole being so that every singer can feel the message of the song that they are about to re-create.

3 "And then, looking at the choir, I give two preliminary beats; the first leads the choir to breathe in absolutely together and they all start on the third beat. I get them to breathe by breathing very obviously myself, through an open mouth. And my mouth is in the shape of the opening vowel. So it's *one, breathe, start.*

"The singing of a song is like an airplane ride. The most important moment is not the journey itself, but the actual preparation for the take-off. Just think how much care and attention is given to that by the pilot and crew, as well as the passengers, and you'll realize what I mean.

EYE CONTACT AGAIN

"It's also very helpful to raise your eyebrows when you breathe for the choir—it gives them just an extra little push."

"Wow!" exclaimed Bob again, looking at the director as he turned another page in his notebook.

"Although many conductors know these truths in theory, not too many of them put them into practice. I've often noticed, for example, that some conductors lower their eyes to their own copy on the first note. That's exactly the moment when they should be making eye contact with the people who are actually doing the singing. And the trouble is they don't realize it! They need someone to take them on one side after a practice to tell them what they are doing.

"Whenever conductors look at their own music they immediately lose creative contact with their singers. And they look at their music for two reasons."

"What are they?"

"One, they don't know the music well enough; they haven't really done their homework. And two, they think that by looking at the music themselves they're actually helping their singers. They're not. Why?" he asked suddenly.

Bob stopped writing and looked up at him. "Because it's only when you make eye contact with a person that you really connect with him or her," he answered confidently, "just as I'm looking at you right now."

"Well done!" laughed the director, getting up to replenish their glasses for a third time.

"I always thought I did look at my choir," he continued as he poured the remains of the bottle into Bob's glass, "but I learned that this was not so, thanks to an outspoken tenor. (Tenors are often outspoken!) I was once conducting my choral society and having a hard job getting them to respond to my beat, and so I said, 'Why don't you look at me?' One of the tenors responded, 'We'll look at you if you'll look at us!' I thought I was looking at them—but I wasn't! I've always been grateful to that tenor for his timely reproof!"

MARKING SCORES
Bob continued writing for a few moments as the director put the empty bottle into his recycling bin. He glanced at Bob and asked, "What should conductors do to avoid losing contact with their singers when they look at their own music?"

"I suppose they could try to memorize their scores—but that wouldn't be very practical."

"You're quite right. What I do—and I commend this to you very strongly—is to mark my scores."

"How do you mean?"

"Buy a set of colored felt-tip pens or colored crayons and mark every important voice-part entry. You can have one color for sopranos, another for altos, and so on. This is particularly important if you're conducting a polyphonic anthem when singers need to be brought in every few measures. Your own color-code will tell you immediately and very clearly what's about to happen.

He got up from his stool to bring a piece of music from a nearby shelf.

"Look," he said, opening the music, "this is the sort of thing I mean."

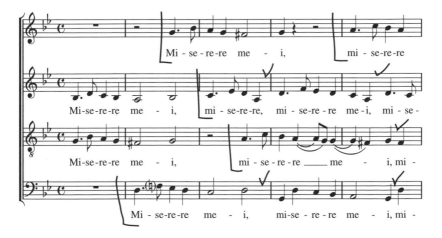

"You should mark your copy so that you can see from six feet away what you have written. In other words what I am saying is that the marks that you make on your score—vocal entries, dynamics, tempo changes and so on—should be so clear that, instead of having to look at your music, and thus lose contact with your singers, all you have to do is to glance at it for a second to remind yourself what is coming up during the next few measures, and then look at your singers again to direct them in what they need to do."

"Golly, that's great!" exclaimed Bob as he put down the director's music and resumed writing in his notebook. "I've sometimes made a few marks in pencil on my scores, but I've always had to look closely at them because they've been hard to decipher when I'm actually conducting."

"The principle of marking in color also applies to conducting an orchestra. Choose one color for woodwind, another for brass, and so on. Of course as orchestral scores often have to be rented one can't actually write on the copy, but you can buy those little semi-adhesive labels and stick them onto the score, suitably marked, and then remove them when the score has to be returned.

BE PREPARED!

"The same principle applies to complicated orders of service. When I was organist of an English cathedral we often had ordinations and other special services. Before each one I used to go through my order of service with colored pens, marking in one color when the choir was due to sing, another color when they had to lead prayers, another when I had to play special music, and so on. It meant that I was wholly confident about my role of leadership because I could see at a glance exactly what I was about to do. And that is the role conductors fill—knowing what they and those under their charge have to do at any one time, and giving directions confidently."

Silence reigned again for a few minutes as Bob wrote energetically in his notebook. He finally looked up. "I suppose I could mark my Sunday service sheet like that, too, although not necessarily in color, because I know what's coming next."

"You're quite right. I always mark my Sunday leaflet—underlining every piece of music that I'm leading and checking that everything is ready in the organ loft and on my conducting stand.

"Nothing is more important than careful preparation before a performance, be it a concert or a regular Sunday service."

22
THE GREAT SECRET

The director put the music back onto the shelf and continued, "Let's take our glasses into the sitting room and relax in more comfortable chairs." And so saying, he led the way into a room whose walls were covered with framed photographs of choirs he had conducted during his long career. They were from all over the world.

"Those are fascinating photos you have," commented Bob as he followed the director into his cozy room.

"Yes, they give me a lot of pleasure, for they remind me of the great privileges I've enjoyed. I've made music with so many wonderful people and I've learned so much from them, and now I'm sharing my experience with you."

"It's very good to be able to talk with you, one-on-one like this," continued Bob as he settled into a low armchair. "Not only am I learning a lot but also I'm getting to know you better."

"You've just defined the Great Secret, Bob," laughed the director.

"What did I say?" asked Bob, sitting up straight.

"You said four things:

1   We are in a one-on-one situation,
2   This enables you to learn a lot,
3   It enables us to get to know one another, and
4   It is very good.

"That's exactly what I do with my singers—and you saw it in action today."

"Yes!" exclaimed Bob, getting out his notebook again. "Nancy Willis taught boys in pairs during one of your practices. Jack Keen had a teaching session with a couple of your teens, and you taught two chorister boys for ten minutes, too. And, of course," he continued, "you're already leading many of your practices with small groups anyway, so your singers are getting a lot of individual attention."

"I wish I'd known the Great Secret when I first began my career," said the director wistfully, "for I would have achieved so much more and my singers would have been much better equipped to enjoy music-making throughout their lives.

"I find that children, and adults too, really enjoy the opportunity to work with me and my assistants in small groups on a regular basis, for by so doing they can learn so much and improve their talents very rapidly."

TWO-ON-ONE

The director took another sip from his glass. "But in practice it's better to work with two singers at a time instead of with one, especially if they are children."

"Why is that?"

"You can induce a friendly rivalry—each one trying to achieve more than the other. That's always a very good principle to use. It's much better for one young singer to demonstrate to the other how a phrase should be sung rather than you trying to show them. Kids love competing with each other, and in that way a singer will remember what he or she has done.

"The other reason is practical, I fear."

"How so?"

"Unfortunately, these days a choirmaster has to protect him- or herself when dealing with children. There's been an increase in unhappy incidents, not only in choirs but in schools as well, and adults can no longer allow themselves to be in a room alone with a child. This is something you have constantly to remember, especially when you're starting in a new job."

"Do you see singers two-on-one in addition to working with your groups of half a dozen or so?"

"Yes, I do, when the schedule permits. Today's schedule was almost continuous, as you saw. One practice following immediately on the heels of another, and so there was no way I could always work with singers in pairs. But I will be seeing two of the senior girls tomorrow at the end of our practice-marathon, and two of our middle-rank boys on Wednesday, whom you've not seen yet. I've made out a roster for the children so that they know whose turn it is every week. And, as you've already noted, this is a good situation; the children love to come early or stay late; they really enjoy their time with me because I really enjoy my time with them!"

PASTORAL CARE

The director put down his empty glass and added, "There's another great advantage in seeing children two-on-one."

"What is it?"

"Well, you defined it already when you said that being here with me enabled us to get to know one another better. In other words, our relationship isn't based solely on musical considerations, but also on other interests—such as your superb cooking. When I'm working with only two students for fifteen minutes before or after a practice, the children not only get to know me better but I also get to know them better, too.

"It's at such times that they feel freer to unload any personal problems they may be wrestling with. My time with them could turn out to be pastorally healing as well as musically educational. Fred Swann, director of music at the Crystal Cathedral in Garden Grove, California, has said that being a choirmaster is being in the people business. You've got to love people as well as love the music if you intend to be a complete choirmaster."

ASSISTANT CHOIRMASTERS?

"You've got the luxury of professional assistants at your church, like Nancy and Jack, who come to help you train the children; I'm virtually on my own at my church, my assistant is very part time—how can I get people to help me?"

"That's a very good point. You'll see tomorrow what I do, because Nancy Willis can only come twice a week to help me train the newer children. I'll have four assistants to help me train the girls tomorrow!"

"Four!" exclaimed Bob, "Where do you get them from?"

"Wait and see!" said the director enigmatically.

23
EIGHT MORE PRACTICAL TIPS

MERIT DOTS

"Tell me about your dots system," said Bob, changing the subject. "I saw that the younger boys all earned a number of them during their rehearsals. How did you start that?"

"Well, my distinguished predecessor used to give merit points to trebles who sang solos or excelled in some other way. He gave them twenty-five cents for each merit. I thought that that was a good idea, but I wanted to extend his system, and so I changed the single merit point, worth twenty-five cents, into a dot, worth ten cents. We could afford that on the music budget and it seemed more useful to give a number of dots instead of only an occasional merit point. The boys and girls quickly accepted this system as a useful way of showing how hard they were trying, and now there's keen competition at every practice to see who can earn the most dots."

"It works out to be pretty expensive, doesn't it?" asked Bob, lying back in his easy chair.

"Yes, it does. A boy or girl could earn half a dozen or more dots per practice, but it's well worth the expenditure. The kids are pleased to get the extra amount of cash in their monthly pay packets."

"That's all very well for you," commented Bob from the deep recesses of his chair, "but I don't have a music budget that can afford such expenditures."

"Well, this is a very good example of what I mentioned to you on Sunday morning after I auditioned the new boy. Adapt appealing ideas to fit your own situation. You'll find that if you present the dots system to your younger singers purely as a means of grading effort and achievement, they'll accept it with enthusiasm...on one condition."

BELIEVE IN WHAT YOU ARE DOING

"What's the condition?"

"That you believe wholeheartedly in what you are doing. I find that if I am enthusiastic about awarding dots, the kids take my lead. If on the other hand I go through a period of not caring, then the kids seem not to care either, even though it means a loss of cash to them. This principle applies to everything you do with people. If you believe in what you are teaching them, if you believe in the values of excellence, if you believe that teaching sight-singing is something really worthwhile, then your children will accept the valuation you put onto things. If, on the other hand, you are in the least half-hearted about any aspect of your role as a choirmaster, then that is the value that all those who work with you will accept. It applies not only to children but also to adults as well.

"And so I suggest that you really make something of your dots system, should you wish to start one. At the end of every month I draw up a list of the top ten dot earners and pin it on my notice board for all to see. I also announce the winners to my kids at their full practice and show my appreciation by shaking their hands. I've also found that the smaller children love to have a copy of the 'top ten dots' list so that they can take it home and show it to their parents."

"Why don't you make a complete list of the dots that every child has earned?"

"For one very good reason. Let me ask you a question, and you can tell me the answer straight away. If I were to do that how would the singer feel who came in last?"

"Oh yes! He or she would feel a failure and you can't do that to a kid—especially in a volunteer choir situation."

"Quite right. We're in the business of encouraging kids, not discouraging them. And so you just pick a few children to honor and then have an encouraging word with the rest to get them to try harder so that they can get their names on the top ten list next month.

"I think the time has come for some ice cream," said the director standing up. "Would you like some, Bob?"

"Yes please," answered his guest as he followed him to the kitchen.

"I've got some rather delicious yogurt ice cream—no fat, no cholesterol," and he got busy preparing the dessert as Bob asked another question.

"I noticed that you asked a lot of questions during your practices today. We talked about that earlier this evening. You said that your aim is to turn ordinary kids into educated, practicing musicians as well as to have a fine choir."

"Absolutely right! One gets a fine choir through teaching them to become practicing musicians. I've said it before and I'll say it again, I have no wish to have a choir made up of parrots who just repeat, mindlessly, what I tell them to do. My kids sing well because they know what they're singing about and they have ownership of the music, because it is they themselves who have worked out how the music should sound. They have just cause to be proud of what they are doing.

"And so," continued the director as he put some fresh strawberries on the top of each helping of ice cream, "my object is to get as much constructive, creative musical instruction into their heads as quickly and as permanently as possible, and the best way to do that is…?" he asked as he led the way back to the sitting room.

"By asking questions, I suppose," answered Bob, following in his wake. "But I don't know why."

"Okay, let me ask you another question and then you can tell me." said the director, handing Bob his bowl of fruity goodness. "If I want you to remember something, is it more likely if I tell you what it is or if you tell me?"

Bob thought for a moment as he tasted his first spoonful of his delicious dessert. "Oh, I'll remember it if I tell you," he answered with a smile. "How very obvious!"

HOW TO GET YOUR SINGERS TO REMEMBER WHAT YOU SAY

"All the best things are obvious. You should know that by now!" grinned the director. "But let me reinforce what you've just said. Some pretty startling figures have been published in educational journals.

"It's been demonstrated by teachers that if they tell their pupils something, only 20 percent of them will remember what they've been told. That's pretty awful, isn't it?"

"Gosh, yes!" exclaimed his guest, putting down his spoon and picking up his notebook. "That means that if I have a choir of twenty singers and tell them to sing a certain phrase softly, only four of them will remember to do it next time. That's pretty depressing!"

"If, on the other hand, you write the instruction on your chalkboard, then 30 percent will remember next time."

"That's not much better," said Bob. "It still means that fourteen singers will have forgotten."

"True. But if you tell them and they also see it written down, the figure jumps to 50 percent. Will that do?"

"No, it won't, for there's still half the choir getting it wrong next time. How can I get it into their heads so that they all remember?"

"This is where asking questions comes in," said the director leaning forward in his seat as he warmed to the subject. "If, instead of me telling them what to do, they tell me..."

"By you asking them the right question," interrupted Bob, with rising excitement.

"Yes, by asking them the right question, then the percentage of those who will remember goes up to 70 percent."

"But what is a right question?"

"Good question," laughed the director. "But we went through all that last Saturday, don't you remember?"

Bob thought furiously for a minute and then said, "Oh yes! Always ask questions so that the students will have to think, but also so that their minds will be focused on the subject you are addressing. And so," he concluded triumphantly, "You always ask 'Is it (a) or is it (b)?'"

"Quite right, young man!" said the director, pleased that some of his teaching was sinking in. 'Is it a half note or is it a quarter note?' 'Were you singing too softly or too loudly?' And, if they get the answer wrong, what do you say?" he asked with a grin.

"You say 'Nearly!'" responded Bob immediately, "which encourages the child to have another try and get the answer right!"

"Okay! Well, having got that sorted out, let me repeat my question: Is 70 percent success satisfactory when you are teaching?"

"It's getting better all the time, but there are still six singers in my choir of twenty who will forget next time. Clearly you haven't finished yet. How can I get them all to remember?" he asked eagerly.

"If they tell you what they should do, and then you get them, immediately, to do what they have said they should do, the percentage goes right up to 90 percent. Choir practices are all about actually doing, not theorizing about doing. It's no good saying to a choir, 'That note was wrong today—sing it right on Sunday.' You've got to get them to sing it correctly now! Singing is a wholly practical matter."

"But tell me, please, how I can improve on the 90 percent figure we've reached, for there are still two people in my choir who won't remember next time!" pleaded Bob.

"You get them to do it again! Repetition is a successful mode of teaching. Repetition is a successful mode of teaching!" and he laughed. "That should bring your percentage up to 95 percent or beyond," the director concluded as he helped himself to another spoonful of ice cream, "and you can't get much better than that."

"Wow!" exclaimed Bob, "that's terrific."

SINGING WITH UNDERSTANDING

"There's an old Chinese proverb which sums the whole thing up nicely:

I hear and I forget,
I see and I remember
I do and I understand.

"The motto of the Royal School of Church Music is I Will Sing with Spirit and I Will Sing with Understanding Also. Their whole organization is geared to help us do just that; I strongly urge you to become a member so that you can enjoy all the benefits that they offer.

"We're in the business of getting our kids, and our adults, to understand what they are doing; to understand the meaning of the notes as well as to understand the meaning of the words. If you're determined to train a choir on those lines, blessed are you indeed!"

PLAYING IN SUB-OCTAVES

"I notice that you sometimes played the tune in sub-octaves today. Why did you do that?"

"I did it so that the children could hear clearly what I was playing. If you play a tune at the same pitch in which the singers are singing they can't really hear it. But if you playing it in sub-octaves, then the singers can hear those lower notes immediately, and you don't have to play loudly, either."

"I've not met any directors who do that," commented Bob.

"Neither have I," smiled the director, "but it's such a simple thing to do and it's wholly practical and it works!"

GIVE THE HARMONIC BASIS

"There's another thing you should do when you're accompanying your choir on the piano," he added.

"What's that?"

"Always play the harmony of a melody you are demonstrating. A tune has no life of its own unless it has a harmonic basis. That's another example of something that most directors don't do—they just play the tune and expect the choir to get it right. A tune often makes no sense unless its harmony is there to give it a firm foundation.

"Of course, you will have noticed that I hardly ever had to do that today. Why?"

"Because all your kids can read music," responded Bob. "They can work out most tunes for themselves without any help from you."

"Yes, that's what makes practices so thrilling for me and for the children, and also the adults," responded the director with enthusiasm. "And I make no apology for pushing this matter of teaching sight-singing down your throat at every opportunity, for it is central to my whole *credo* as a choirmaster, and many directors don't do it!"

WALK AMONG YOUR SINGERS

"There's another thing I noticed you did today, which few other choirmasters do."

"What's that?" asked the director with interest.

"I'll turn the tables on you this time by asking you the right question so that you can give me the right answer," laughed Bob.

"Okay, shoot!"

"Did you spend the whole of your practices behind the piano?"

"Oh no! I often got up to walk among the singers—to look them straight in the face as they were singing so that I could hear what they were doing and to encourage them to continue working hard."

"Did you confine yourself to walking along the front row of the choirdesks?" asked Bob, pressing home his initiative.

"No, I also walked along the back rows so that those who were farthest from me when I was playing the piano also knew that I wanted them to do well."

"Why did you do that?"

"I did it to keep alive my personal interest in every singer, to let them know that I really cared how they were doing. It's so easy for singers who are sitting in back rows to let their attention wander and to feel no real contact with the choirmaster. If you make the effort to exercise your right to walk around the entire practice room, back rows as well as front rows, and to look choir members in the face as they are singing, then they will immediately feel a lively contact with you, which will last for some time after you've returned to your place behind the piano. They will pay more attention to what you say and so their standard of singing will improve immediately."

"That may work for kids, but you wouldn't do it with your adults, would you," observed Bob.

"Oh yes I would, and I do!" retorted his host. "It takes a measure of courage on the part of choirmasters to walk up to adults who may be older than they are and look them straight in the face as they are singing: it repays enormous dividends. But you must be encouraging in the way you do it, not judgmental. The singers must feel better for your visit, not worse!

"Of course," continued the director as he collected Bob's empty dessert bowl, "it is a threatening situation for singers to have someone walk up to them as they are singing and to listen to them for a few seconds. But that's what choirtraining is all about. It's all to do with challenging your singers to do better and better, and it seems to me that there's no greater challenge than to put yourself on a one-on-one situation with every singer in your choir at least once every practice. Try it for yourself and see what happens!"

WHO IS IN CHARGE OF YOUR CHOIR?

"I don't know if I dare," responded Bob. "Some of my singers are old enough to be my parents, or even grandparents!"

"Who's in charge of your choir, you or they?"

"I am, of course!"

"Well, accept your responsibility, however much it may cost you. You'll never know unless you try it!"

The director stood up again and asked, "Would you like some coffee?"

"No thanks, it'll keep me awake all night and it's already late. I think I'll go to bed."

"I agree," responded the director. "I'll put these plates in the dishwasher and come to bed myself, for tomorrow is another busy day."

"What's your program for Tuesday?" asked Bob as he followed the director into the kitchen.

"I've got a staff meeting, which will last for most of the morning, and then there'll be some paperwork to get through. But I could come home for lunch and then take you down to the church for our five hours of rehearsals." .

"Five hours!" exclaimed Bob. "Who are you rehearsing tomorrow?"

"Well, there are three hours of rehearsing the girls choir, then, after a break, I have two grueling hours with my chamber choir. I shall be pretty exhausted after all that and so we'll come straight home afterwards."

"Right! I'll see you in the morning then. Thank you for a tremendous day; I've learned so much and written so many notes that I'll need the whole morning to sort them all out. Sleep well!"

The director smiled as he tidied up his kitchen. Bob was a wonderfully responsive guest who, clearly, had a great future as a choirmaster. Both of them had thoroughly enjoyed the day's exchanges. He looked forward to an equally constructive time on the morrow when he would share more practical secrets about choirtraining. He turned the light out and walked upstairs. The day had been very good.

♪ TUESDAY ♪

24
CHURCH STAFF MEETINGS

STAFF PRAYERS

The director's bedside alarm rang at 7:00 the next morning; he rolled over in his bed and hastily turned it off. "It mustn't wake Bob in the next room," he thought.

He got up and padded down to the kitchen to make himself a cup of tea, which he took into his sitting room; he had work to do. It was his turn to lead the church staff prayers that morning and so he marked in his bible and prayer book the lessons, a psalm and prayers set for next Sunday's services which he was to read. He studied them carefully, noting a few passages that puzzled him. "I'll get the clergy and lay staff members discussing those points this morning," he thought. "The only way to bring these fifteen-minute worship sessions alive is to involve everyone and get us all talking to each other."

He made his way back to the kitchen and helped himself to his own peculiar mixture of six cereals, orange juice, nonfat yogurt and grapes, which he stirred together into a gooey mess in a breakfast bowl. "It's a good thing Bob's still in bed, the sight of this might make him want to throw up!" While he was eating it, he boiled an egg, made some toast and prepared a thermos of cocoa to see him through the morning's business.

Half an hour later, clothed and in his right mind, he was just about to creep out of the house when the spare bedroom door opened and a tousled head appeared.

"Good morning, Bob," said the director in an unbearably cheerful voice, "did you sleep well?"

"No!" croaked his visitor, "I stayed awake until 3:00 A.M. reading your book on sight-singing. I was so interested that I couldn't put it down. I read it through twice, nonstop. I feel pretty awful right now, but I think I understand how simple it is to teach kids, and adults, to read music."

"I wish more choirmasters realized that," smiled the director looking up the stairs at his unkempt guest. "We'd have much finer choirs in this country, and elsewhere, if they realized how easy it is to achieve.

STAFF MEETING

"Well, I'm just off to lead the staff prayers at church and to chair the weekly staff meeting."

"Chair the staff meeting?" echoed Bob in amazement, "Why doesn't your minister do that?"

"Oh, he does, when his turn comes around. But he's introduced the great idea that each member of the core staff, not only the clergy, but also the leader of the church school and the office supervisor, take turns chairing the full staff meeting. It really gets us involved in everything that's going on. There's an unspoken competition between us to see who can chair the shortest meeting! I hold the record at present, but there's so much to discuss this morning I'll also probably hold the record for the longest!

"We always spend the first five minutes deliberately saying appreciative things about each other—such as last week's sermon or how well the choir sang an anthem—it's a great way to get goodwill flowing. You know how important it is to begin a practice well; the first few minutes define how the rest of the rehearsal will go. It's the same with our staff meeting, or any meeting, come to that. You might want to see if you can introduce the idea of circulating chairmen to the staff meeting at your church!"

"I don't think our minister's ready for that," smiled Bob—it was too early to laugh—"but I can see that it would get you all pulling together in a constructive and cooperative way."

"That's what all church staffs should do and be," said the director as he opened his front door. "I must hurry or I'll be late. I'll be back for lunch and we can talk some more," and he closed the door quietly behind him as he made his way to the garage. Bob also closed his door behind him and retired back to bed; he had some sleeping hours to catch up on.

25
BASIC SINGING TECHNIQUES

Four hours later the director walked through his front door to find his guest in the kitchen preparing lunch.

"Well," commented the director, "you look better than you did first thing this morning!"

"Yes, it's amazing what an extra couple of hours sleep will do," responded Bob cheerfully as he stirred a saucepan of delicious vegetable soup. "I found these ingredients in your fridge," he said, "I hope you don't mind."

"Be my guest!" laughed the director, sitting on one of his bar stools. On the counter top were two plates of tuna salad with cole slaw and tomatoes and a couple of glasses of freshly squeezed orange juice. "Let's get started."

"I'm looking forward to seeing you work with your girls' choir this afternoon, for I really need to know how to get children to sing easily," said Bob as he brought a couple of large mugs of steaming soup to the counter top.

"Well, you saw a lot of that yesterday when I was working with the boys. It's just the same when working with girls."

"Yes, but could you outline for me the basic essentials of how to get kids to sing easily—how to produce their voices so that they make a lovely sound?"

"Certainly! Get your notebook out and I'll run through them—they're very simple. I learned many of them from watching Frauke Haasemann when she and I led a course together. She was marvelous."

RELAXING TECHNIQUES

The director took a quick sip of soup and began. "Singers must always be relaxed. So many children, and adults, tend to tighten up when they're singing. The first few minutes of your practice should be spent in helping your singers to let go of all tensions.

"They should stretch their arms up high to try to reach the ceiling and then bend right down to touch the floor, dangling their arms loosely. This, like most exercises, should be repeated several times.

"Then they should roll their shoulders forwards and backwards in circles. This helps to get blood to the vocal cords, and they need blood to work! By the way, eating before a practice takes blood away from the vocal cords. Next, lift one shoulder to an ear, then the other. Roll the head right round several times, first one way and then the other.

"Children and adults love these exercises. What's more, everyone is equal in this regard."

"How do you mean?"

"In any choir there are those who have fine voices and those who are less gifted. But in these relaxing exercises everyone can do them equally well. Doing them together gets the practice off to a good start."

He drank a little more soup and continued, "I often find that, when singers seem to have a problem in singing higher notes, it's due to tightening up."

"What do you do when that occurs?"

"I get them to bend over slightly so that their arms dangle loosely in front of them and then I ask them to sing a gentle *Oo* from a note or so below where they began tightening up. I then gradually raise the pitch. They should imagine that the sound is going straight through the top of their heads. It's important that they are thoroughly relaxed everywhere, especially in their necks and jaws, for that's often where the tension occurs. If they stick their jaws out, that's a sure sign of tension."

POSTURE

Bob snatched a mouthful of tuna salad and resumed writing as the director continued.

"Your children, and of course your adults, need to stand well."

"What about sitting?" interposed Bob. "Many choirs rehearse sitting down."

"True. It's best if you consciously mix standing and sitting, as long as the singers do both well. My choirs prefer to stand through all their practices.

They have movable, adjustable choir desks in the practice room. When your singers sit, you must ensure that they sit forward in their chairs, with their bottoms away from the back rest. Too many singers slump when they sit down, and that is not helpful for good vocal production."

"That's not easy to accomplish, is it?"

"No, it isn't. You will have to decide if you really mean it when you say 'sit tall,' for they will push you time and time again by sitting back in their chairs. But if you once establish that sitting tall is what you expect, then you will tend to get it.

"Singers must stand firmly with their chests held proudly, but not stiffly, shoulders down and pulled a little way back. Hands should not be behind their backs, for that makes the shoulders tense.

"The head should feel that it is resting gently on the spine with plenty of room to move.

"Faces should have a happy expression with eyebrows raised, and the jaw should feel heavy—it should hang down of its own weight. Again, I must stress that jaws, or chins, should not stick out; if anything, they should be held a little in to ensure that they are relaxed.

"When singers hold books they should be held away from the body in such a way that the singer can see the page, see the conductor, and allow plenty of room for the sound to be unobstructed.

"You'll have to polish all these points time and time again, for most singers will tend to relapse into a lazy slouch unless they are prodded!"

BREATHING

The director took a long drink of orange juice and continued, "Singers succeed or fail through their breathing."

"What do you mean?"

"Well, think of the organ; if the wind supply is unsteady or inadequate, no matter how good the pipework is, the instrument will make a nasty noise.

"And so singers must, from their very first practice with you, be taught to breathe well. I cannot over-stress this. In very large measure, your success as a choirmaster hangs upon it. Singing is all about producing long phrases in one breath sung with lovely tone—and it's all based on good breathing technique.

"When you ask children to take a deep breath you'll find that they almost always raise their shoulders and become tense. This has to be overcome very quickly, otherwise you'll get nowhere with your new singers.

"Good breathing is based upon breathing low, right down in the diaphragm. Singers need to be taught to feel their diaphragms. Frauke used to say in her classes that it was like a trampoline under the lungs. Singers should put one hand on their tummy and the other hand on their side and feel the trampoline moving as they breathe in deeply.

"I tell the children that it's like having a balloon down there, which they must fill with air. First they need to exhale, getting rid of all the air, like blowing out candles on a birthday cake. They will feel their hands going in. And when they breathe in deeply, as low as possible, they will feel their hands moving outwards."

"I would imagine that most children can do this pretty quickly," commented Bob as he divided his time between writing and snatching a bite of lunch.

"Alas, that is not the case. You'll almost certainly have to spend a lot of time with new children at every practice until they've really got it.

"I find that it's often helpful for a child to feel your tummy when you're breathing. That's one of the matters that you, as a new choirmaster, will have to be very careful about. It's okay for the child to touch you, but it's not okay for you to touch the child.

"Another helpful thing is to get the child to lie down flat on the floor to practice breathing. It's almost impossible to breathe incorrectly when you're lying down. Once a child realizes what he or she is doing and how the tummy is going in and out, up and down, it's only a short step to get them to do that when they're standing tall."

The director paused for a minute, for his soup was getting cold and he'd hardly touched his salad.

He continued: "Once children can breathe in and out correctly you need to show them how to use the technique they've acquired."

"Give me an example."

"Get them to breathe in low and deeply, and then exhale on a hiss, as you count. Get a spirit of competition going between the children to see who can hiss for the longest time. Start with counting up to ten, one count per second, and then gradually increase it. I've found that some children can reach thirty or even forty in one breath, and that's very exciting.

FORMING TONE

"And then you need to begin forming tone."

"How do you do that?"

"Get the children, while they're still concentrating on their breathing technique, with hands on their tummies and at their sides, to sing a continuous Oo for ten or more counts."

"Should you start on a low note or a higher note?" asked Bob.

"I'd begin on G above middle C, and then go up, by half steps to D while the children are singing Oo for counts of ten or more. From D, I change to the vowel Aw and then to Ah as they sing even higher.

"By singing Oo really well, they find that they have to push their lips forward into a trumpet shape. It's almost impossible to sing badly if your lips are pushed slightly forward. So many children in other choirs pull their lips backwards as they try to sing higher; they look as though they are being strangled and they certainly sound as though they are! Forward lips help to correct this problem.

"Too many choirmasters start their children's warming up exercises so low that kids sing with chest voices nearly all the time and cannot sing the high notes that God had equipped them to use. Being a kid in a choir is all about singing top Gs easily, and they won't be able to do that if you start them on middle C!"

He collected their empty plates and cups and took them over to the sink as Bob continued to write. "That was delicious—thank you. Would you like some coffee?"

"Yes please," said Bob, not looking up. He had learned so much during lunch time that he wanted to make sure he got it all down in writing.

The director busied himself with kettle and coffee grinder as he said, "By the way, another useful thing I learned from Frauke is that singers should breathe in with their mouth shaped to the vowel that they are about to sing. That's a wonderful thing to know. And she also said that one should inhale quickly with a faintly surprised look on the face—raised eyebrows somehow seem to help tone formation. I've tried it with my children and it really works.

"Another useful tone formation technique is consciously to hum the *M* or the *N* when they sing 'Moo' or 'Noo' for warm ups. 'Mmmmmm-ooo' and 'Nnnnnn-ooo' are useful devices to get children to sing with open throats and to cultivate head resonance."

"What about the chest voice?" asked Bob as he watched the director pouring boiling water into his coffee maker.

"The chest voice should be brought into operation below F above middle C. Children should sing the vowel *Ee* to cultivate this and feel the vibrations on their chest. The chest doesn't vibrate when they sing with head tone. But I would caution you not to get into chest tone until the children can sing with head tone really well."

"Why?"

"Because so few children sing with head tone in the choirs that I've encountered. They find that singing with a chest voice comes more easily because that's the way they've been taught. They find themselves trapped within the interval of a ninth or so, from middle C to D, because so many choirmasters think that that is what a child's voice should do—and they are wrong, wrong, wrong!" He began to do the dishes in the sink very vigorously to get rid of his frustration. "You'll find that so much of the music that is published for children's voices these days is composed within this range—and so much of it is rubbish! I'm editing some real music for children's voices, which explores the higher notes, as well as the lower ones. But I feel like I'm fighting a lone battle at present," he added sadly as he poured two mugs of steaming coffee and brought them to the counter top.

HOW CAN CHOIRMASTERS
ENCOURAGE THEIR CHILDREN TO REMEMBER?

"I suppose that children easily remember to put their breathing techniques into practice once they start singing songs," observed Bob as he took a deep drink of coffee.

"No, they won't," said the director. "That's something you will constantly have to bring to their attention throughout every practice, especially in their early days in the choir."

"Oh well, I must remember to tell them, over and over again, what they should be doing."

The director, with great self-control, put his coffee mug gently on the counter, for he felt like throwing it at his guest. "My dear young man, will you never learn?" he said quietly but very firmly. "That is exactly what you will not do. I thought we'd been through all that last night, or has your disturbed sleep erased it from your mind?" He stood up. "I'm going to lie down for an hour to prepare for the marathon of rehearsals I'm leading tonight. Why don't you look through your notes and try to remind yourself of at least some of the basic essentials that we've been discussing." And, so saying, he took his coffee mug with him upstairs leaving a bewildered Bob behind him wondering just how a choirmaster can remind his singers to breathe well, and do everything else that they should be doing, without telling them!

26
HOW MANY PRACTICES?

An hour later the director emerged from his bedroom looking refreshed and ready for the rigors of the remainder of the day. He found Bob still sitting in the kitchen, revising his notes. "I must apologize for walking out on you as I did," said the director as he filled a kettle, "but I was feeling a little tired after a long morning. I shouldn't have done that."

"That's okay," said Bob. "You really made me think. I *can* help my kids remember, without actually telling them, all the things they have to do."

"Great!" responded his host as he cut a couple of slices of cake. "I won't even ask you what the answer is, because it's so obvious, isn't it!"

"It certainly is, and I won't forget it now," said Bob gratefully.

"Have a cup of tea before we go and a slice of cake to keep you going," said the director, carrying a steaming mug and a laden plate to his guest.

"Thanks." He took a bite of cake and asked, "How many practices do you have for the girls each week?"

"We have only one. I wish it could be more, for the girls are so keen, but there just aren't enough days in the week to fit them in. However, I pack so much into their rehearsals that we achieve a great deal and they sing really beautifully."

"How often do they sing in church?"

"Twice a month. The boys sing every Sunday, with the men, so they rehearse twice a week. They also progress twice as fast as the girls because of the number of hours they put in. If I had even more assistants I would be happy to increase the number of rehearsals the girls have—it wouldn't be difficult to arrange, and their standard would shoot up even further. But let's get going," and he led the way out of the house to his car.

"The more practices you have the better your choir will be," he said as he backed his car out of the driveway. "A few years ago, I directed a week's course for the children's choirs of one of the most prestigious churches on the West coast. They have an enormous church with a superb program. I was very impressed. However, the minister only allowed their children's choirs to rehearse once a week, on Sunday mornings. He told their director that he couldn't have the children at any other time."

"That must have been very hard for the music director," commented Bob as the car sped along a straight country road lined with trees and pleasant houses.

"Yes, it was. He couldn't achieve much with those children for they sang in church only once every month. But I managed to get quite a lot done with them during that week and encouraged them to reach standards they'd never dreamed possible.

"At the end of the course one boy, whom I helped, came over to me in floods of tears and said, 'Oh, sir, what can I do to get better?' My heart went out to him, for he was very gifted and so keen."

"What did you do?" asked Bob as the car entered the town.

"Well, I'd discovered an article that the minister had written in which he'd said that everything was possible if you believed that it could be done. I wrote a letter to the choirmaster, quoting what his minister had said. I recommended that he double the number of practices for all his kids, and to tell his minister that he was only following his lead!"

"What happened?"

"Well, a couple of months later I had a call from the choirmaster who said that he was now holding four practices every week for his children, and that they could come to any two of them. 'But they're so keen,' he said, 'that most of them come to all four!' I was thrilled, and so was he and so, of course, were his children."

"Wow!" exclaimed Bob as the car pulled into the church parking lot, "that's given me a lot to think about, for my kids have only had one rehearsal a week. I must see how I can get them in more often."

"If you lead your practices in the way I've been showing you and also spend a lot of time with children in pairs, working with graded training cards and also giving them worthwhile music to sing, nothing can stop you," said the choirmaster with a broad grin as he locked the car and led the way into the choir room. "That sums up my whole *credo* for training children. "

27
GIRLS' PRACTICES

For the next three hours Bob watched as the director led three separate practices for girls.

TWO ASSISTANT CHOIRMASTERS FOR THE NEW GIRLS

First he had four new girls to whom he gave training cards. He introduced the basic principals of singing, starting with breathing. He spent five minutes showing them how to breathe correctly; three of the girls did very well, but the fourth seemed to have problems. Her tummy went in when she inhaled and came out when she exhaled and nothing that the director could do seemed to be able to help her. However, he complimented her on her effort and on the way she was standing, which made her feel good about the situation.

He then introduced them to the concept of the G clef, much in the same manner as he had done with the new boys the previous day. He was in the middle of explaining a point to them when two more girls walked in. They were only a year or two older than the new girls.

"Hello Emily, hello Lea," he said. "How good to see you. You're just in time to help Kate with her breathing. Why don't you take her into the next room and show her how simple it is to breathe. And then, when you can do it," he said to Kate, "come back again so that you can show me. Off you go." And the three girls ran off looking excited.

Wow, thought Bob from his place at the far end of the room, those must be two of the extra choirmasters the director was talking about last night. What a great idea to use older girls to help the younger ones. I must remember that!

The practice continued for ten more minutes and then the three girls returned. The director stopped what he was doing with the other new girls and asked Kate to show him how she should breathe. She did it well. Everyone was delighted, the director, the other new girls, Kate and also her two young teachers.

"Well done, everyone!" said the director. "Now, Emily and Lea, I'd like you to take Sarah and Susan out to teach them the names of the notes on the spaces in the treble stave. Kate and Allison know them already, for they have piano lessons." And the girls went off with their mentors, leaving the director free to teach the other two girls.

The remainder of the practice continued in the same way; the director gave the older girls simple teaching tasks to fulfill with one or two younger girls while he continued teaching the others. The time flew by and it soon came time to stop. Every new girl had passed at least one test and they all felt very excited about the progress they had made, and the director shared in their pleasure.

THE BEST WAY TO LEARN

The director delivered the new girls to their waiting parents and told them how well they'd all done, which the parents could see quite plainly, for their daughters were glowing with delight. Then he came back into the practice room for his next rehearsal.

"You see what I mean about having assistant choirmasters ready to help out?" he said to Bob as he drank a cup of cocoa from his thermos flask.

"Yes, I do; it worked wonderfully," said Bob with a smile.

"The best way to learn is…is to do what?" he asked.

"The best way to learn is to teach!" responded Bob immediately. "Those two girls learned a lot themselves by helping your new recruits. They really know how to breathe now, and also what the names of the notes are on the treble stave."

"Yes, and it makes them so enthusiastic to feel that they are part of my teaching team. They can't come early every week, but there's nearly always some who do, and I can always make use of them."

WARMUPS FOR MIDDLE-RANK GIRLS

The next practice was with twelve girls who'd been in the choir for one or two years, including Emily and Lea, who were giving a very good lead to all the singing. Bob noticed that, after the relaxing exercises, the director asked the girls on his left to sing the B-flat above middle C to *Oo*. They did, and it was right, without the pitch being given on the piano.

"Wow!" thought Bob, observing closely what was going on.

The four girls on his left sustained the *Oo* as he said to four girls in the center, "Sing me a D," and they did, sustaining the interval of a major third with the first set of girls. "Sing me an F," he commanded the remaining girls on his right, and they immediately completed the triad of B-flat major to *Oo* breathing whenever they had to.

What a great sound that is! thought Bob, and he hasn't played a note on the piano yet.

"Up a half step," commanded the choirmaster, and the triad changed to B major. "And another to *Aw*,"—C major, "and one more,"—C-sharp major.

"Right, let's have some scales, starting with E major," and the choirmaster led the girls into that scale, singing to a clear *Ah* downwards and upwards, sustaining the last note for four counts. He then got them to sing scales in triads, in the same way that the chorister boys had the previous day. They didn't succeed quite as well as the boys, but then, they were younger. However, every girl tried very hard indeed, and the director showed that he was pleased with them.

TWO ASSISTANT CHOIRMASTERS
FOR THE MIDDLE-RANK GIRLS

During the warmups, two older girls had crept into the room and were looking on admiringly. "Now the two head girls are here," the director told the junior girls impressively. "Aren't our young ladies doing well today?" he asked them.

"They certainly are," said Jenny. Bob remembered that she'd been presiding at the ice cream stall two days before. Her companion nodded in agreement.

"Come along, Jenny and Maya, and see what we're doing. Then I'll ask you to take out one or two of the girls to give them your special help."

The practice proceeded on its way with the director spending a lot of time on two or three hymns and a page or two of a simple anthem while the two head girls walked round looking over the shoulders of the young singers and helping them when they needed it.

During the course of the practice, it was clear that several of the girls were experiencing some problems, either being unable to follow notes wholly accurately with their fingers or not being quite sure how many beats a dotted-half note was worth. Whenever that occurred, the director asked one of the head girls to give some one-on-one instruction to the girl who needed it. Invariably the girl returned a few minutes later wreathed in smiles, both from the new knowledge she had gained and also, even more importantly, because she had had the personal attention of one of the head girls for five minutes.

He also asked the head girls to take several singers for tests. "Jenny, why don't you take Clare for her clapping rhythm test. I think she's ready to pass it. See if you can get her through it in ten minutes." Clare took her training card and eagerly followed Jenny out of the room. She had been in the choir for nearly two years and was clearly well on her way to becoming a senior singing girl.

Throughout this practice, as with the practice for the youngest girls, the director made a point of giving a dot to every girl who showed that she was trying particularly hard or who had succeeded in singing a couple of measures correctly by herself. Girls who'd been taken out for special instruction automatically received a dot, and they earned an extra dot when they successfully demonstrated what they had been taught.

The director was careful to mix solo singing with singing in groups and singing all together, so that every girl felt wholly involved all the time. Not a moment was wasted and, by the end of the practice, every girl felt that she'd learned something new and was one step nearer to being promoted to the next grade up.

When the practice was over and the young girls going out were being replaced by the senior girls coming in, the director drank another cup of cocoa and came over to speak with Bob. "Aren't the girls delightful?" he asked. "Really, they are such a joy to work with, for they are so willing and you don't have to spar with them as you do with boys!"

"Your two head girls are great, too," observed Bob who been greatly impressed by the maturity of Jenny and Maya. "And how the little girls loved to be with them."

"Yes. I feel that they can learn as much, or more, from the head girls as they do from me. There's an element of hero worship, which can be harnessed so positively."

REHEARSING SENIOR GIRLS

The director screwed the top back onto his thermos flask and said, "Well, this next practice is one of the finest of the week."

"I thought the others I'd seen were pretty good," responded Bob in amazement.

"Yes, but these older girls are very special. They're made up of senior singing girls, and junior and senior choristers. You'll see that we mix the girls up so that an older girl stands next to a younger one. Teaching singing is like teaching Christianity. It's better caught than taught!

"They can all read music, of course, for they've been in the choir for at least three years, and many of them have really beautiful voices. They're also very busy with school and sporting activities, and of course six of them are in the men and boys' choir—you saw them last night at our teens' rehearsal. Those girls sing in both choirs, and they spend at least six hours here every week. Most of them are in high school, but one or two are younger—they've shown by their application and achievement when they were in the group that's just left that they can hold their own with the older girls."

The director went to his chalk board and wrote a list of music that they were to rehearse, plus the names of those who would be late or could not come that night. And so the practice began.

The director got the girls singing Oo in triads as he had the previous group, and Bob noticed that he went round all the girls looking them straight in the face as they were singing. Bob thought, He's saying, in effect, "I know you're here, and you know that I know you're here, and that I appreciate your presence." What a great thing to do! And he made a note in his rapidly filling notebook.

The girls were wonderful indeed. They sang a great range of music, from a couple of simple hymns, a Bach aria, through a Lassus motet in two parts with half the girls singing the tenor part an octave higher (they read it almost 100 percent accurately the first time), to a fairly complicated anthem by Stanford that kept changing key and meter. The last twenty minutes were spent reading through much of Britten's *St. Nicolas* cantata, which they would be singing with the other choirs at Christmas. The girls had their own special parts to sing, which were rather tricky because they were so fast and came at awkward moments in the composition.

And to think that those girls can sing all that music almost perfectly right away because the director spent a year or two teaching them to read music when they were younger, thought Bob admiringly. Teaching sight singing certainly pays enormous dividends and makes the leading of practices a real joy. There's nothing that those girls cannot do—except, perhaps, sing bass!

TWO ON ONE

After the practice was over, Bob watched as the director spent fifteen minutes with two of the younger girls, Kathe and Elizabeth, who needed a little extra help. He began by asking them to sing a few scales to give them confidence. "That's a lovely mouth, Kathe," he said. And then he complimented Elizabeth on the beautiful sounds she was making.

Even though they'd been singing hard for an hour, both girls still showed enormous enthusiasm and gave the director their full attention as he went on to explain to them the intricacies of dotted-eighth notes and leaps of a minor seventh, which had occurred in one of the anthems they'd been singing. He noticed that the director first explained the theory of each concept to them very simply and then immediately got them to turn it into practical singing. By the end of the fifteen minutes the girls had mastered what they'd been unsure of earlier. They left the room happily, picking up their school bags that were full of books for their homework.

28
FOUR MORE PRACTICAL SECRETS

STANDARDS OF ATTENDANCE AND PUNCTUALITY

"Well, I think we deserve some food," said the director rather wearily. It had been a very busy three hours. "I've got to get back my energy for the last session tonight. My chamber choir is the most demanding group of singers I have ever met!"

"Why is that?" asked Bob as he followed the director out of the music building.

"Because they are so incredibly talented; many of them are professional musicians in their own right. One of them even has a doctorate in choral conducting—how do you think that makes me feel? Some of them have at least an hour's car journey to get here after a hard day's work, plus the return journey afterwards, and so I must make it thoroughly worth their while. I can only do that if I am in top form physically, mentally and musically, and so let's go get some calories!"

They walked along in silence and reached some traffic lights, which were against them. "I noticed that you make a point of informing each choir which members would be late and who would be absent," Bob observed as they waited at the curbside.

"Yes, punctuality and regularity of attendance are two of the cornerstones to what we do here," answered the director shifting from one foot to the other, because he was very hungry. "If you allow attendance to slip and become indifferent to punctuality, then the whole spirit of your choir will begin to break up."

CONSULT YOUR MINISTER WHEN
DIFFICULT DECISIONS HAVE TO BE MADE

"Several of my choir members in Seattle have told me that they can only come occasionally to practices," remarked Bob as the lights changed and they began to cross the road. "What should I do about that?"

"You should think very carefully indeed about that from every angle and consult your minister as well as respected members of your choir, for it will affect them all. Never take any major action without consultation, especially when you are in a new job, for you won't know the factors that are involved."

"How do you mean?"

"Well, one of those who cannot come may have been a generous donor to the church, perhaps even giving the organ or a stained glass window. You cannot throw people out of your choir who have shown such devotion to the church. But equally," he continued, as he led the way down a long flight of stairs into a restaurant, "you cannot run a successful choir program with members who don't turn up to your rehearsals or services even though they've shown themselves generous in times past. This is where your minister's wisdom and experience come in. Listen to what he says and agree between you what should be done.

ONLY THE ACT OF VOLUNTEERING IS VOLUNTARY!

"But as a matter of principle," he continued as a waitress showed them to a quiet table in the corner of the room, "singers who join choirs should join wholeheartedly, knowing what is involved. Dr. Lionel Dakers, former director of the Royal School of Church Music, has said that the only voluntary thing about joining a volunteer choir is the act of joining. After that you should expect 100 percent from all your singers."

"But you didn't get 100 percent tonight," observed Bob as he perused the menu. "Several of the girls were away and some others came in late."

"You're quite right. This is where you have to exercise judgment and bend with the wind. I don't mind singers being late occasionally or missing occasionally as long as they tell me beforehand. All kids these days are very busy indeed and if I insisted on an unyielding 100 percent from them, they would very soon find that they couldn't manage it, and leave."

CREATE A CHOIR WHICH IS WORTHY
OF STRONG ALLEGIANCE

The waitress brought glasses of ice water and filled their mugs with coffee, which they began to drink appreciatively.

"If, on the other hand, a young singer comes up to me and says, 'I've been given a part in the school play and I can't attend practices for the next two months,' I would say to her, 'Well done! Give yourself wholly to your play and forget the choir, and then, when the play is over, come back to us full-time. We'll keep your place for you and be proud of what you are doing at school.'

"On no account say to her, 'Come to the choir as often as you can while the play is in production—we'll understand.'"

"Why wouldn't you say that?"

"Because I'd be saying in effect, 'The choir is of secondary importance and we'll be happy to accept you whenever you aren't doing something more worthwhile.'

"No, the choir is of prime importance in my life and in the lives of the children, the teens, and the adults who come here faithfully week by week. I'm determined to keep up that standard. I tell those singers who have other interests to give themselves wholly to that special interest, be it school play, swim team or tennis. After it's over they can come back and resume giving themselves fully to the choir again, because that's the sort of choir we have— one that's worth giving your full attention, energy and dedication to."

"Wow!" exclaimed Bob, "That's a great thought!"

"Yes it is. Never let your standards of attendance or punctuality slip, or the esteem in which you hold your choir and all its members. The more you esteem them, the more highly they will think of you and the choir you lead.

"Now," he said as the waitress approached for the second time, "what will you have to eat?"

29
HOW TO CREATE A CHOIR

An hour later they found themselves back in the airy practice room where several adults were already moving the choir desks into a semicircular format away from the piano.

"Let me introduce you to Ivor and Katherine, who are two founder members of my chamber choir," said the director. Bob chatted with them while the director busily wrote a new list of music on the chalk board so that the singers would know what they were about to rehearse and the order in which they would sing them.

The room gradually filled with men and women, mostly in their twenties or early thirties. But there were also three high school students from the teen choir of the previous evening, including one of the head girls who'd also sung an hour earlier.

"Tell me about these people," said Bob when he could snatch a quick word with the director who had been chatting informally with a number of his choir as they came into the practice room. "Who are they?"

"They're superb singers who have regular jobs, such as a medical doctor, an attorney, an advertising executive, a public radio personality, a couple of linguists, several Ph.D. students, and a number of directors of music of churches who have Master's degrees in music. Some of them drive fifty miles to be here and they are enormously proud of being members of such a choir. Several leading musicians have said that we're one of the finest choirs in the U.S. today!"

"Golly!" exclaimed Bob. "I see that you've also got three of your high school students here."

"Yes! They're so good that they can hold their own with the professional standard adults whom we've accepted for membership. Everyone has to audition to get into this choir, and we limit the number of singers to twenty-nine: eight sopranos and seven of every other voice part. Every singer is vital to the success of the choir, and they know it."

HOW TO CREATE A CHOIR

"How did you form this choir?"

"I started with only a dozen singers whom I'd chosen from my church choirs, and from some of their musical friends. I told them that my aim was to build one of the finest choirs in the state. From the very beginning they knew that high standards would be expected."

"How exciting for them," commented Bob.

"Yes. It also meant that their horizons were high and wide from their first rehearsal. They were all on my wavelength."

"What did you sing for your first concert?"

"I chose simple music that we could sing superbly with the numbers we had at that time. After our first concert, which I made sure had press coverage and a photograph, the word spread rapidly and more singers applied to join us."

"Did you have an upper number of singers in mind?"

"Yes. I wanted six singers for each vocal part, but in practice we found it better to increase that number slightly, for singers sometimes have to miss concerts through sickness or for business reasons. We needed the larger numbers to cover us for such emergencies. It took several years before we achieved exactly what we wanted, but the process was fun, and every practice and every concert was a thrillingly creative time as we continued to raise our standards."

"How do you audition singers for this special choir?"

"I screen the applicants first, looking for good sight-singing ability and also for a voice that blends well. Having the right personality also comes into it. For a small, closely-knit choir like this, everyone not only has to blend musically, but they also have to like each other. I ask applicants if they think that they can put up with me; if they laugh, then that's a good sign! If I feel that a singer might fit in with us, I invite him or her to join us for four rehearsals."

"That must be pretty intimidating," remarked Bob.

"It can be, but you must remember that an audition is a fifty-fifty situation. Not only are we seeing if the singer fits in with us, but also the singer is seeing if he or she would really like to become part of our choir. It has to be handled tactfully but, if potential new singers are told what the process is before they audition, it generally works very well."

"How do you make the final choice?"

"The choir is run by an elected committee of its own members, and it is they who make the decision.

"And so," concluded the director as he prepared to begin his fourth rehearsal of the day, "if you want to form a new choir, decide what sort of choir you want, find a nucleus of singers who will help you, and give yourself fully to achieving your aim.

But now," he said, "keep your eyes and ears open and you'll see what it takes to train a choir to the very highest standards. If I've got any energy left after this practice we'll talk about what you've observed."

With that Bob retired to a corner of the room where he could see and hear everything that went on. He turned to a fresh page in his notebook, laid two pencils and a pen ready beside him and watched as the practice began.

30
ADVANCED CHOIRTRAINING
TECHNIQUES

PLACEMENT OF SINGERS
The director took his place on the low rostrum with all his music in order and a pencil on hand. As the clock in the practice room neared 7:30, the singers, of their own accord, began to take their places around him, standing behind two rows of music desks placed in a semicircle. Bob noticed that the men and women alternated as a general rule, instead of having all the sopranos and altos in the front row.

He's told me about that already, thought Bob, for he did it with his teen singers yesterday. I expect he's got these singers standing in SATB single-voice quartets so that every singer can hear the other three vocal parts around him or her. He was quite right!

At exactly 7:30 the director said, "Good evening; thanks for coming; let's begin! We'll start with the Parsons motet, 'Ave Maria.'"

A - ve __ Ma - ri - a,

He doesn't waste words, thought Bob, he was welcoming, polite, brief and efficient, and he only said everything once.

CONDUCTING
The director waited for a few seconds while everyone found their place. "Sing it to a quiet *Oo*", he said. He then looked towards a rather jolly looking tenor who blew a note on his pitch pipe. The director raised his arms, embraced the whole choir with a gentle sweeping glance, waited for

five more seconds (I can feel the whole choir coming into focus, thought Bob), conducted two gentle beats, the second of which coincided with the whole choir breathing in, modeled by the conductor, and the choir began singing.

Bob had never heard anything so beautiful. They hit the first note as one, making the most exquisite sounds, and they watched the conductor almost every measure. All the sopranos and altos sang with a straight tone. They remind me of the sound of a fine English Cathedral choir, he thought. He also noticed that the conductor hardly ever looked at his music, but spent most of his time looking at the singers, from side to side, bringing in the occasional voice-part with a gentle indication of his left hand. The director conducted with loose, flexible wrists, which made them capable of expressive nuances, and he kept his palms turned upwards for much of the time in an encouraging gesture.

Most choral conductors I've seen conduct with their palms facing downwards, which gives an impression of no. This man conducts with them upwards, which gives the message yes!

He also seems to feel the music through his whole body. He conducts not only with his hands, but also, when the music becomes emotional, with his elbows—he can indicate a crescendo by stretching his arms out from the elbows; it clearly works. He also sways with the music from head to foot, without actually throwing himself around the rostrum. He's committed to the music with his whole being and the choir seems to catch this wholehearted commitment from him.

Also, he doesn't conduct with both hands at once in a contrary "windmill" motion, as so many choral conductors do; he beats time with his right hand while giving indications of expression, or bringing people in with his left. When the choir has to sing a long note he holds up his left hand for the duration of the note while conducting the beats with his right, so that the choir can see exactly when they should come off.

TONE

Bob also noticed that the choir sang in long phrases of four or more measures at a time, which gave the music a lovely sense of continuity and flowing growth.

Clearly these singers are all highly trained; they know how to breathe and how to sing through a phrase really legato so that it comes alive. The singers made gentle crescendos through every phrase and then quieted down as it came to an end. It's rather like gentle undulations of the sea, thought Bob. It gives the music tremendous power and, at the same time, it's so alive.

After the choir had sung a couple of pages very quietly to *Oo* the director said, "Change to *Aw*," and they did. The tone expanded with the change of vowel and became even more expressive. Two pages later, as they were approaching a section which had a number of low notes the director got the choir to sing to an *Ee*, and immediately the tone became richer still. A page later, as the music became more lively, the choir changed yet again to an open *Ah*, which enabled the singers to sing with an even freer tone. As the end of the anthem approached the director said, "Words!" The choir immediately began singing the text and it transformed the sound they made.

It's as though the whole anthem suddenly sprang into color, thought Bob. But even though they are singing the words, the tone remains consistent, for they know how to produce their voices. The quality of their sound has its own personality, rather like a set of stops on the organ, but it is tremendously expressive. All the singers sing right through a phrase—they don't bump from one note to another or from one word to another; it's as smooth as a highly polished table.

EVERY SINGER IS IMPORTANT TO THE CONDUCTOR

Bob then saw the director get down from the low platform on which he was standing, and walk around the front row of the singers as he continued to re-create in himself, by expressive gestures, the music they were singing. And then he did the same with the back row, while the singers continued to create lovely sounds. Every singer was aware of the conductor's interest in each individual and tried a little bit harder, knowing that each member of the choir was important to him.

SINGERS LISTEN TO THEMSELVES AND EACH OTHER

He resumed his place on the low rostrum as the choir approached the final cadence. He slowed them down so that everyone could listen to the last few chords clearly, and he sustained the final chord for a long time, looking round the choir at each singer. They're really listening to the sound they're making—it's so gentle and it sounds exquisite! I wonder what he'll say now, for I wouldn't know what to do after that, it sounded perfect to me.

WATCH THE CONDUCTOR

"Good," said the conductor. "Most of you are watching me very well, but there were some untidy moments at the alto and bass entries at the bottom of page four. Start at the top of page four, second measure."

He was very specific there. He pointed out exactly what the fault was and what they should do to remedy it: they should watch him more closely. And he gave them a run up to the passage that needed attention. Wow! He's not giving them the note—they've got to work it out for themselves!

The director waited for a few seconds until everyone had found the place, embraced them with a sweeping glance, conducted two beats and brought them in.

He's looking directly at the altos and basses here, observed Bob, and they're looking at him. That was super!

"Good," said the director again. "Let's start from the beginning."

PRONUNCIATION OF CONSONANTS AND VOWELS

One of the singers put up her hand to inquire about the exact pronunciation of one of the Latin words. The director turned to an attractive soprano and asked her to tell the choir precisely how it should be pronounced. That must be one of the linguists, thought Bob. What's she telling them to do? "Be careful to get the *l* forward in the mouth when you sing 'mulieribus,'" said the soprano; "Americans tend to get the *l* too far back in the throat."

"Thank you, Vicky," said the conductor. "Everyone say 'mulieribus' as Vicky modeled for us." (Great! thought Bob.) "No," said the conductor, "it didn't have the clarity Vicky projected." (Whoops! I must raise my standards and listen more closely!) "Say it again for us please, Vicky." She did and the choir listened harder to what she was demonstrating and succeeded better the second time they imitated her.

"There's another thing," said Vicky, taking advantage of the director's invitation to improve the pronunciation. "What is it?" asked the conductor. "I can hear some people near me singing 'bene-*dick*-tus' instead of 'bene-deek-tus.'" "Everyone say 'bene-*deek*-tus,'" commanded the conductor, and they did. "How was that, Vicky?" "Much better, thanks." "Thank you!" said the conductor gratefully.

"While we're on that word," he continued, regaining his initiative of leadership, "I want everyone to sing a liquid *d* on '-deek-tus.' Some of you are making a percussive sound on it, turning it almost into a dry *T*. You should actually sing the pitch of the note on that consonant. Sing me a scale of D major up and down to the consonant *D* with no vowel sound, all together," and they did, enjoying the process. "Good. We'll start at the bottom of the previous page to get that right in context."

Golly, thought Bob as the choir put into practice what they had just been told. I didn't realize that you could sing the pitch of a note on a consonant. I must discover if there are other consonants you can do that on; clearly, if you can, the tone of the choir will improve enormously. He thought for a few minutes, going through the alphabet, and discovered that there were a number of consonants on which notes could be sung.

He turned a page in his notebook and wrote, *A superb choir ensures that the pronunciation of vowels and consonants is absolutely identical for every singer. This means that they need a model to copy, then practice what they have been shown until it is right. The conductor has to ensure that he has a high standard of what he regards as right. "Nearly right" is not good enough! The more you ask of singers the more they will give you.*

"Now you'll have noticed that the composer has written this motet so that the climax comes in measure 52 at the top of page eight," continued the conductor. Everyone turned to the place to see where he meant. "And therefore I would like a generally continuous crescendo from page one right through measure 52, with one or two exceptions, after which we diminuendo for the next six measures."

Bob thought, I've never heard a choir make a crescendo for eight pages; how is he going to achieve that?

DYNAMICS

"Therefore everyone mark page one *pp*; measure 12 starts *mp*; measure 21 is *mf*; measure 31 we quieten down for a while—mark it *mp cresc.*; measure 40 is *mf*; measure 47 *dim*; measure 49 is *mf cresc.* to *forte* by measure 52, from where we diminuendo gently to measure 58." He waited, having given these instructions slowly, until everyone had marked their scores.

The jolly tenor put his hand up. "Does that mean that we take no notice of phrasing within a page?" he asked. "No, of course not, Robert!" answered the conductor with a smile. "It means that you have to grade the expressiveness of your singing so that the overall effect of those eight pages is one of gradual musical growth. Please sing every phrase with a rise and fall of expression as only you can!" Robert smiled gratefully at the compliment he had been paid.

"But first," said the director, "we need to know what it feels like to sing at these different dynamic levels. Sing me the first chord of measure 7 to the vowel *Ah* first at *pp* then *p* and so on, so that we know what we're aiming for. Listen to the sound you're making."

That's great! thought Bob. He doesn't ask them to do anything unless they really know what it is he wants. And he watched as the conductor achieved, by trial and error, the exact quantity of sound he had envisaged for every dynamic.

"Hey, people!" exclaimed the director when they were singing the chord forte,"Don't change your tone with the change of dynamic. You are tending towards a harsh, tight tone as you get louder; keep the same sound while getting louder and continue to make it creatively musical. Listen to each other. Let's try making a continuous crescendo on that chord from pianissimo to forte, keeping the tone and the musicality constant." They did, and the difference was remarkable.

"Okay, we've got it," said the director with a satisfied smile. "We'll start from the beginning, pianissimo." They did, and it was very beautiful.

ALLOW THE CHOIR TO SING!

Bob noticed as the practice continued that the conductor allowed his choir to sing quite long passages without stopping them. It used to drive me crazy when I sang in a choir and the conductor kept stopping us. This man clearly knows that choir members love to sing, and yet he's directing them all the time. He often saves time by talking to them as they are singing. "Tenors, sing a little softer, I can't hear the altos!" "I need more bass in that measure, this passage needs firmer support." "Altos, that entry was untidy—we'll do it again in a moment." "Sopranos, you are making the most exquisite sounds—keep it up!"

ALTERING WRITTEN NOTES

Bob also noticed that he frequently asked the choir to shorten the length of written notes at the ends of phrases. "Tenors, at the end of your first phrase on the word *Maria,* change the last note from two-beats to one-beat and add a one-beat rest afterwards; make a diminuendo on it so that you soften to silence; don't end on a 'click' as some operatic tenors are wont to do!" And he smiled, knowing full well that several of his tenors loved singing opera. "Let's practice it."

He never asks them to do something without immediately getting them actually to sing it. Many choirmasters would have pointed out what they wanted, but then expected the singers to do it later on; this man insists on overseeing every point he makes. That's why they're so good. He has very high standards, and he ensures that everything comes up to the standards he has set. It must take a lot out of him—I'd be dead on my feet by this time!

FIRST NOTES

As the practice continued, the conductor made much of the way that the choir sang first notes of phrases. If a phrase began gently, he conducted gently, if it began energetically he conducted his preliminary two beats energetically.

Bob also noticed how he corrected faults, and mixed in a little humor to sweeten the pill. "Tenors, some of you are scooping up to the first note; aim your pitch right in the middle of the note and listen to what you are really doing. Sing it for me." They did, and Bob thought it was good. "No, several of you are still scooping like octogenarian Russians. Focus on the note that Robert gives you and visualize your own note before you start to sing it. Get your larynx into the right position and take a breath on the vowel you are about to sing. That way all your singing equipment will be ready to go."

Whoops, again! thought Bob, I'm not listening as closely as the conductor is to what the choir is actually doing; I must listen much more carefully and raise my standards.

Robert again blew the note on his pitch-pipe. The conductor waited until all the tenors were focused and then he brought them in. "That was better, but I can still hear a small scoop. That won't do. Sing the note to me six times in succession." The tenors did, at one short note per second; for the first two the sound was untidy, but for the last four they were absolutely together. Everyone, including Bob, knew that they were right and that the practice could continue.

Bob noticed that the conductor continued to explain what he wanted with few words. So many conductors I've heard talk far too much. This man knows that the choir has come here to sing, not to listen to him talk, and so he keeps instructions down to a minimum, immediately focusing in on what he wants.

In fact, continued Bob, as he wrote yet more in his notebook, I can define exactly what he does:

1 *He tells the choir what needs correcting.*
2 *He tells them what they ought to do to put it right.*
3 *He explains how they can correct it, and*
4 *He then gets them to do it by looking at them inspiringly as he conducts, and he stays with that one point until he is fully satisfied.*

Getting the tenors to sing the first note on pitch was a good example of his technique. They know he won't be satisfied until it is wholly right and that's why they drive such long distances—to achieve something really worthwhile. They wouldn't bother coming if his standards were only "That's nearly right."

UNDERLINE IMPORTANT SYLLABLES
Bob wondered how the choir knew to which note they should crescendo in any one phrase. He soon found out.

"Underline very lightly the first syllable of *gratia*—make sure you insert an *s* when you sing 'gratia'—it should sound 'gratsia.' And then underline strongly the first syllable of *plena,* for 'ple' is the climax of that short phrase; you must crescendo towards it and diminuendo away from it. Let's go from the bottom of page two at the tenor entry." The choir sang a couple of pages and the difference in their interpretation was immediately obvious. The music came alive in a new way and the meaning of the words pulsed through the notes.

"That's better," said the conductor, stopping them with a gentle wave of his hand. "But notice that some of you are giving too much stress to the second syllable of 'gra-TI-a' because it's set to a dotted rhythm. Lighten it, and it will sound more gracious." The choir sang the passage again and the conductor said over them, while they were still singing, "That's right! Let's go on."

There were a lot of melismas (many notes to one syllable) in this motet. Bob noticed that the choirmaster encouraged his choir to sing very legato. He said, looking at them as they continued to sing, "Imagine that you are a choir of well-oiled cellists playing with lots of rosin on your bows; really enjoy the sensation of moving forward through these passages. Crescendo as you reach a climax and then diminuendo gently away from it."

That calls for a lot of breath control, thought Bob. Now I can see what he meant when he said that singing is all about producing long phrases in one breath sung with lovely tone—and it's all based on good breathing technique. It's really coming alive here!

MEAN WHAT YOU SING—BY FULLY UNDERSTANDING THE MESSAGE OF THE WORDS
"There's one more thing we need to achieve with this motet tonight," said the conductor. "Although you are all singing very beautifully with lovely tone, blend, balance and expression, the essential meaning of the words is not coming through. Look at the opening words, *Ave Maria,*

'Hail Mary.' Imagine that you are the angel Gabriel coming to Mary to ask her if she's willing to become the mother of God. Get into Gabriel's frame of mind. He would be gentle and loving and oh so courteous—re-create that mindset so that our audience can feel it, too. We'll sing just the first couple of pages. Now, here you come flying down from heaven and you see Mary sitting quietly and you say…" and Robert gave the note once more. The conductor looked at everyone as though he and they actually were Gabriel. With great feeling they sang the words that changed the course of history. They were so caught up by what they were doing that they went on singing to the very end, after which there was a profound silence. The singers themselves had been moved by what they had done and there was no little sense of awe at what they had achieved together.

Fantastic! thought Bob.

31
MORE ADVANCED CHOIRTRAINING TECHNIQUES

Later that evening, the director drove Bob home. He was clearly worn out by his succession of rehearsals, but Bob ventured to ask him a few questions about all he had seen and heard.

STRAIGHT TONE

"I noticed that your sopranos and most other singers sang with a straight tone. Why is that?"

"Because that is the sound I want and, to my mind, that is the only way to get a real blend of voices.

"If your choir is made up of singers who have a vibrato, they must, by definition, stick out from the rest. There's no way you can get an even sound, perfectly tuned, if your singers vibrate!" he continued with a smile. "The essence of a vibrato is that it wavers above and below the pitch of the note and that standard of intonation is not good enough for me. I love a vibrato in a solo singer—the sound is most attractive and expressive—but choral singing has a different set of rules."

"Not many American choral conductors would agree with you," commented Bob.

"I know!" said the director with a sigh. "But I always find that when my chamber choir gives a concert attended by choral conductors (and we've enjoyed the privilege of singing at two national choral conventions recently), everyone is entranced by the sound the choir makes and the choirmasters wish they had similar voices in their own choirs!"

"Are your singers capable of singing with a vibrato if they want to?"

"Yes, indeed! Many of them can change gear when they are asked to sing a solo and the sound that comes out is really lovely. It floats distinctly over the rest of the choir because it is being produced differently; but that underlines what I said about a vibrato making blend impossible."

"How do your sopranos change from straight tone to a fuller tone with vibrato?"

"I asked one of my leading sopranos how she did it, and she told me that it was tied up with having a superb breathing technique, coupled with the ability to sing with a head voice when straight tone was required. Again, the straight tone comes more easily when singers sing softly—and that is in itself a great way to achieve blend."

INPUT FROM SINGERS

"They are an outstanding group of singers," commented Bob. "Clearly you've got no discipline problems with them as you sometimes may have with your children."

"Quite right, Bob. They come because they really want to work, and the only discipline problems I have arise from overenthusiasm."

"How so?"

"Well, many of them are choral conductors and professional musicians in their own right. They all have their own views as to how an anthem should be rehearsed. Sometimes the suggestions they make are very useful, such as Vicky's input on pronunciation tonight. At other times we nearly get into arguments as to what should be done with a passage, and although I greatly respect their views, there comes a time when I must put my foot down and say, 'Thank you, but we'll do it my way.' They are gracious enough to accept that and we get back to a well-ordered rehearsal.

"Sometimes a singer who is worried about a certain point will take me aside during our break, or after the practice, and put her case to me. This I find very helpful, for we have the time to talk the matter through, and the net result is that both I and the choir are enriched by what she has to say. If you've got gifted people in your choir, use their gifts for the benefit of the whole body, but ensure that it's done in such a way that it harnesses your goodwill rather than challenges your authority."

THE PLACING OF VOICES

"I also noticed that halfway through the practice, when you needed a firmer sound from the second basses, you moved one of the basses from the back row to the front. I was amazed that such a small move made such a big difference."

"Yes, the practical importance of where singers are placed within a choir is something that not too many choirmasters have recognized yet. We experiment a lot with various placements in my chamber choir. Every configuration leads to a different overall sound. One of my sopranos is particularly good at working out a placement plan, and so we try what she suggests and then amend it until everyone is happy; happy with where they are standing within the group and happy with the singers who are around them. I also need to be satisfied with the resulting tone of the choir.

"Of course," continued the director as the car neared his home, "tall singers tend to be placed in the back row and shorter ones in front. Those with more powerful voices are in the back, and the softer singers in front. But it is important not only that a soprano can hear the alto, tenor and bass singers around her, she must also be able to hear the other sopranos who are near her. Placement takes a lot of careful thought.

"You'll find that this principle will also work with your church choir."

"How do you mean?" asked Bob again.

"Don't place your strongest singers together, for they'll only compete with one another to see who can sing loudest. If you have all your sopranos together—and I hope you won't, but will try dividing them at least into halves—place a stronger singer standing next to a quieter singer and constantly remind them that they should sing so as to be able to hear each other. This will encourage the weaker singer to sing out more and the stronger singer to modify her tone."

FINANCING A NEW CHOIR

"How do you go about raising money to pay the singers in your chamber choir and also to buy music?" asked Bob.

"I confess that I am very fortunate," answered the director, "because all my singers give their services entirely free."

"There can't be many choirs of your high standard who do that," commented Bob with awe.

"You're right. I've said it before and I'll say it again, they come because I make it worth their while to come."

"By aiming at the highest standards possible," interrupted Bob.

"Right again! But the matter of finance is vital to the success of any venture. Here again, we've been very fortunate in having a Board of influential citizens who meet three or four times a year and advise us about such matters. You need to get in touch with Chorus America *(see details in Appendix B)*, which is a body dedicated to helping choirs such as ours."

THE EYES

"Where did you learn your choirtraining techniques?" asked Bob, changing the subject as they continued their journey home.

"From many people all over the world! But when I was a student I had the good fortune to study for two years with Dr. Boris Ord, director of music at King's College, Cambridge. He also taught David Willcocks, his successor, and I've learned much from him, too. That was a long time ago," he said nostalgically.

"In those days, King's chapel choir had a quality about them I couldn't define—they sang superbly in tune and every note was vibrant with life. Boris was a stern disciplinarian when in front of his choir; a delightful teddy-bear of a man when he was off-duty. There was a certain something about their whole approach that I didn't understand. I couldn't quite place what special quality Boris possessed until I asked Dr. George Guest. 'Boris had a piercing glance when he conducted,' he told me, 'It was almost mesmerizing. No one under his gaze dared to sing a note in any way other than superbly, with their whole being committed to their conductor and the choir.'

"I've never forgotten that," concluded the director, "and so I spend as much time as I can looking directly into the eyes of my singers as I conduct them, to inspire them with my concept of how the music should sound."

"Wow!" exclaimed Bob, "I've never heard that before. I can't wait to try it on my own choirs back home."

CREATIVE CONDUCTING

"There's even more to it than that," said the director, summoning up an extra reserve of strength to deal with all the points they were discussing.

"What?"

"A distinguished organist told me once that all French organ music, from Franck onwards, should be played as an improvisation—that the music should be sown so deeply into the performer's mind that he feels he can play it because he wants to rather than because he has to. That's fantastic advice, for it opens up a whole new concept for playing French music!"

Bob was so excited by this gem that he wasn't even able to murmur a faint "Wow!"

"And so I apply that principle to my conducting whenever I can," continued the director as he put on a burst of speed to beat a set of traffic lights that were about to turn red. "When I have a superb choir before me, with everyone looking at me, I feel free to change the interpretation of an anthem or motet during a performance, without telling them beforehand. It's a thrillingly creative thing to be able to do, for the singers also realize that they are creating music rather than just repeating the techniques that they had rehearsed during previous weeks. But you can only do it if everyone looks at you, because…because, why?"

Bob enthusiastically responded, "Because you look at everybody, all the time, and demand their immediate response!"

"Right! It reminds me of a story told about the great English orchestral conductor, Sir Thomas Beecham. At the end of a rehearsal before a concert someone said to him, 'Sir Thomas, you forgot to rehearse the Mozart symphony!' 'No I didn't, my boy. They know the notes so well that I shall make them perform it superbly tonight!'

"He, too, like Boris Ord," said the director as the car approached his house, "had piercing eyes and a gargantuan gift of musicianship which could command all those under his care."

THE FINAL QUESTION!

The car rolled into the director's driveway and he turned off the ignition with a sigh. It had been a long day.

"There's one more question I must ask you," said Bob as they got out of the car and made their way to the house.

"Okay, just one, for I'm going straight to bed," said the director as he unlocked his front door.

"In all our talks so far you've stressed the vital importance of asking your choir questions to encourage them to think and to participate fully in your practices. And yet you didn't ask any questions during your chamber choir rehearsal; why was that?"

The director closed his front door and leaned against a wall. "What an intelligent question that is, young man! It never occurred to me until now. Let me think why."

He thought for a long half-minute and then said, "I ask questions in my other choirs, especially in my children's choirs, to stimulate their interest and to educate them into thinking creatively. They need to be educated in what singing in a fine choir is all about, not only technical skills such as sight-singing, the production of beautiful tone, good breathing, good stance, and the need to concentrate for long periods, but also the whole spirit of approach to choral work. Included are such elements as dedicated enthusiasm for detailed rehearsal in order to achieve excellence, and total commitment of mind, body and spirit to the whole group through the music they are making together."

He paused for breath, and continued, "All those qualities were present in my chamber choir tonight. There was no need to stimulate them to try hard, beyond my own total dedication to them and to the music we were singing. For it was from their patent goodwill and my own leadership everything else flowed.

"I must admit that, occasionally, one or two of the singers relapse into less than excellence in attitude of mind—often because they are tired after a hard day's work or for some equally valid reason. Then I coax them into trying harder with a quiet word or a small joke.

"But I expect them to think, and to think creatively. You noticed how I spent a minute getting the tenors to sing the opening phrase of the first motet by cutting the final note short and softening to silence. What did I expect the other singers to do?"

"You expected them to do exactly the same whenever they, in their turn, sang the same phrase."

"Exactly right. I aim at defining a principle—such as the exact length a breath or how to sing a phrase—only once, and I expect everyone to take note and follow suit.

"I think the secret of my approach can be summed up in the phrase 'never be predictable.' I learned that from my dean when I was director of music of an English cathedral. He was a superb after-dinner speaker and he shared with me how he did it. 'I tell them a funny story,' he said, 'and while they're still laughing I hit them with a very serious point. They don't know where they are—I've got them in the palm of my hand and can do anything with them.'"

"But you are predictable in expecting them to listen to you when you say things just once. And you are predictable in always expecting high standards," commented Bob, a little puzzled.

"Quite right! But don't be predictable in a boring way. Your choir should never think, 'Oh, we know what he's going to say, so we needn't listen.' Be unpredictable in the way you describe things. Have at your finger-tips a host of teaching techniques which can illuminate the problem you are dealing with.

"For example," continued the director, "if the choir is singing a passage too slowly and heavily, I could say, 'you remind me of an elephant with a stomach ache! Sound more like a butterfly that's rejoicing in the Spring!' They all laugh, but they get the idea and immediately lighten and quicken their approach.

"So, my friend," said the director, poking Bob in the tummy with his car keys and hitting him lightly on the head with a copy of a Howells anthem that had lain on a nearby table, "never be predictable. Goodnight!" and with that he bounded up the stairs with a sudden burst of energy and was not seen until the following morning.

"Wow!" said Bob, predictably.

♪ WEDNESDAY ♪

32
WORKING WITH COLLEAGUES

"What are the plans for today?" asked Bob at breakfast the next morning, through a mouthful of toast and marmalade.

"Well, I've an hour's paperwork to get through, but then I should be free until lunch time," said the director as he filled his thermos flask with coffee. "Perhaps you might like to play the organ while I clear my desk, and then we can spend the rest of the time talking. I've three rehearsals with the new and middle rank boys this afternoon, and then, tonight, there's a meeting of the choir support committee that you must see."

CHOIR LIBRARIANS

"That sounds great," enthused Bob as he prepared to follow the director to his car.

"We've got to get through a lot of music this week," he said as the car edged its way out of the driveway. "You'll have appreciated how much work our librarian, Deane Parker, does to keep the music program vital and active; we couldn't exist without him."

"Yes, I noticed that all the music is in the singers' cubbies and that on your notice board there's a list of all the singers with their cubby numbers next to them."

"Yes," answered the director as the car sped along the now familiar country road, "it all comes under the heading of good order and courtesy to one's choir members."

"Please explain what you mean," asked Bob, trying desperately not to be predictable.

"Well, so many of our singers come from well-ordered, neat and comfortable homes. Why should they come to a practice room that is untidy and uncomfortable? I admit that I am one of this world's untidiest creatures, but I make a real effort, as far as the choir is concerned, to ensure that the practice room is kept in good order. I try to polish the top of the piano every so often and clean the piano keys, for they quickly get dirty, especially when little boys and girls play it."

"Does the librarian look after all the music on his own?"

"No, he has the help of three high-school singers who collect the music after services, sort it into numerical order, for every copy is numbered, and put each anthem back in their appropriate boxes. It's very good for these young people to have this training. It helps them to realize the importance of order in their lives, which stands them in good stead for their future. They are also made to feel that what they do is integral to the success of the music program, and they love it!

"Deane also has the help of a member of the adult choir for their music—she is a treasure and, like all librarians, wholly dedicated to what she's doing."

"I notice that you don't waste time at any of your rehearsals by giving out music."

"You're quite right. We plan our whole program a year ahead, as you have seen from our choirbook. Deane knows exactly what music to put out each month, and what needs collecting after it's been sung."

"Do you keep strictly to what you've planned?"

"No," laughed the director, "I sometimes change an anthem because I've chosen too much to learn or the clergy decide that one of the services will have a special theme that Sunday. I meet regularly with Deane to ensure that we both know what's coming up and can plan accordingly."

CONSTANT VIGILANCE

"It must be pretty easy to keep the music in order, when you've got such a splendid team of librarians," observed Bob as the car approached the church.

"No, it most certainly isn't," responded the director, turning into the parking lot. "The matter of human frailty is all too present when it comes to keeping our practice room tidy. We find that singers sometimes take music home to practice it, and then forget to return it until several months later. Some copies get left around the vestries after services and others just disappear. Much of Deane's time is spent in putting stiff covers onto copies to preserve them as well as ordering new sets of music when we need them.

"Periodically he checks through everyone's cubby to clean out music that's been left there by accident—you'd be surprised at some of the mess that singers accumulate in their music folders! It's a constant battle to keep the place clean and tidy and, I must admit, we don't always succeed. Deane needs my continual support to help him keep the practice room really tidy.

"It's the same with all the other facets of choir life," he continued as he got out of the car, "the care of the robes, punctuality, regularity of attendance, and so on. It is the director who sets the rules and it is he who has to see that those rules are being kept. Adults, like children, will test your boundaries, either consciously or unconsciously. If you don't comment on lateness or on an untidy pile of music in one corner of the room, things will continue to deteriorate. So I always have to check that I'm doing my job properly so as to encourage everyone else.

"Well now, young man, you go and play the organ, and I'll see you in an hour when I've conquered my desk work—unless something intervenes to stop me!" and, so saying, each musician went his separate way, looking forward to their next meeting.

THE ORGAN LOFT

Bob really enjoyed his hour on the organ for it was a fine instrument. He noticed that the organ loft was very tidy. I wonder if that's due to the director or to Nancy Willis? he thought. He remembered other organ lofts he'd been in which weren't neat and realized how important it was that good order should reign as much in the organist's private domain as in the choir room. It makes life much easier if things are where they ought to be!

He saw a box on a nearby shelf with the words *Swell-box* written in red ink on the lid. Being inquisitive, he opened it. Inside was a collection of miscellaneous objects: the organ tuning book; some scotch tape; three pencils, two of them colored; a pencil sharpener; an eraser; a packet of paper clips; a pad of yellow semi-adhesive notepaper; a polishing cloth; some tissues; and several packets of candy. What a great idea! he thought as he absent-mindedly helped himself to some candy, There's everything here that an organist needs for services or practices. I must get one myself!

THE SEXTON

Bob so enjoyed the organ, as well as the candy, that he stayed in the loft much longer than he intended. While he was there the sexton came to empty the trash, which was full of last Sunday's orders of service. He remembered what the director had said when he'd first arrived about the importance of getting to know other members of the parish, so he spent five minutes talking with the sexton and found him a fascinating man. His name was Derek. He'd been a motor mechanic and a carpenter, was fluent in Spanish and his wife had once appeared on a TV quiz show. "Did she win anything?" asked Bob. "Yes, an electric organ," answered Derek with a laugh. "We don't know what to do with it because neither of us plays the thing!" and with that he left Bob to continue his playing while he went about his business of keeping the church clean and tidy. Both felt good about the time they had spent chatting together.

UNOFFICIAL SEXTON!

A couple of minutes later Nancy Willis came up to the organ loft to find some music that she needed to practice. Bob told her about his meeting with the sexton. "I'm glad we've got a full-time sexton at my new church," said Bob, conversationally, as Nancy rummaged through her collection of Bach's works, "because we only had a part-time sexton at my first church when I was a student. I spent an awful lot of time moving chairs before choir practices and locking up afterwards."

"My dear Bob," said Nancy with a laugh as she found the piece she'd been looking for, "all choir directors have to be unofficial sextons, and unpaid at that. We're often the first to arrive and the last to leave; it goes with the territory!"

"What?" exclaimed Bob.

"Oh yes! We musicians spend a fair amount of time moving furniture, turning on the heat before a concert, and turning off lights afterwards.

"Many of us find that we learn so much more after we've graduated than we did when we were students," added Nancy. "But you will find that, if you give a lead in the matter of moving pianos and tidying up after practices, others will be happy to give you a helping hand."

"Thank you," said Bob. "I'm glad you told me that."

"Happy to oblige," said Nancy as she gave him a farewell wave before disappearing down the organ loft stairs.

33
SINGING IS GOOD FOR YOU

A few minutes later, Bob walked toward the music building over a well-trimmed lawn, rejoicing in the warm sunshine that fell on the honey-colored stonework of the church. It was a good place to be, and he relished the feeling of well-being flooding his soul.

He found the director on the phone. "Yes, Mrs. Callahan, I'm delighted that Peter and Ellie have settled in well at their new schools; we find that our choir children do particularly well academically because they receive so much training in the art of concentration during our practices. I look forward to seeing you all on Sunday. Thank you for calling.

"Hi, Bob!" he said, turning round in his swivel chair, "That was a potential new choir-parent who's bringing her children to see me next Sunday. Her family have just moved here and they're looking for a church to join."

IMMEDIATE FOLLOW UP

He gave Bob a steady look and asked, "What must I do about it right now?"

Bob thought for a moment and said, "You need to make a note in your calendar so that you remember, next Sunday, that they are coming to see you."

"Quite right," said the director, following his advice. "But what else do I need to do?"

Bob thought furiously for several moments, but nothing occurred to him.

"Well, sit in that chair and watch what I do," responded the director, somewhat disappointed that the careful teaching he was giving to his visitor was not always bearing immediate fruit.

Bob watched as the director wrote a letter to Mrs. Callahan in which he said again how much he looked forward to meeting her family on Sunday, and he enclosed with it a leaflet giving details of the choir program. He then wrote a memo to the minister giving him particulars of the potential new members of the church. He also wrote a note to the church school superintendent, for he knew that Mrs. Callahan had some even younger children who might welcome the opportunity of joining the pre-K group.

"Oh dear!" said Bob, as he watched the director fulfill these obvious tasks, "There's an awful lot to do in response to such a small matter."

"That's okay," responded the director kindly. "You'll find that good communication really does pay off."

SCHOOL WORK

"You told Mrs. Callahan that singing in your choir helped children's academic work," remarked Bob, getting out his notebook. "When I was a student and had a part-time church job, the parents of my choir children often said that singing in my choir interfered with their kids' school work."

"If you run your choir program really well, by stretching your children's capabilities at every practice—inspiring them to achieve a lot through a well thought-out and clearly defined training program, their powers of concentration will improve wonderfully, and their parents and teachers will notice it and thank you for it.

"I've been in this profession for many years," he continued as he tidied the remaining papers on his desk, "and a recurring theme has been a continual stream of reinforcement for what I've been doing, both from parents and teachers. A director of education told me that participation in a comprehensive and demanding choir program, such as we have here and which I hope you will promote in your church, can be a very positive experience with regard to developing children's mental capacity and increasing their powers of concentration.

THE BRAIN

"Do you know about the functions of the left- and right-hand side of the brain?" asked the director, offering Bob a cup of coffee from his thermos flask.

"Yes. The left-hand side deals with logical concepts and the right side has to do with our artistic nature."

"Quite right," responded the director, taking a well-earned drink of coffee himself. "The right side is creative, encompassing visual, imaginative and musical concepts."

"Wait a minute!" interjected Bob, putting his cup down suddenly and spilling some coffee on the floor in his haste to write in his notebook. "Singing in a choir therefore involves both sides of the brain; the left side deals with mathematics, which includes rhythmic concepts and also the use and meaning of words, and the right side controls melody, phrasing and expression. Wow!"

"Correct! A recent survey by an educational testing center," said the director, refilling Bob's cup, "reported that the students who get the best grades in school were those who have several major outside activities. What a positive thing it is, therefore, for children to have as one of their major extracurricular activities, the opportunity to sing in your choir, for there they continually exercise both sides of their brain.

"Do you know," he said, leaning forward in his chair, "that we humans use only three percent of our potential brain-power! But do you also know that deep breathing exercises, such as we have at the beginning of our practices, not only stimulate the brain but also relax the body? One of my choir parents actually said that being in the choir helped her son to excel in his swimming at school because he'd had so much training in deep breathing," and the director paused for a moment, for he was out of breath himself!

CHILDREN ARE INTELLIGENT!

"Children are capable of achieving far more than many teachers can conceive," he continued, leaning back and looking at the ceiling, as though for inspiration. "It breaks my heart when I lead workshops for choir children and find, time and time again, that girls and boys who have given three or four years' service to their choirs still have no idea about some of the basic essentials of how to sing effectively, let alone how to read music." He raised his eyebrows in a gesture of despair.

"The world is divided into two groups of people: those who are succeeding and those who are failing." He leaned forward suddenly and added, "And both those are continuing processes. Children at a recent workshop I directed were clearly programmed to fail and to continue failing. It took me an hour to begin to enable them to believe that they really could do what I asked of them. My heart went out to them for their choirmaster hadn't even bothered to turn up—he had something better to do than to waste a morning learning how he could improve his choirtraining. And so I knew that those children would easily slip back into their failure mode the next time they came to choir. My own children, on the other hand, are geared to success—and that's not boasting, it's just a plain statement of fact. They succeed because it's so much more fun to win than to lose—and it's so simple to achieve if, in the words of Sherlock Holmes, you follow my methods!"

He paused for a minute and then said, unexpectedly, "Children, by the time they are three years old have learned a foreign language!"

"A foreign language?" echoed Bob incredulously.

"Yes, it's called English!" laughed the director. "In South Africa, where I've frequently directed choir courses, many children do even better: they can speak both English and Afrikaans!

"And so if children can master a foreign language in their very early years, think how much they can achieve while their brain-capacity is still increasing. Like muscles, a child's brain actually improves the more it is used, and it develops best when both sides are being used together. The brain can store an almost limitless amount of information and also learn how to put that knowledge to practical use. You just have to look at how skilled children are on computers these days to see what I mean; they're far quicker than adults who have comparable training.

"Have you been to Sea World?" asked the director, suddenly sitting up.

"Yes! I was amazed at what dolphins and whales could do." Bob paused while the director looked at him. "Wait a moment—you're trying to tell me something, aren't you? If the trainers at Sea World can get those animals to perform so superbly, for the incentive of a bucket of fish, how can we get children, who are far more intelligent, to reach the greater heights of musical achievement?"

"Yes, indeed! I was amazed myself when I asked some students who visited my practices, as you are doing, what motivated my children to do well. They said that the children tried hard because my approval was important to them. I wasn't aware of that until they told me."

"Their success is important to them because it is so important to you," observed Bob generously.

"Thank you! If you really care for each child under your care, and feel that everything you teach is of vital importance, then you will succeed.

"From birth to the age of twelve," continued the director, shifting his position again, "children's brains are expanding, then they gradually plateau until the age of eighteen, after which their capacity for learning is fixed. A child's learning capacity should be stretched, therefore, from birth through eighth grade. It's so vital to begin training children when choirmasters have this glorious window of opportunity, through a demanding educational program while the singers are young, with a system of carefully graded training cards and a lot of two-on-one teaching. Never waste their time, or yours, with puerile games that may entertain but certainly don't educate."

LONG LIFE

He rummaged in a drawer for a moment, and drew out a sheet of paper. He folded it neatly in half and put it into his pocket. (What's that? wondered Bob.) The director continued, "There's even more to it than that! If children are brought up in the right way by inspiring choirmasters, then they are more likely to spend all their adult lives praising God through their skilled music-making.

"A doctor has recently reported that people who go to church every week are six times less likely to have heart attacks than those who have no spiritual basis for their lives, and another doctor has discovered that people with more education tend to live longer than those with less. And so," the director concluded, standing up to stretch himself, "singing in an educationally-oriented church choir is demonstrably good for you, mentally, spiritually and physically. What better incentives could you have than that?"

"Golly!" exclaimed Bob as he scribbled ever more illegibly in his notebook, "What a great message that is to get across to the parents of potential new singers; I can hardly wait to get back to my own church to start on all this. It's so exciting!"

"Let's go and have some lunch," said the director, leading the way from his office and out into the glorious sunshine, "and choose some food that will be healthy for us." It was indeed good to be there.

34
CHOIR CEREMONIES

HEAD BOYS AND GIRLS

The director took him to a diner at the far end of the town where they served all-natural food. As they walked along in the early fall sunshine, past attractive shops that were clearly doing good business, judging from the number of people who were coming and going, Bob said, "I notice that you place a lot of reliance on your senior girls and boys."

"Yes. I couldn't run the choirs without them. Their example in leadership is such a vital role model for the younger children who look up to them. The matter of good role models is so important these days when there is no shortage of the other kind.

"As you will have seen," he continued as he waved to a choir parent on the other side of the road, "we keep our children right through high school; I cannot begin to tell you what that does to the younger children who have such pressures upon them at school where many of their contemporaries think that singing in a church choir is 'sissy.' When our twelve-year-olds see seventeen- and eighteen-year-olds who excel in sporting activities singing with them in the same choir, they know that it's worth their while to continue.

"There's a major difference in ages between the head boys and the head girls. The head boys have unchanged voices—so they tend to be around twelve or thirteen years old. The head girls, on the other hand, are seventeen or eighteen years old, for they are in charge of all the girls, from the youngest to the oldest. The teenage altos, tenors and basses don't need a senior in charge of them."

"How do you appoint your head choristers?"

"It's usually pretty obvious who the next one will be. It's helpful to have a deputy who is set to succeed when the head retires; sometimes you can have two deputies if the numbers in your choir warrant it. But when the succession is not obvious I discuss the possibilities with the outgoing head girls or boys and listen carefully to their advice. If the decision is still not clear, I take a secret ballot of the more senior singers and this usually clinches it.

"I make sure, he concluded, "that I always treat the head choristers with honor, especially in front of their peers, so that their authority is strengthened. Sometimes," he added, "a new head boy or girl has to be instructed in the art of giving orders and how to be helpful to those under their care. Regular meetings with them, especially in the early days of their new responsibilities, are very important."

PROMOTIONS POLICY

"What do you discuss with them?"

"I ask them how they think things are going and how individual singers are doing. Their input is invaluable here, for they are, by definition, closer to their younger peers than I am. I consult with them when I think that a singer is due for promotion."

"I thought you promoted singers when they had completed one of your training cards," Bob observed as the diner came into view.

"I do for the newer children but, because of the schedule I have to follow here, there's no opportunity to organize training cards for the upper grades."

"How do you decide whether or not a singer is ready for promotion, then?"

"This is where the system of merit dots is so useful. If a boy or girl within a group regularly earns more merit dots than their colleagues then, clearly, they are doing better than the others and so should be considered for promotion.

"By the way," added the director, "the young men are not given dots—they've outgrown that system."

"What about the older girls?"

"I keep it for the girls because the age-range of the senior girls' choir is wider than for the teenage men."

They went up a short flight of steps and entered the diner. It was full of customers, but they found a small table at the far end, which had just been vacated, and sat down. "I never promote singers on this assessment system without the full backing of the head boys or head girls. When a singer rises from one rank to the next he or she should have shown, not only to the head choristers but also to their peers, that they are worthy of promotion; and so the whole system is held in respect by all the singers."

ADMITTANCE AND PROMOTION CEREMONIES

"You mentioned something a couple of days ago about formal ceremonies. Can I see what you do?"

"Most certainly! I knew we were going to talk about this today and so I brought a copy for you to keep," and so saying, the director drew out of his pocket the mysterious sheet of paper he'd put there half an hour before. On it were printed not only the ceremonies of admission to the choir but also upgrading ceremonies.

"Let's order lunch first and then you can look through it," he said as a waiter approached them. "What will you have?"

Bob looked at the menu and chose tuna salad with cottage cheese and garlic bread, plus a freshly squeezed orange juice. "And the same for me, please," said the director as he handed Bob the ceremonies sheet.

ADMISSION OF A BOY/GIRL TO THE CHOIR OF
FIRST CHURCH, HOMETOWN

The choir stands. The senior boy/girl present stands ready with a surplice. The Director of Music (DOM) presents the candidate to the Priest/ Officiant (P/O). The candidate is already vested in a cassock.

DOM: Reverend/Sir/Madam, I here present to you N. to be admitted by you into membership in our choir.

P/O: Do you consider this boy/girl to be suitable through dedication and ability to become a member of our choir?

DOM: I have examined him/her and think him/her so to be.

The P/O addresses the candidate.

P/O: N., do you wish to become a member of our choir?

Candidate: I do.

P/O: Will you try your best at all times to become a more worthy member of our choir through good attendance and effort?

Candidate: I will.

The Candidate kneels before the P/O who takes his/her right hand and says:

            N., I admit you into full membership of the choir of First Church; May you sing heavenly praises to your life's end.

All: AMEN.

The senior boy/girl then vests the candidate with a cotta.

P/O: Let us pray for N., that his/her time in our choir may be blessed in the knowledge and love of God and of his Son, Jesus Christ our Lord in the power of the Holy Spirit through the exercise of the gift of music.

All: Bless, O Lord, us thy servants who minister in thy temple; Grant that what we sing with our lips we may believe in our hearts; And what we believe in our hearts we may show forth in our lives, through Jesus Christ our Lord, AMEN.

The candidate stands and all bow to the Priest/Officiant. The Director of Music then leads the Candidate to his/her place in the choir.

P/O   Come, let us sing to the Lord:

All: Let us shout for joy to the Rock of our salvation.

UPGRADING CEREMONY

The choir stands. The candidate stands before the Priest/Officiant with the Director of Music and the senior boy/girl present, who shall have the appropriate medallion ready.

DOM: Reverend/Sir/Madam, I here present to you N., who, by reason of his/her diligence and loyalty has been found worthy of promotion to:

> Junior Singing Boy/Girl
> Senior Singing Boy/Girl
> Junior/Senior Chorister
> Team Leader
> Deputy/Head   Boy/Girl   in our choir.

The P/O takes the candidate's right hand and says:

> I hereby raise you to the status of ___ in our choir. May the Lord bless your going out and your coming in from this time forth for evermore.

All: AMEN.

The senior boy/girl present then places the medallion and ribbon over the candidate's neck. All bow to the Priest/Officiant and return to their places.

THANKING CEREMONY
for those leaving the choir

The Officiant, standing with the Director of Music, faces those leaving (after the DOM has formally introduced them) and, taking each one by the hand says,

> N., on behalf of the minister, church council, staff, congregation, and choir of First Church, I thank you for your years of loyal and faithful service to the worship of Almighty God in this place, and we pray that he will be with you wherever you go and whatever you do in his Name. Amen.

ADMITTANCE TO THE CHOIR ALUMNI ASSOCIATION

The Chairperson or other officer, says to those being admitted:

> N., as Chairperson of the Choir Alumni Association I have pleasure in welcoming you into full membership of the Association, with gratitude for all you have done for the music of First Church.

> We pray that you will find the fellowship to be an enduring blessing in your life and that you will want to support your colleagues past and present by continuing to exercise those gifts of music and Christian witness that have marked your year(s) of service to us in this place.

The Chairman shakes hand with the new alumnus and gives him/her an alumnus tie/scarf.

"Wow!" exclaimed Bob, when he had finished reading. "I should imagine that when you admit children to the choir they must think it a most important day in their lives if you make as much ceremony about it as this."

The director paused as the waiter brought their lunch to them. "Yes, indeed," he answered after taking a sip of his freshly squeezed orange juice. "You see," he continued, "they know they've fully earned the right to become members of the choir because they've been working hard at their admission tests for several weeks or months. It's with a real sense of fulfillment that they take part in the ceremony (which the head boy or girl rehearses with them beforehand). Also their parents and grandparents get excited about it and they turn up with cameras to capture the scene. It's always a special occasion for everyone."

"When do these ceremonies take place?" asked Bob swallowing a mouthful of delicious tuna.

"Here, we do it five minutes before the end of a preservice practice in church. The minister likes to preside whenever he can, but when he can't be present I ask one of the senior choirmen to be the officiant. They are only too happy to help out. Sometimes, when the child of one of the choir adults is due to be admitted I ask that parent to preside; it gives both parent and child a great thrill to enter into this new relationship.

"But you should discover the best occasion at your new church for such ceremonies. When I did this in England, for example, it was held during evening service, and so the whole congregation was involved in the process. Find out what works for you and alter the wording to fit your circumstances. I do think it is important," he concluded, "that the new singer is asked, formally if he/she wants to join the choir, and then to make a formal promise in front of everyone that they will try hard once they're admitted."

THANKING CEREMONY

They ate silently for a few minutes as Bob digested what he had just learned. What a great system this was! He looked at the bottom of the second page and asked, "What is this Thanking Ceremony and Choir Alumni Association?"

"Saying thank you is one of the most important lessons in life. 'Thank you' oils wheels of communication and encourages further participation. When a child, or an adult, has served with honor for any length of time in our choir and finds that he or she has to leave, it is a basic courtesy to say thank you for all that they have given to us. I like to do this formally, in front of the whole choir, and if it is appropriate, reinforce it informally in the vestry afterwards or in someone's home at a party. But I find that the formal 'Thank you' means a great deal to everyone—to those who are being thanked and also to those are doing the thanking.

"The ceremony explains itself, as you will see. It's particularly important when a boy's voice changes and he is about to join the young men in the back row of the choir. This thanking ceremony can be seen as a rite of passage from boyhood to manhood, with the implicit promise that the church will continue to nurture him through his high school years.

"In my formal introduction I say, 'Reverend Sir, I here present to you William Smith, head boy, who has been a member of our boys' choir for five years and participated with honor in the English Cathedrals' Tour two years ago, and who, today, is singing treble for the last time!' That really brings home to the boy, and to all those who are watching, that this is a rite of passage from being a boy to becoming a young man. And then the officiant adds the words to the end of his thanking paragraph '...and I welcome you as a member of our teens' choir,' and everyone applauds. It's a moving moment."

THE CHOIR ALUMNI ASSOCIATION

"What about the Choir Alumni Association?"

"This goes hand in hand with the rite of passage I've just mentioned. A boy is admitted to the association when his voice changes. A girl is admitted when she graduates to high school after having served for at least three years, and adults may be admitted after they've served with us for one year.

"This is another of these structures that folk value if they have to work to qualify for membership. We've had a long and noble musical tradition at this church, which started many years before I came. Those who have sung with us in years past are proud to be associated with us. The association came into being to encourage fellowship with past singers, who sometime pop in to see us, and college students who love to come back at Christmas to sing with us.

"We have a perfect treasure of a choirman, Dr. Jurgen George, who took on the responsibility of organizing this association several years ago. Already we have the names and addresses of over two hundred former singers, and we keep them informed about what's going on here with a bi-annual newsletter. They, in their turn, let us know what they are doing, and their news is included in the next letter.

"We find that a lot of alumni who are now college students join us for our Christmas services—they love coming back to us and we so enjoy seeing them all again. They also join us at the end of the season when we have our choir Sunday. Most of them are home by then, and it gives us the opportunity to field a really large choir. We also have an annual dinner in Dr. George's home and, gradually, our fellowship is increasing."

"What great ideas!" exclaimed Bob, pushing away his empty plate to make more room for his notebook. "How do you fund the association?"

"We ask all alumni members, except students, to contribute annually to help with the costs of postage and printing and the manufacture of alumni ties for the boys and scarves for the young women. Do you think that we get a good response?"

"With an organization such as you have here," responded Bob as he folded up the ceremonies paper and put it safely in his pocket, "I would imagine that the answer is yes."

"Alas, you're not right this time," answered the director, wiping his mouth. "It's the hardest job in the world to get money out of people, especially when they live far away, even though they are keen to remain members."

"And so how do you fund it?"

"The choir support committee is generous enough to underwrite any losses we may have at present. I foresee that situation continuing for a few years until the association has really got going. But, judging from my experience with similar organizations in England, the matter of wringing money from lethargic pockets is something that will remain with us."

And so saying he got up from the table and led the way out of the diner, paying the cashier on his way out.

I was rather hoping to enjoy a healthy ice cream, thought Bob, but I'd better not say anything as he's paying!

35
CHILDREN'S CHOIRS

"Would you like the most delicious ice cream you've ever tasted?" asked the director as they went down the steps from the diner. Bob choked for a moment, because of what he had just been thinking, and said, "Lead me to it!"

They continued walking for a few minutes in silence as the afternoon sunshine beat gently down on them. The director waited for Bob to ask him another question. He didn't have to wait long.

SEATING
"You give a lot of importance to the placing of your singers in your adults choirs."

"Yes. As you will have seen when I moved a bass in my chamber choir, it enables me to get the blend and balance that I want."

"Does it work for children's choirs, too?"

"It most certainly does," responded the director firmly as they ran across a road, causing an approaching car to sound its horn. "And it works for a number of different reasons:

"First, in practices you can place your good singers next to less experienced ones. The younger children seem to catch some of the techniques that the older children practice. It's similar to the saying I've already mentioned that 'Christianity is caught, not taught!' he said with a laugh, as they turned into a side street. "They learn how important good breathing is and how to sing high notes really easily. They catch from their elders how to concentrate for long periods, to follow the music, and to look at the conductor.

"Having new children on their own in a choir of more experienced singers leaves them out in the cold and helpless. And so the placing of children is very important in that regard."

They turned down another road, which was lined with a row of attractive new shops. "Now you can tell me the second reason why you should consider exactly where your children should be placed," he continued with a grin as he led the way into an ice cream shop that was decorated like an English pub. "Let me ask you the right question, but first, choose what ice cream you'd like."

Bob surveyed the abundance of ice creams displayed before him and chose an exotic mixture of caramel crisp with honey and sugar-coated almonds, topped by fresh raspberries. "I'll have a nonfat chocolate yogurt," said the director, "topped with strawberries.

"Now then," resumed the director as they watched their confections being assembled, "when you are conducting a children's choir practice, which singers do best, those nearest you, or those furthest away?"

"Didn't we discuss this idea on Sunday?"

The director laughed, and said, "I'd completely forgotten! Yes, you're right." Their conversation was interrupted for a moment as they were handed enormous helpings of ice cream, which Bob offered to pay for. "Thank you, Bob. But it does no harm to say things twice. Why?"

"Because repetition is an aid to memory. You've mentioned that, too!" he added with a caramel-covered smile.

"Do you know," the director continued as he relished the first mouthful of his nonfat dessert, "I watched a most experienced choirmaster recently when I was on the West coast. He was rehearsing in the church's large, airy hall. He had a superb choir of boys to whom he taught sight singing and, being a trained singer himself, he got them to use their voices in the most creative ways.

"But there was something wrong; there was a barrier of communication between them. He couldn't see what it was even though it was obvious to me. I had to think how I could get him to see it without offending him. After the practice I complimented him on everything he did and then said, 'I notice that you've got your boys on the stage, but you are on the floor, several yards away from them. I just wonder why that is?' He paused for a minute and then said, 'I never thought of that, thank you!' And for the next practice he had his boys on the floor level seated on chairs arranged in a semi-circle round his piano. The improvement was amazing, but not unexpected."

They finished their ice creams slowly, in silence, appreciating every last mouthful.

SOME FAULTS SHARED BY CHILDREN'S CHOIRS

"Well, this won't do," said the director, standing up and putting their empty ice cream dishes in the trash. "I've got a full afternoon of practices with our new and middle-rank boys, so we'd better get back." He turned to the young man who'd served them and said, "Thank you—they were great!" "Come again," he responded. "I certainly will," replied the director with a smile as he followed Bob out of the shop into the sun-filled street.

"What have you learned as you've gone round the country leading children's workshops?" asked Bob as they made their leisurely way back to the church.

"Apart from all the things I've already mentioned to you, such as finding that many children can't really sing, can't read music, have no idea how to concentrate for long periods and don't give themselves fully to what they are doing?" asked the director with a grimace.

"Oh, it can't be as bad as that!" exclaimed Bob as they crossed a quiet road.

"There are glorious exceptions, of course, but I fear the general run of children's choirs often fits into the categories I gave you just now—and it's all because choirmasters have no concept of how to stretch their children's many abilities. That seems to be my mission in life at present—to demonstrate how clear, focused teaching of children can bring out so many talents that are just waiting to be cultivated.

"Training children," he continued, as they walked across a grassy square leading to another attractive row of shops, "can be the most rewarding of all musical experiences. I love working with my kids and they, apparently, enjoy working with me. That's why they come to all my practices so faithfully and sing so much music so well."

SING FOUR MEASURES IN ONE BREATH

"Okay," responded Bob. "But you haven't told me any new points that children's choir directors should pay attention to."

"Oh, that's easy! If there's one fault shared by nearly all children's choirs I've heard, it is their apparent inability to sing more than two measures in one breath."

"Really?" exclaimed Bob. "I thought that many choirmasters spent a lot of time training their children to breathe correctly."

"You're right, they do! But they don't follow through their admirable teaching by applying it to the music they get the children to sing. It's as though there were two compartments to their practice schedule. In the first part, children do their warmups, which are generally quite good. And in the second part, the children are taught to sing songs and anthems, which are sometimes less than good.

"I've found that, whenever I've conducted children's choir festivals, I've often had to try to get them to sing twice as many notes in one breath. They do it for the rehearsal, of course, for I really concentrate on getting them to respond to me 100 percent. But why do you think, when it comes to the performance, that hardly any of them remember?"

SINGERS NEED TO LOOK AT THE MUSIC CREATIVELY

They walked on for a few paces, turning a corner into the main street and dodging a number of shoppers who were also enjoying the afternoon sunshine. "I suppose because they'd rehearsed the music in the old way so often with their choirmasters at home that they couldn't make the change," responded Bob.

"Absolutely right!" said the director, pleased by Bob's increasing perception. He'll make a great choirmaster, he thought to himself. "But," he continued out loud, "there are several other reasons they can't make the change."

"What are they," asked Bob, helpfully.

"Because they've not been taught to read music, they are not trained to look at the copy creatively. Whatever fresh markings you've asked them to make may just as well have been in Greek for all the good they did them. Also, the children had not been taught to think creatively when they are in practices, let alone when they are giving a performance. They quickly return to their zombie state, repeating, like parrots, what their choirmasters have taught them during the preceding months. My children are not zombies and they certainly aren't parrots," he continued, as they turned into Church Street. "And let me remind you again that my children are all local children—some of them could not match pitch when they came to me first, but now they are among my most reliable soloists—purely because I know how to teach them and am prepared to spend a lot of time with them to enable every one of them to succeed."

He turned to Bob, as they went through the practice room door, "And you now know all you need to know, through the practical advice I've given you and the training method I've shown you, so that you, too, may succeed."

"I know," said Bob gratefully. "Thank you."

36
REHEARSING BOYS

"Come in and watch what happens for the next four practices. I've got our new boys again for forty-five minutes; then the novices, who are the next grade up; followed by forty-five minutes with the junior singing boys, whom you haven't seen yet; and finishing with an hour with the senior singing boys, whom you also haven't seen. I must just nip upstairs to get my thermos flask, for I'll need reviving in the middle of all this!" and he sped away, leaving Bob to make himself comfortable on a stool at the far end of the practice room, where he could see, yet not be in the way.

NEW BOYS AND NOVICE BOYS AGAIN
The rehearsals for the new boys and for the novices were conducted in the same way as on Monday. All boys received a lot of individual attention from the director, who looked every boy in the face when he was trying to sing a passage on his own. The boys were gathered around the piano, very near to him. Occasionally, when a boy was experiencing a

152

problem, the director either got up from his stool and went over to the boy, or else asked the boy to come and stand next to the director, so that he could be shown what the problem was.

He was talking about that this afternoon—how important it was to have one's singers near you, especially those who need more help, thought Bob.

Bob noticed, again, that the director never solved a problem for a boy; instead he enabled the boy to solve the problem for himself. "Was that second note right, Shelton?" "No." "What did you do wrong?" "I held it for only one beat." "Well done! For how many beats should you have held it?" "Two." "Great! Try it again." And more often than not the boy got it right.

He also noticed that the director spent only about ten minutes on any one subject. Ten minutes on breathing, ten minutes on singing scales, ten minutes on one hymn, ten minutes on another, so that the boys would not get bored with any one subject. But Bob noted, with approval, that the director never left one subject, be it breathing or singing a verse of a hymn, unless every boy had achieved at least one new thing during that period.

His system is geared to success, and it shows, thought Bob.

MORE EXPERIENCED CHILDREN TEACH LESS EXPERIENCED

Mrs. Willis wasn't able to be with them that afternoon, and so the director had to lead boys in taking their tests on his own. At least he did to begin with, but near the end of the novices' practice a small boy wandered in and stood near the director. "Hallo, Sam!" he said, greeting the boy with a broad grin, to which Sam responded. "I'm glad you came early because I want you to help Nathan with his breathing. Take him outside and show him how he should breathe, and then when he can sing up to ten counts in one breath, bring him back in again. If he can do it right, you'll both get a dot."

Sam did as he was asked, watched by Bob, who thought that Sam couldn't be more than six months older than Nathan, and yet here he was helping the director to train the choir! Some girls did the same thing yesterday, thought Bob. What a great way to involve children in the learning process. They clearly benefit so much through teaching, and their enthusiasm for everything the choir stands for must increase.

Ten minutes later Sam and Nathan walked in and waited for the director to finish what he was doing with the other children. "Well, can you do it, Nathan?" he asked, giving the two boys an encouraging look. "I think so," said Nathan. "Okay, show me. Take a breath as you've been taught, really low, and then sing one through ten on this note," and he played an A for him.

Nathan tried very hard indeed, but only reached the count of nine. "That was terrific, Nathan," said the director. "You nearly did it. Try it again, but sing more softly this time." The boy sang again and reached the count of eleven before running out of breath. "Wow, that's super, Nathan! Well done—and congratulations to you, too, Sam. You'll make a great teacher. Let me give you a dot each." The two boys swelled with pride and pleasure in their achievement and in the director's evident pleasure in what they had done.

Bob thought, He put into practice several of the things we've been talking about today. When Nathan didn't succeed in his first attempt he didn't say 'no,' he said 'nearly,' leading the way for a second chance. And then he told Nathan how he could succeed, so that Nathan was encouraged. And all the time he showed his pleasure in the effort that both boys were giving. He's always positive in his approach, which leads to a positive response from his kids. That man's got loads of patience. I wish I had!

After the novices' practice had ended, Bob walked over to the director. He was refreshing himself with a cup of coffee while writing on the board a list of music that the junior singing boys were about to rehearse.

"It really works!" said Bob enthusiastically.

"What really works?" asked the director as he finished writing.

"Having young children help you train the newer ones."

"Of course it does! When I teach children something, they know they can do it and they remember it. The only thing they have to do then is to do it better and better, and there's no more practical way of achieving this than by getting them to pass on their knowledge to those who are following them." He turned to Sam who was still standing there. "You saw how impressed my friend was by what you did this afternoon, Sam. Can you come early again next week and help me some more?"

"I can't come too early," responded Sam, "because I don't get out of school in time. But I'll get here as soon as I can," and he smiled.

"That's great!" enthused the choirmaster. "You can be a great help with some more of the novices who aren't as good as you are, yet!"

The door opened and seven more boys walked in.

"Here come the other juniors," said the director, "right on time to begin their practice."

Bob took the hint and resumed his seat, but not for long. The director called on him to take boys out, two at a time, to work on some of their tests to earn their way to become senior singing boys. This is great, thought Bob. The director wasn't going to let me see the other training cards, but here I am actually using one.

GOOD TEACHING COMES FROM YEARS OF EXPERIENCE

He spent the next forty minutes in a nearby vestry where there was a piano as well as a small chalkboard, helping pairs of boys to learn the names of the notes on the bass staff so that they could relate them to the notes on the treble staff. He also taught them how to clap a dotted eighth and sixteenth notes, polished a page of an anthem that the other boys had been learning and tried to get two more boys to understand the principle behind basic key signatures.

He found it very hard work, for he hadn't yet acquired the skill to always be able to focus in on the exact problem that individual boys were experiencing. But he remembered to tell each boy at the end of their ten-minute sessions that he'd earned two dots, which pleased them all, including Bob. They all showed progress and were glad of the opportunity to work with him.

I feel the same way, he thought, as he sent the last boy back into the practice room. I've shown some progress, too, but I haven't yet got the experience to spot exactly what each boy should be working on at any one time, or how to ask the right question so that the child can work out the answer for himself, rather than listen to me tell him. But I'll keep at it and, with practice, it'll come.

TRAINING CARDS FOR NOVICES AND JUNIORS

As he was about to return to the practice room Bob noticed, under a pile of music on top of the piano, two unused training cards, one for novices to become juniors, and the second, which he'd just been using, for juniors to become seniors. Great! he thought. I'm sure the director doesn't know they're here. He'd been wanting to find out just how the training was graded to enable boys and girls to continue to increase their abilities once they'd qualified to become members of the choir.

He brought out of his pocket the first training card that he had been given, probationer to novice, and compared it with the two he'd just found.

Hymn singing progressed from being able to sing one verse of a hymn correctly after rehearsing it, to singing one verse of three familiar hymns after rehearsing them, and then to singing one verse of three familiar hymns correctly without rehearsal. Hmm, he thought, these children are clearly encouraged to think for themselves. It isn't easy to sing a verse of a hymn absolutely right, even with rehearsals, for they have to get the tune right, the words clear and also breathe in the right places. It's a real test for the older children to sing a verse of a hymn correctly without rehearsing it.

Clapping rhythm went from whole, half and quarter notes, to dotted halves and eighths, and then to dotted eighths and sixteenths. Those boys I've just been helping were very enthusiastic about clapping rhythm. It was fun!

Sight-reading went from singing four measures with notes moving by step, to the introduction of the interval of the third "cuckoo," and then to singing the melody of three unknown hymn tunes correctly after two or three attempts.

Knowledge of time signatures and key signatures was introduced progressively and there were some aural tests, such as singing a four-measure melody after it had been played twice and also singing the lower of two notes. The singing of simple and more demanding anthems was also included.

The more experienced children were expected to recite the creed, and some other parts of the service, from memory. That would open the way for the director to give his children some direct Christian training, he thought. It's one thing to be able to say the creed from memory, but it's much more important to be taught to understand it.

Bob noticed that, in all tests, the children could make as many attempts as they needed in order to be able to pass them. They had to complete every test on a card before they qualified for promotion. What a great system! He hesitated for a moment and then put the other two cards in his pocket. I'm sure the director won't mind, he thought as he made his way, cheerfully, back into the practice room where he found another group of boys assembling for their rehearsal.

37
REHEARSING SENIOR BOYS

These were larger children, six senior singing boys, who were one rank below the choristers. Bob found them an interesting group; clearly they were more accomplished than the boys he'd heard that afternoon. The director spent less time on warmups with them, for every boy knew how to produce his voice well. The director used a couple of hymns as warmup tone producers, getting the boys to sing them to *Oo* when the pitch was low, and to *Aw* when the notes were higher. Again, the director didn't give them the first note. They were all eager to try to pitch it themselves and, more often than not, they were right.

REHEARSING A NEW ANTHEM
The boys rehearsed three anthems that they would be singing that Sunday. Two of them they knew, but one was unfamiliar, and Bob noticed, with interest, how the director got them to tackle the new work.

After getting the pitch of the first note from them, he played the key chord and then asked them to sing the whole anthem through, slowly, to various vowels, as he played a light accompaniment on the piano.

He's asking them to sing vowels so that they can concentrate on the notes and not get sidetracked by having to look at the words as well, thought Bob. He's getting them to do one thing at a time—something that they can do, rather than cannot. The director didn't play the melody line except when there were awkward leaps. Then he played the tune lightly in sub-octaves, so that the singers could hear clearly, but otherwise he just gave them the harmonic structure and let them work out the tune. They were pretty successful, and the director showed that he was pleased with them.

ENCOURAGING INDIVIDUAL EFFORT
Occasionally, they encountered a particularly tricky passage that he used to enable each boy, in turn, to try by himself. "You can have two

attempts at this," he said, "until someone gets it absolutely right, when they'll get a dot. Okay, Jake, it's your turn first." Jake made a valiant effort, but stumbled at the point where the music was awkward. The director asked him to explain what the problem was, which he did, and then to have a second try. This was a little better, but still not wholly accurate. "You're nearly there, Jake," said the director encouragingly. "I think you've made it easier for Wilson to get it right."

Then Wilson had his two tries. He got the difficult bit right at his second attempt, but made a mistake on an easier part. "Well, between you, you've got the whole thing right. All I want is for someone to do it right nonstop. Zach, you have a go." Zach, who was smaller than some of the other boys, grinned and sang it absolutely right, which brought a burst of applause from the boys and a dot from the director.

What a great spirit of competition there is here, thought Bob. All these boys are pretty equal in accomplishment and so they enjoy seeing who can do best when it's their turn. As the practice proceeded Bob saw that every boy enjoyed a moment of glory when he sang something right that the others had not, and so the practice was both happy and productive.

They went through the new anthem three times in all. The first time slowly, to varying vowels, getting the notes right. The second time, equally slowly and continuously with the words, and the third time a little faster, but practicing it in more detail. They would sing a page or so and then the director would ask the right question to enable them to sing it better next time. "Did we start together?" "No, because we weren't watching you." "What letter is missing on the word *let*?" "*T*." "Why did you come in too early on page three?" "We didn't count the rests correctly." At all times the director built up the boys' interest in what they were doing by focusing their attention on one issue at a time and getting them to solve the problem themselves.

EVALUATION

The hour sped by on wings of achievement, and by the end the boys and the director were exhausted. Just before he dismissed them, he asked them to put their music in neat piles in front of them and to stand up straight. "Now tell me," he said as he walked towards them, "how do you think that practice went?"

Bob, from his seat at the end of the practice room thought, why should they tell him how it went? Surely he should tell them what he thought of it. Uh, oh! I think I'm about to learn something! He listened more closely as the boys and their director evaluated what had happened during the hour.

"The beginning of the practice went well," said one boy, "but halfway through we weren't trying so hard." "I agree, Wilson. Why was that?" "Perhaps we were tired after a long day at school," replied a diminutive boy. "That's a good thought, Tim." The director looked at all the boys and asked, "Who's had a long day at school?" and several boys put up their hands, including Tim. "I see," said the director, "Well, that's a very good reason for feeling tired. But I was pleased with you all as a whole, for we got through a lot of music, and so I'm going to give you three extra dots each." This pleased the boys considerably and the director read out the number of dots that each boy had earned; Tim and Zach came out on top with seven each, and the other boys weren't far behind.

TWO ON ONE AGAIN

"Now it's Martin's and Wilson's turn to see me for fifteen minutes, isn't it?" he asked as the other boys were leaving. "Let's look at that new anthem we were rehearsing."

The two boys stood on either side of the grand piano so that they could see each other and be close to the director at the same time. Bob noticed that the director gave each boy a singing lesson as well as a rehearsal in how to sing the anthem more accurately.

They began to sing the first page together, but the director soon stopped them and asked Martin to sing it by himself. "How's your mouth, Martin?" "It's closed," the boy replied. "Well, you know what to do about that, don't you? Try again." And Martin did try again, but with not much greater success. "Wilson, show Martin what an open mouth is like. You sing the first page for me." Wilson's mouth was better than Martin's, but his tone production was not as easy on the higher notes, and so the director got Martin to show Wilson how to do it better. And so the short practice went on, with one boy excelling at one time, and the other excelling next. Both boys felt good about their time with the director and went off with two more dots each, having accomplished a lot in a very short time.

38
HOW TO ENSURE GOOD BEHAVIOR

"It's food time again," said the director, predictably. "We've got to be back here in seventy-five minutes for a meeting of the choir support committee. It's the first one of the season and so, instead of holding it at church, our chairperson generously invited us to her lovely home. We'll talk about it over dinner."

"Do you always meet in the chairperson's home?" asked Bob as the walked out of the practice room.

"No, only for the first and last meetings of the season," answered the director as they left the music building. "For all other meetings we gather in one of the church rooms. We try to book the most comfortable, although we find that we get more business done if we're sitting round a table."

On their way down Church Street, Bob changed the subject and asked, "All your boys and girls are wonderfully well-behaved. Don't you ever have problems with them?"

"My goodness, yes!" exclaimed the director, "but not nearly as many problems as some choirmasters.

"You see," he continued, "you have to make up your mind what your standard of acceptable behavior is, and then stick to it. Some choirmasters expect their children to walk into practices in absolute silence: that's not for me, for I prefer a more informal approach. Other choirmasters allow a great deal of chatter during practices, as well as inattention, lateness, and unexplained absences. That's not for me either!

CHOIRMASTERS WHO HAVE TO REPEAT INSTRUCTIONS!

"Many choirmasters don't realize," he continued, "that their choirs train them in how practices are run, rather than vice versa."

"How do you mean?"

"If a choirmaster has to say something three times before her choir takes any notice, it's because they've trained her to accept that mode of communication. 'We won't take any notice of you until you've said it three times, because we know that you will say it three times!' Similarly, if your kids spend a lot of time playing around in your practices or making noise, it's because you have sent the message that such behavior is acceptable. It's no use saying, 'I can't do anything with them,' for you are the leader and it is you who should set the standards of behavior and attention that are comfortable."

TESTING THE BOUNDARIES YOU SET

"How do you set a standard and keep to it?" asked Bob as they crossed the road.

"I have to confess that I learned this skill fairly recently, much to my shame," said the director with a grimace. "It always used to bother me that, when I gave a group of children an order, there was always at least one kid who didn't obey it. I used to think I was at fault and that I lacked the necessary firmness of tone to make my wishes known." He stood still and looked at Bob to drive his message home. "That wasn't the case at all. All I lacked was knowing how to deal with the particular situation."

"Tell me about it," prompted Bob as they continued walking along the main street.

"I was watching a television program a few years ago; it had nothing to do with choirtraining, but the man was talking about children. He said, 'When you set a boundary for a child, he will immediately cross it...' I said 'Amen, brother!' for that had been my experience for years. However, he went on and flooded my soul with light. He said, '...he will immediately cross it in order to see if there's a boundary there!'

"I cannot tell you how much that meant to me, for it completely changed the course of my life, my relationship with children and also, be it said, with adults."

SETTING A BOUNDARY IN PRACTICE

"Give me an example so that I can understand more clearly what you are talking about," asked Bob.

"Well, the start of our full practice on Thursdays used to be a contest of wills between me and the rest of the choir. They're a very lively bunch: men, teenagers and boys. They were always there on time but I had the greatest difficulty in getting them to stop talking so we could actually begin the practice. I had to bang the top of the piano and call for order at least three times before they even began to quiet down.

"But after seeing that program on TV, I knew what I should do the next time."

"What did you do?" asked Bob, stopping in his tracks so that he could give his whole attention to what the director was about to say.

"Well, I had to begin by getting their attention in the old way. Eventually they became quiet and I then told them that that was no way a choir of their standard should start their rehearsals. 'Your singing is respected throughout this country, and beyond,' I told them, 'but I am glad that no one knows what it takes to get your attention! Next week we shall begin this practice in an entirely new way.'"

Bob found a bench nearby and sat on it as the director continued. "I told them that the following week they would come into the practice room in the usual way; go to their cubbies to get their music and go to their places and talk to their friends. 'However,' I continued, 'when the time comes to start the practice I will play on the piano, a slow arpeggio of D major, during which you may finish the sentence you have begun, and then turn towards me, ready to begin the practice. Is that okay?'"

"You asked them if they agreed?" commented Bob, looking up at the director.

"Yes, it was very important to have all the singers on board with me, for this was a make or break situation."

"What did they say?"

"They didn't say anything, they were so taken aback by what I'd just said. They just nodded their agreement in dead silence."

PRACTICE WHAT YOU WANT THEM TO DO

"Well, I bet you started the practice immediately, having gotten their attention," said Bob with a smile.

"Nearly," said the director, and waited.

"You mean, no, don't you?"

"Yes, I do. You've forgotten that the essence of leading a choir practice is to get them to do right away what you have asked them to do, not to ask them to make a mental note and do it right next week. So, what did I do?"

"You rehearsed them in getting quiet while you played the arpeggio of D major!"

"That's better! Yes, I told them that we would practice what I just said. 'In a minute I shall ask you to start talking to your neighbors again and then I will play the arpeggio of D major, during which you will complete the sentence with your friend and then turn to me, ready to begin the practice. Okay—talk!' and they all broke into loud conversation, testing me to see what I would do."

"What did you do?"

"I let them talk for at least half a minute; it's difficult to maintain a frenzied conversation for more than a few seconds, so I let it die down naturally. But then, I played a long arpeggio on the piano, clearly and deliberately, so everyone could hear it."

"Did everyone stop talking?"

"Everyone except two adults on my extreme left-hand side."

"What did you do then?"

WHAT TO DO WHEN YOUR BOUNDARY IS CROSSED

"That's a very good question. Why don't you come up with the right answer while we go into the restaurant. You can tell me your solution, once we've sat down." And, so saying, he led the way into a small cafe that specialized in making delicious pancakes. They found a table at the far end of the room, were given menus and a glass of ice water by the waitress and left to themselves for a few minutes.

"Well," said the director, "what did I do?"

"You could have done one of two things," answered Bob, confidently. "You could have started the practice, because most of the singers were giving you their full attention, or you could have played the arpeggio again to try to get those two adults to stop talking."

"Wrong and wrong again!" said the director not unkindly. "I didn't think you'd get the answer right for, whenever I've put this problem to choirmasters at workshops I've led, those two solutions are the ones that are invariably put forward."

"Why are they wrong?" asked Bob.

"Because I said I wanted everyone to be ready to begin the practice, not just most of them, and because I said that I would play the arpeggio only once. I didn't say that, if it didn't work the first time I'd play it again, and if it still didn't work I'd play it a third time. No! I had set my boundary very clearly and I was not going to move it. The arpeggio would be played once, and everyone would stop talking."

"But everyone hadn't stopped talking, had they?"

"Quite right. And so this is where a schoolmaster technique comes in."

WHY SOME CHILDREN MISBEHAVE

He leaned forward and said, "Most children misbehave because they want the teacher's attention. The easiest way to get the teacher's attention is to be slightly naughty. 'Frank, sit up straight. Frank, I told you to sit up straight. Frank, how many times have I got to tell you to sit up straight?' Who's the winner there, the teacher, or Frank?"

"Frank is," laughed Bob. "He's got the teacher doing exactly what he wants."

POSITIVE REINFORCEMENT

"Right again! Good teachers know about these schoolboy tricks and so they circumvent them by ignoring mildly bad behavior and reinforcing good behavior. 'James, you are sitting up well, and so are you, Elizabeth,' by which time Frank knows what he's got to do to get teacher's attention. He sits up straight and waits for her to notice him which, if she is wise, she will do."

"And so," said Bob, echoing the question that the director had asked him a few minutes earlier, "what did you do?"

"I reinforced the good behavior of the vast majority of the choir by looking to my right and gradually going round counter-clockwise catching everyone's eye and saying, 'Thank you...well done...this is good.'"

"What happened when you got to the two adults who were still talking?"

"Fortunately for them, they stopped just as I was about to look at them. I gave them a glance that showed them I knew what they had been doing—they'd been testing me, you see—and then we began an absolutely first class practice. I owed it to them all to be in top form, to show them my appreciation for what they had just done."

DISCIPLINE IS A SERIOUS MATTER

"But supposing the two adults hadn't stopped talking?"

The director became serious for a moment and said, "If that had been the case, I would have blasted them to kingdom come, looking them straight in the face. 'Don't you realize that you are wasting everyone's time? I asked you all if what I intended to do was a reasonable course of action and no one disagreed with me. If you wish to continue wasting everyone's time like this I shall have to ask you to leave the choir. Please see me afterwards when we can talk about it!' When it comes to firm discipline," the director continued, "you have to do it with great serious- ness and go straight to the point. And," he added as an afterthought, "if you threaten to take a course of action when a child misbehaves, such as, 'If you do that again I'll have to ask you to leave the room,' you must carry through what you have threatened. Don't move that boundary, or you will be left playing the child's game instead of vice versa, and that is bad, not only for you but especially for the child."

"Wow!" commented Bob, who felt the force of the director's firm resolve, even though he hadn't been the one who had been talking.

"You'll have noticed that I used peer pressure. I didn't say, 'You are wasting my time,' but 'you are wasting your colleagues' time.' That's always a good way to approach things—especially with children, who seek the approval of their peers."

UNUSUAL BEHAVIOR PATTERNS

The director paused for a moment and then continued, "You should also be on the lookout for unusual behavior. This often occurs, not because a child wants your attention, but because there may be a problem at school or at home. It's up to you to notice this and call the parents to see if you can be of help.

"Also," the director added, "the spring is a time when the sap starts to rise and young men and women get particularly hyperactive. It's a good idea at such times for you to bring this to their notice and ask them to deal with it themselves. If you have cultivated a good relationship with them, they will want to please you and will try to act as responsibly as they can.

"The three most threatening words in the English language are, 'See me afterwards.' They put the fear of God into children and adults alike, but you should only use them when you really have to."

"I see, now, what you mean by deciding firmly what your boundaries are, and sticking to them," said Bob.

DON'T BEAR A GRUDGE

"There's one further thing one should beware of when dealing with so-called badly behaved children," said the director.

"What's that?"

"Let me ask you a question." Here we go again! thought Bob. But the director's questions do help me to remember the right answers. And so he smiled and said, "Fire away!"

"If you've experienced a real problem with a child or a teen at one practice, what should your attitude be to him at your next practice?"

"That's obvious! I should tell him that I shall be watching him carefully to make sure he behaves better this time."

"Oh dear," sighed the director as he leaned back in his chair. "Would you like to reconsider your answer?"

Bob was surprised at the director's response, but he couldn't think of any other course to take.

The director took a sip of water, leaned over the table and looked Bob straight in the eyes. "Being a member of the church means that we are in the business of redemption," he said seriously. "If a sinner can't find forgiveness with us, where can he go?"

"Do you mean that I have to forgive this child?"

"If you have dealt with him lovingly and firmly the previous time and gotten rid of the problem—yes I do! As God in Christ forgives us our sins, so we must forgive those who sin against us."

"As it says in the Lord's Prayer," said Bob, anxious to earn his way back into the director's favor.

"Right! But how many of us actually put into practice the matter of forgiving others? If we don't forgive others, then God cannot forgive us!"

"Do you mean that I've got to play God in this situation?" asked Bob incredulously.

"Yes I do. For a very practical reason." The director leaned back and took another sip of water.

"If that child comes to your next practice and you still treat him as a naughty boy, there's no way that he can get out from under your condemnation. He has not received your forgiveness. Your role is indeed to play God as portrayed by the father welcoming back the prodigal son. The son was received with unconditional love. You must do the same with your returned prodigal singer! Only then is he free to try his best—and he will because he knows that you really love him. You will have motivated him to want to please you. You showed him tough love when you dealt with his problem at the last practice. You now show him unconditional love when he returns to you.

"In playing God," added the director, "you can choose either to be a judge or a redeemer. Which will it be?"

Bob blinked his eyes and murmured, "Redeemer!"

DISCIPLE YOUR SINGERS

Host and guest looked at each other across the table and smiled with a new understanding. "When all is said and done," concluded the director, "your best way to ensure discipline is to let your infectious devotion for the task in hand enthuse all your singers to want to learn from you. The root meaning of discipline is to learn. A disciple is one who learns! Make disciples of all your singers."

"I'll try!"

The waitress came over at that point to take their order. "Do you like pancakes, Bob?"

"Yes, I do."

"Well, let's have a strawberry, a banana and a cranberry pancake each, and coffee, please," he asked the waitress, who made a note of their request and left them in peace again.

BOUNDARIES ARE AREAS WITHIN WHICH TO EXCEL

"You need to realize that a boundary is not a negative concept, but one which is wholly positive," continued the director, taking a sip of water, for he'd been doing a lot of talking.

"Go on," said Bob, again writing in his notebook.

"Think of the game of tennis. The reason it is such a superb game, and so many first rate players compete in it, is because its boundaries are so clearly defined. If a ball falls an inch within the line, it's counted in. If it falls out by an inch, or even less, it's counted out, however good the stroke was that got it there. Everyone understands those simple rules and abides by them. There are no exceptions.

"It's the same with the way I run my choirs. I say, in effect, to the children, 'If you come here and do exactly what I want you to do, then you will succeed, because I know better than you do what's good for you and, what is more, you will enjoy it, as a player enjoys a really hard game of tennis, for

I'll help you to win. If, on the other hand, you come here and decide not to stay within these very clear boundaries, then I cannot help you to excel.'"

"And your boundaries are very simple," commented Bob. "The children must be punctual and try hard right through your practices. That's all you ask of them."

DISCIPLINE SHOULD BE POSITIVE

"Well put!" exclaimed the director. "As long as they try hard, I'll see to it that their efforts bring success. Everything one does regarding discipline should be positive. Kids need guidance as to what is or is not acceptable behavior. 'You may talk when I have finished speaking.' 'When you need to go to the bathroom, ask me.' After you have reprimanded someone, turn it around by asking, 'How can we deal with this next time?'

"There are two ways of helping children to do their best which I find most useful," added the director.

"What are they?"

"The first is, how to give an order. Orders should never be open-ended."

"What do you mean?"

"Never say, 'Go fetch your music from your cubbies,' because there's no end product and no time boundary."

"What should you say?"

"You should give your orders in three parts—one: when the order is to be carried out; two: what the order is; and three: how it is to be completed.

"And so," continued the director, "you should say, '(one) when I have finished speaking, (two) I want you to fetch your music from your cubbies, (three) and when you have put it in a neat pile in front of you and you are standing still, I'll know that you are ready to begin.'"

"That's so clear!" exclaimed Bob.

"And the other helpful hint I can give you is how to handle the situation when a child is behaving so badly that you have to send him out of the room."

"That doesn't happen too often, does it?"

"No! But that's all the more reason for handling the situation with care."

"What do you do?"

"There are again, three stages. One: If a child is being a continual nuisance the time will come when you have to say to him, 'Carl, you are not being helpful to the other boys! If you choose to do that again, I'll have to ask you to leave the room so that the rest of us can get on with our work.'

"You see that I'm using peer pressure here," added the director. "The boy is not getting in my way, his behavior is getting in the way of the other children.

"Two: Almost certainly he'll misbehave again."

"To test your boundary," observed Bob with a smile.

"Right! And so what do I do when he crosses that boundary?"

"Three: You have to send him out—you don't move the boundary to give him another chance, because that would be playing his game and not yours."

"Well done! You're learning fast, young man," commented the director with a grin.

"But," he continued, "the way that you send him out of the room is of crucial importance. You can't banish him to 'outer darkness' permanently, for you aren't giving him the opportunity to redeem himself."

"What do you do?"

"As it was his decision to misbehave, so you must allow him to make the decision to behave better next time."

"And so what do you say?"

"I say, 'Carl, you must leave the room to allow the rest of us to get on with our work. But when you decide that you want to be helpful and to join in again with the rest of us, you may return.'"

"Wow!" said Bob, predictably.

"And more often than not, within a few minutes Carl will come back into the room, a reformed character!"

"And you welcome him as though nothing had happened," said Bob, remembering that a choirmaster is in the business of redemption, not judgement.

"Well done, young man, you've got it!"

"Let the child see that it is solely his, or her, decision whether or not to stay within the boundaries you have set. If they choose to exclude themselves, that is their responsibility until they decide that they wish to come back in again. And so," the director concluded, "continually ask yourself how you can help the difficult child to understand what is best for him—and that is to choose to come within your boundary, for there, and there only, can he excel. My dean used to say that a difficult person is a person with a difficulty. He also said, 'To understand all is to forgive all.' Help that child, or indeed that adult, to recognize what their problem is so that they can start to solve it.

"But here come the pancakes. Let's relax a little before we start talking about tonight's meeting," and they both dug into large platefuls of delicious pancakes topped with a mound of whipped cream.

39
WHY HAVE A
CHOIR SUPPORT COMMITTEE?

A few minutes later, after they had consumed a pancake each, Bob asked, "Tell me about your choir support committee."

"I couldn't run my choir programs without the active help of our choir parents. A strong support team is essential to the success of any venture, and you can see it clearly in the organization of choirs. You see," he said, as he tackled his second pancake, "there are so many facets to the life of a choir, beyond the weekly practices and services."

"What are they?" asked Bob, who was half a pancake ahead of his host. "You tell me!"

Here we go again, thought Bob. He's making me do the thinking when I'd hoped to get away by making him do my thinking for me! He paused for a while and then said, "I suppose someone has to organize the car pools that bring the children to the church."

"Yes, the parents look after that themselves very well. What else needs to be done to keep the choir going?"

Bob thought for a little longer and said, "Well, it can't be organizing the copies of music, because you've got a fine team of librarians."

"True," he responded unhelpfully.

This man's really making me sweat, thought Bob. I'll certainly remember the answer once I've found it. After a few more moments he asked, "Who looks after your choir robes?"

CARE OF ROBES

"Ah! That's better. We have a team of parents who take care of all of that. They ensure that all the robes are washed and ironed at the end of the season, sorted out into sizes and hung neatly on racks in the vestries ready for the start of next season. And then, when the season begins, teams of parents come to our opening practices to fit all the children and teens with new sets of robes.

"These parents also ensure that the parents of each child sew into his or her robe the child's name."

"Why? Wouldn't a number be just as effective?"

"It should be in theory, but in practice it doesn't work out like that. If a child accidentally takes someone else's robe there's no quick way to find out who it is. A name in the robe settles things very quickly. You'll find that it is not easy to get all parents to cooperate in this way. You may well find that you have to appoint a robes-person to look after this side of things for you.

"All this takes an awful lot of time and trouble on the part of these helpful parents, but it is absolutely essential if the choirs are to look good in church. And then, of course, as Christmas and Easter approach, they ensure that all singers take their robes home to be washed again. They also inspect them regularly to check that they're kept in good order, and if a robe is torn it's sent back to the child's parents to be mended. Halfway through the year some of the children have grown so much that they need larger robes, and our team of parents takes care of that, too.

THE DIRECTOR'S SUPPORT OF VOLUNTARY ACTIVITIES

"It's an enormous job to look after all our robes, continued the director, as he took another mouthful of delicious pancake. "It calls for endless hours of sacrificial work by many highly dedicated parents. And they do it all so willingly—if I show them strong support at all times. The active support of the choirmaster for all matters to do with the choir is essential if these voluntary activities are to flourish. Tell me," he asked unexpectedly "how I can show my support?"

Bob finished his final helping of pancake, pushed his plate away, and answered, "You write them letters of thanks; you make appreciative remarks to them as often as you can and you're there ready to lend moral support whenever parents come to fit robes."

"My word! that was a well thought-out answer," said the director admiringly. "I can't think of anything to add to it except, perhaps, that you need to ensure that the young boys and girls, in particular, hang up their robes neatly every week to keep them in good condition. You see," he added with a smile, "there's so much more to running a successful choir program than just knowing how to breathe and conduct four beats in a measure!" and they both laughed.

"But you'll see at tonight's meeting how many non-musical activities there are that help the choir programs to flourish." And so, after Bob had insisted on paying the bill, they began to walk back to church.

40
FINDING A CHAIR FOR THE CHOIR SUPPORT COMMITTEE

"I don't have a choir support committee at my church," said Bob as they made their way along the main street, which was lined with shops whose windows were filled with attractive displays. "How can I start one?"

CONSULT WITH YOUR MINISTER
"Well, you must first discuss it with your minister. I can't stress strongly enough that you need to work very closely with your minister in all things and especially when you want to start something new. He must be the first person on your list of those to consult, for he knows the parish better than you do and so should be able to offer you more help and," continued the director as they came to traffic lights, which were against them, "his is the final responsibility for all things to do with the church. He needs to be able to exercise that responsibility by enabling you to carry through your best ideas."

As they were waiting to cross the road, Bob got out his notebook and began writing. "What should I ask him when discussing a choir support committee?"

FINDING THE RIGHT CHAIRPERSON
"That's a very good question," responded the director as the light turned green and they crossed the road. "First of all, you need to sit down

and think what needs such a committee could fulfill. You'll get a lot of input from tonight's meeting when you see our agenda.

"Secondly, you'll need his input as to who should chair the committee."

"Shouldn't I chair it?" asked Bob, experiencing difficulties with writing and walking at the same time.

"You could if you want to give yourself a lot of extra work," laughed the director. "But it's far better to get someone whom you respect, and who is respected by the other parents, to chair it for you. This is a case of two heads being better than one, for your chairperson will be able to give you insights that you might not have."

THE FUNCTION OF THE CHOIR COMMITTEE CHAIRPERSON

"Such as what?"

"Such as how the other choir parents are thinking about certain issues; such as whom to ask to head up special projects, such as when it's time to get robes washed for Christmas and also to keep an eye on other practical matters. These are components of your choir program that you won't really have time to think about if you're really doing your musical job well."

The church parking lot came into view and the director got his car keys ready. "One of the most useful functions a good choir chairperson can fulfill," he said as he unlocked his car, "is to act as a frank and friendly advisor to the music director."

"How do you mean?" asked Bob as he slid into his seat.

"You will find that there are times when you are not aware of how your actions affect choir personnel and their families. You may have arranged to have practices when the schools are holding concerts. Someone needs to tell you, and the choir committee chair is the person to do it. You will certainly overlook something that you ought to have done. And it is the choir support chair who should take you on one side and have a quiet word with you about it."

The director drove out of the parking lot and down a side road to some shops.

"The chair should be the sort of person you can consult about courses of action you propose—such as, is it a good thing to take all the girls away for an overnight singing weekend or should you take the seniors only. The chair can give you a different perspective from that of your music staff so that you can arrive at a well-considered decision."

The director stopped his car outside a flower shop and got out. "And so," he continued, as he locked the car and led the way inside, "both you and your minister need to feel comfortable about who is to head up your choir support committee, for he or she will play a vital role in your music program for several years."

HOW TO APPROACH A POTENTIAL CHAIRPERSON

He chose a bouquet of brightly colored fall flowers and, after paying for it, led the way back to his car, still talking. "Once you and the minister have agreed on a likely choice, you need to write to that person to ask if you may call to discuss it."

"Couldn't I phone him or her?" asked Bob as he slid into his seat again.

"You could, but because this is such an important matter I would recommend that you write to the person of your choice, briefly setting out the need for such a committee and asking if he or she would be willing to consider heading it up for no more than two years. Better still, ask if you could call to discuss the matter with them."

"I would have thought that, if one has found a really good chairperson, you'd want to keep them in the job for longer than two years."

"Ah!" exclaimed the director as he drove round a succession of roads, which were lined with lovely houses, "you're much more likely to get a really good person to be your chair if you tell them that it is for a strictly limited period. You won't find people volunteering to help you if it is open ended.

"If you've chosen a really competent and efficient person, he or she is bound to be involved in many other activities. They would be more willing to help you if they knew it was for a limited period. You should tell him or her that their great experience is needed to set up this brand new committee that will play such a large part in the life of the church."

He stopped the car outside a lovely house where other cars were also parked. They got out and made their way to the front door. "Take your time with this person and arrange with him or her to meet the minister and yourself before a decision is made. Once they accept the position, the three of you should work very closely together to set up and meet with a provisional committee, draw up a constitution and get the thing moving."

He rang the doorbell and waited. "But all this will spring, initially, from your own enthusiasm, your own leadership and the specific needs you have defined for the formation of such a committee. And," he concluded as the door was opened by their hosts, "tonight's meeting will give you a lot of ideas as to how you should begin."

41

CHOIR SUPPORT COMMITTEE AGENDA

"Margaret, I'd like you to meet Bob. He's from Seattle, and he's spending a week with me absorbing our choir program. Bob, this is Margaret and Stephan Silver; she's the delightful chair of our wonderful committee and he's her splendidly supportive husband."

COMMITTEE MEMBERS
Their hosts welcomed them both, graciously accepting the director's gift of flowers, and led them into the dining room where a number of adults had already assembled. They were sampling a tantalizing array of

cakes and sandwiches, with wine, coffee and tea on the sideboard. The director introduced Bob to them all, one by one, as further committee members arrived, including Nancy Willis, the associate director of music; Rena Elvin, the head boy's mother, who was also the committee secretary; two members of the adult choir; and Dr. Jurgen George, the chairman of the Choir Alumni Association. Bob met the parent of a twelfth-grade bass and also two mothers of three choirgirls.

"My daughters are twins," said one of the mothers, "No one can tell them apart, not even the director!"

"And my daughter only joined the choir at the end of last season," chimed in the other mother. "She's a senior at high school, and wishes that she'd joined much younger because she loves it so much."

Maya Jones, the deputy head girl, was also present; she represented the teens on the committee. The junior warden, who also happened to be a choir parent, came, and also one of the clergy, the Reverend Margaret Rose. Last to arrive was Frank Stevens, the chairman of the concerts' committee. He came because the choirs were heavily involved in the series of concerts that his committee had arranged for the season.

After twenty minutes of food and chat their hostess called them into her large sitting room to begin the meeting.

Bob sat quietly in a corner watching all that went on and taking many notes. He was given a copy of the agenda for that night, which he read carefully and put into his notebook. The director was quite right, he thought. The vast range of subjects covered during the next hour and a half did give him more than enough ideas to begin his own choir support committee when he got home.

CHOIR SUPPORT COMMITTEE (CSC) AGENDA

Welcome to new members
Minutes of the last meeting
Financial statement
Allocation of responsibilities for the season:
    Care of boys' robes
    Care of girls' robes
    Care of teens' robes
    Care of adults' robes
Allocation of parents for:
    Men and boys' choir weekly suppers
    Girls' choir breakfasts
    Receptions in the church hall after monthly Evensongs
Appointment of chairs for:
    Choir stall for the church Christmas Fair
    Choir stall for the annual rummage sale
Venues for parties:
    Parents of choirboys

Parents of choirgirls
Adult choir parties (3 per season)
Afternoon tea for parents of new boys and girls
Director's reports:
Last summer's choir camps
This year's choir personnel, including new singers
Outline of special events this season
Check dates for singing outings and book CSC-funded buses well in
advance for:
Men and boys' choir
Girls' choir
Adult choir
Who would be chaperones for children's outings, and who
would provide soft drinks and cookies for the journeys
Money raising efforts:
Choir photographs: provisional dates
Choir recording: provisional plans
Other plans: When, what, why, and who to chair
Scholarships for young singers to attend singing camps next summer,
funded by CSC
Arrangements for open practices to be attended by:
Parents of the girls
Parents of the boys
Report by the Concerts' chair
Report by the Choir Alumni Association chair
Any other business
Confirm dates of meetings for the remainder of the season

Thanks to the efficiency of Mrs. Silver and the enthusiastic offers of
help from all members present, the meeting ended on time and everyone
went home, excited at the prospect of all the good things that lay before
them this season. Bob left the house in something of a daze after all he
had seen and heard.

42
CHOIR SUPPORT
COMMITTEE LOGISTICS

MAINTAINING CONTACT WITH THE CHAIRPERSON
By the time they'd got into the director's car and were driving back to
his house, Bob had recovered enough to ask some questions.

"How often do you see Mrs. Silver?"

"Every week! As she's a choir parent I see her when she brings her children to church for practices, but I also see her, officially, at least once a month when we discuss the agenda for our next meeting. These chats are essential to the well-being of our choir programs here, for it is then that we discuss pastoral matters regarding choir families as well as our day-to-day organization.

"You see," continued the director, "if you are running a really worthwhile music program in your church, much of your time will be spent thinking about the music. You will need someone whose focus is more on the choir families themselves, and the chair of the choir support committee can be that person, especially if he or she is a choir parent. She will meet other parents in the church parking lot when they bring their children to choir, and many warm friendships will spring up. The choir support chairperson can pass on to you the good things that other choir parents are saying about the program—and that is encouraging, for we all blossom when we're given encouragement. But she should also pass on to you the criticisms that others are making."

"Why?" asked Bob as he filled yet another page in his notebook.

"Because the only way we can grow is to discover what we are not doing well, or even doing badly. Her input at these times enables the director to rectify the situation. If she knows of hurt feelings among choir families and doesn't tell you, then how can you bring healing? We learn from our mistakes. Without constructive criticism we tend to get self-centered and not realize, sometimes, that we may be straying from the path we had set ourselves.

"The chairperson, if she is really conscientious, will also take it upon herself to deflect unconstructive remarks and bring them to you in a positive form so that you can, together, see how situations can be remedied."

"Surely people wouldn't say unkind things about you behind your back if you are really doing your job well," remarked Bob.

"My dear young man!" exclaimed the director. "I'm afraid you may be in for a nasty shock. Yes, there will always be some people who misunderstand your motives and say things about you and your work that they wouldn't say to your face. This is where the chair of your choir support committee can be so helpful, if she is a really dedicated person who can handle conflict. She can bring to you some of the things that people are saying about you, but she can turn them around so as to spare you the unkind details. And then, together, you can work out how best to deal with these problems."

"Your chairperson really is vital to the success of what you do, isn't she," remarked Bob.

"Yes, she is. She's a sort of personal counselor—someone whom I respect and trust, and who feels the same about me. We meet once a year to discuss how things have been going. I tell her how she can be even more helpful to me, and she does the same for me. I've even set aside a cubby for her in the choir room," continued the director, "where I can leave notes for her as ideas occur to me. She is central to so much of my thinking here."

CHOOSING COMMITTEE MEMBERS

The director made a right turn into a winding country road as Bob turned a page in his notebook and asked, "How are members of the committee elected?"

"They're not! They volunteer to be members of the support committee, knowing full well that such a voluntary act carries with it the responsibility of participating fully in the activities we organize. Having such a large program, as we do here, it's very useful indeed to have as many active folk as possible on the committee.

"We find that most of the parents, once they join the committee, tend to stay during the years their children spend in our choirs—and this is mutually beneficial. A child will be more likely to remain in the choir until graduation if her parents are actively involved in helping to organize the program. And if a child is keen to sing, her parents will catch this enthusiasm and be equally enthusiastic to remain with us.

"Some choir support committees in other churches prefer to have parents and adult singers elected for a limited period. It's up to you to decide with your minister and chairperson how best to organize your own committee."

INVOLVING NEW PARENTS

They drove a little further down the dark road. The lights of houses hidden among the trees shone out to mark their way. "I notice that you have arranged a reception for the parents of new boys and girls. Why is that?"

"That's a very good question! One of our choir parents remarked, several years ago, that it took time to learn how to become an effective choir parent in our demanding program. She suggested that it would be very helpful, at the beginning of a season, to invite all the parents of new young singers to meet with a few more experienced parents. We could tell them how the program works and what would be expected from them during the time their children sing with us. The experienced parents would answer their questions and tell them how rewarding it was to belong to our choir program. And the whole thing would take place in the context of afternoon tea in the home of one of our choir members. We make sure that the minister is present, both for his support and for his input."

"What a great idea," exclaimed Bob. "I must certainly organize a meeting for our new parents as soon as I get back. It might be a good way of starting a choir support committee."

SPECIFIC PLANNING FOR NEW PARENTS' MEETING

"I suppose that it's fairly simple to get all the new parents to come to the tea," Bob remarked, when he had finished writing.

"No, it's not! It's not easy to organize any kind of group, for there are so many pressures on parents and children alike, these days."

"How do you go about getting them there, then?"

"You really have to push it. For example, what we do is:

1   "Send out an attractively printed invitation, with RSVP. Tell them, briefly, the point of the meeting, where it will be held, and for how long it will last. (3:00—4:30 P.M. on Sunday is a good time, for it is long enough for your business and short enough to allow parents to do something else in the evening.)

2   "Follow that up with a phoned invitation a couple of days later.

3   "The day before the party we call them again to say, 'Looking forward to seeing you tomorrow. Do you need a ride? We'd be happy to arrange for someone to pick you up.'"

"That's rather overkill, isn't it?" remarked Bob.

"Alas, it's not. There's so much junk mail these days that we all find it hard to differentiate between what's important and what isn't. Also, even with the best intentions in the world, we all forget engagements at some time in our lives and finally, Sunday afternoon is generally regarded as a time for families to be at home—but it's the best time for the sort of gathering that I'm talking about, because almost everyone is free then."

"What happens when the new parents arrive?"

The director continued:

4   "Have name tags ready, with the name of each parent in one color and the name of their child in another.

5   "Allow thirty minutes for afternoon tea, when everyone may visit and introduce themselves to each other. The hosts should provide a choice of tea and coffee, with cakes, cookies and sandwiches. Members of your choir support committee should be brought in to help with this.

6   "Start the meeting with your minister giving a welcome and saying how important the music program is to the church.

7   "You come next, telling them, in an attractive way, what the choir is about."

"What is it about?" interrupted Bob.

"It's about bringing up children in the best atmosphere possible in one of the loveliest buildings in the town, where they are loved and cared for by trained staff, both clerical and lay. By the way, remember to give a little of your own background, for parents will be interested to learn more about you.

"It's about training them to be practicing musicians, with weekly, free instruction not only in how to sing beautifully, but also in how to read music. This is a gift that will remain with them for the rest of their lives.

"It's about performing regularly some of the world's greatest music—assuming that your musical diet is not made up of kiddy songs!

"It's about opportunities to sing concerts with orchestral accompaniment and singing visits to great cathedrals.

"It's about involving the children's parents in all these opportunities so that their families may grow together in an positive environment free of the destructive influences that are so prevalent these days."

"Wow!" said Bob.

The director continued: "Encourage the new parents to ask questions at any time during this session. There's nothing more guaranteed to send people to sleep than being talked at for half an hour nonstop.

8   "Let a couple of experienced choir parents say what the choir program means to them and their families.

9   "The chair of the choir support committee should outline what the committee is all about and why the new parents should become involved. There are so many worthwhile support tasks that need doing. And please note," said the director, "that licking stamps and folding letters are not tasks likely to attract new members—those should be reserved for long-time members whose loyalty to the cause has been proved!

10   "After more questions and general discussion, you should bring the meeting to a close with thanks to the parents for coming and thanks to your hosts.

ALWAYS FOLLOW UP IMMEDIATELY

"And," continued the director, "make sure that you finish punctually. What will you do after that?" he asked unexpectedly.

"You help your hosts clear up."

"Good! What will you do the next day?"

Bob thought for a minute and then said, "I will write a thank-you letter to the hosts and also a letter to the parents who came, thanking them for coming and saying how much I look forward to working with them and their children." And he smiled, knowing that he'd given the right answer.

"Well done! You're learning fast, young man." The director smiled too, as he continued to drive in a leisurely manner to his home. "But make sure that your letters to the parents are personalized—that's easy to do on your wordprocessor—include the name of their child and add a brief sentence applicable to that family alone. All this will show that you really care about them. You will be fulfilling your promise made to them at their meeting that they and their family will be entering a loving and caring community.

"It would be good if the chair of the choir support committee wrote or called the new parents, telling them when the next choir support committee meeting is, and asking if they'd be interested in helping with a certain task. Get the new parents involved immediately while they are still malleable. If you wait too long they'll have found other interests to occupy their time."

"Gosh!" said Bob, "That sounds like a great idea. Thanks!"

OPEN PRACTICES—AN AID TO RECRUITMENT

"Tell me about the open practices."

"I often used to think, as I rehearsed our boys and girls, how good it would be if their parents could see just how wonderfully well they are doing. My associate at that time then said the obvious: 'Why don't you arrange one practice a year when the parents can be there? One for the boys' choir and one for the girls'!'

"And so we did—and it worked splendidly. We have all the boys at one practice and all the girls at another, getting the new singers to share music with the more experienced. I then conduct an hour's practice. We rehearse music for the next few Sundays, and I ask the parents if they've noticed just how well the girls or boys did this or did that, so as to keep them interested during a working rehearsal. We end with the parents singing a verse of a hymn while the children sing a descant. And then we all go home.

AIDS TO RECRUITMENT

"The chair of our choir support committee provides name tags for everyone and she takes the opportunity to recruit parents for some of our programs. It's also a good way to recruit new singers. Parents feel that they can bring along their friends who have children and may be interested in joining us, and younger brothers and sisters come along, too. I get them involved if at all possible."

"Do you serve any refreshments?"

"We used to, but we found that it took too much time out of a busy evening for parents—especially those who have just come home from work and need a good meal, not just a snack."

CHOIR PARENTS' AND ADULT SINGERS' SUPPORT OF THE WHOLE CHURCH PROGRAM

"One final comment," said Bob as the director's car neared his home. "I noticed that the junior warden was there."

"Yes," answered the director with enthusiasm. "You'll find that, if you organize a really lively music program in your church, the parents and spouses of many of the singers will be elected to office in the church, and this, of course, can be a great help to you. I've been here for eleven years and for nine of those years either one or both church wardens were either choir parents or adult singers. Nearly one third of the current church council has similar strong connections with the music program and you will find that this will happen for you, too."

He drove the car into his short driveway and got out. "This has been a good day," he said, as he led the way back to his darkened house.

"Yes it has!" agreed his guest. "I can hardly wait until tomorrow!"

🎼 THURSDAY 🎼

43
BOYS' CHANGING VOICES

"What's the program for today?" asked Bob as he ate a slice of toast and marmalade and tried not to look at what the director was eating out of his cereal bowl.

"It's our big choir practice evening—from 4:15 through 9:30, but we start the day with a meeting of our music staff in my office, so let's get going!"

Fifteen minutes later they were bowling along in the director's car. "I noticed that you have a lot of high school young men in your choir. How do you encourage them to stay on when their voices change?"

"That's a good question, Bob. Children, especially boys, tend to drop out of choir programs at the onset of puberty, and that's such a shame, for they have so much to give, and we can offer them so much in return."

BE GENTLE WITH YOUR TEENAGERS

"Well, how do you go about it, then?"

"The golden rule when dealing with boys who are going through puberty is to be gentle with them.

"Dash it!" he exclaimed, "there's a traffic jam up ahead—we're going to be late, and there's nothing we can do about it!"

His car ground gently to a halt and the director turned off his ignition. The road ahead, as far as they could see, was filled with stationary vehicles. Clearly there'd been an accident and they would have to wait it out.

"Never mind," said Bob soothingly, "what were you saying about being gentle?"

"Oh yes! In the words of St. Paul, 'Be kind to one another, tenderhearted, forgiving one another as God in Christ forgave you.'"

"Why, what do you mean?"

"When a boy reaches that stage in his life he finds that he is getting a whole new range of equipment. It's like trying to drive a car after you've been used to a bicycle—he doesn't know what's what. It's an exciting but unsettling experience for him, and he won't show how he feels. He's particularly sensitive to personal remarks, such as, 'Altos, you're flat again!', especially if there are girls around. Puberty doesn't happen like this to girls—their voices get better and better (a prime reason for keeping them in your choir program!). Young men's voices are like an unbroken horse—full of promise, but untamed—and they can't do anything to speed up the process."

PHYSICAL SIGNS OF IMPENDING PUBERTY

"How can you tell when a boy is approaching this time?"

"His shoulders begin to broaden, his speaking voice lowers, and, of course, he gets some hair on his upper lip. As regards his behavior, he could go either way; he could show increased maturity or greater insecurity, which might lead to an outbreak of bullying on his part."

"What are the musical signs?"

"Surprisingly, his voice could suddenly get better and better for a short time. It could get richer and fuller or, on the other hand, it could deteriorate. He might experience difficulty in singing upper notes and complain that it is beginning to hurt. Also, he may find it difficult to sing in tune as well as he used to, and it is all because he's getting this new equipment that he can't control."

ALL TYPES OF VOICE-CHANGE ARE NORMAL

"Do all boys' voices change in the same way?"

"No, indeed they don't," smiled the choirmaster. "Some change very quickly. A boy could sing a solo in his treble voice one week, and find that he's turned into a bass by the following week. Another boy may find that the change is imperceptible and that his voice gradually slides down in pitch over a period of a year or more. Yet another boy may find that some of the notes in his middle range disappear altogether, while his upper and lower registers remain intact."

"Which is the normal way for a voice to change?"

"Every way is normal." The director turned to look at Bob, for the traffic remained at a standstill. "When all this is happening to a boy, it's important for him to realize that all these changes are completely normal. He'll be feeling very unsure of himself and you need to reassure him that he's okay.

ONE ON ONE

"And that leads me to another point," said the director, detecting some movement of vehicles ahead.

"What?"

"The time has come for you to have a gentle word with him, one-on-one. He's naturally upset at losing a beautiful voice that he's been cultivating for several years. In England this change is called the 'breaking of the voice,' and it's very much like that for him. He's had this fine bicycle all his life and now it's broken; it just won't work any more. This is where being a male choirmaster is particularly useful, for you can talk to him, man to man. He'll appreciate that. You might say:

"'You're finding it hard to sing; do you know what's happening to you?' Then let him talk to you about it and listen sympathetically.

"'Try singing these notes for me.' Play a note or two around G below middle C and, whatever noise he makes, be sure to admire what he achieves, even if it's very restricted. Remember, he won't show what he's feeling; he'll keep an impassive face.

"'You're turning into a very nice bass (or alto).' It's very reassuring for him to have someone compliment him in this new situation for, as I've said, he has very little control at this early stage."

WHEN SHOULD THE CHANGE BE MADE
"Do you tell him that he must now leave the boys' choir?"

"Most certainly not! This is a very good example of how one can treat him gently. He's given four or five of his most formative years to your boys' choir—it is not for you to tell him when he should leave. It's his call. And so I say to him that he might like to talk with his parents to discuss when he might like to think of joining the young men. Put it positively: not that he's leaving one choir, but that the opportunity is coming when he can qualify to join another. And then ask him to get back with you in a few weeks' time. That will give him another chance to enjoy a one-on-one with you, which you will both appreciate."

KEEP YOUR SINGERS SINGING
RIGHT THROUGH HIGH SCHOOL
The cars immediately ahead of them began to move. The director turned on his ignition and began to inch his way forward.

"This is where our Thanking ceremony is so useful, for we make the change from boy to man a positive thing. We thank him for what he's done as a boy and now welcome him into the young men's section where he will be an accepted member of a new peer group, and that is very comforting for him."

"And so you keep your new young men singing right through, do you?"

"Yes, I most certainly do!" said the director as his car gradually picked up speed. "Some choirmasters disagree with me here, but I know that it's vitally important to keep this young man within the fellowship of the church while he is going through this personally unsettling time. We can offer him security when he is feeling insecure. We can offer him friendship when he doesn't quite know who he is, and we can show him that he's becoming an even more valuable member of our musical team at a time when he could very well feel worthless."

CONFLICTING INTERESTS
"But high school students get more homework to do, don't they?"

"Yes, they do. And they have more pressure on them to play sports and join in other activities. This is where you need to ensure that your choir program is really worth staying in. If you give them demanding music to sing and insist on high standards so that they can recognize that their musical prowess is increasing, week by week, you will have the edge over many other extra-curricular activities.

"On the other hand, you will also have to bend with the wind."

"How do you mean?"

"You'll find that when the tennis season comes round, for example, the young people who excel in tennis will naturally want to compete. It's important for them to be able to do this and it's important for you to show your support by enabling them to participate." He looked further ahead and added, "Oh dear, there seems to have been an accident. I hope no one was hurt."

Bob waited for a minute and then continued with their conversation. "The choirmaster can also go and watch his young people playing sports, can't he?"

"That's a marvelous thing to do, well done! The kids so appreciate your presence at their sporting activities or when they're appearing in a school play. Really make time to go and see them, and make sure that they know you're there."

"And also write them a letter of appreciation afterwards," said Bob.

"My word, you're learning fast, young man!" answered the director with a concerned look as they approached the scene of the accident.

CHANGE OF VESTRY

"But," he continued, as they passed several policemen who had gathered around a car that had hit a telephone pole, "there's something else that sounds silly, but it means a lot to a lad who has just left the boys' choir. You can change the place where he hangs his robes. He'll now be with the men and so his physical position in the vestry will echo the physical changes in his body.

"But you should be on the lookout to help him make the change more easily. Some young men still want to hang around with the boys, and that isn't necessarily a good thing. He needs to be weaned away from them so that he can identify himself in every way with his new peer group. It doesn't often happen like that, and so, when it does, you just need to show him a little extra tender loving care and, perhaps, get one of your other young men to take him under his wing to make him feel more welcome in his new role. Your senior choirman could act as a sort of godfather to the young man if you ask him—they'll both appreciate that."

GIVE TEENS MORE INDIVIDUAL HELP

The director smiled with relief as the car continued to pick up speed. "I think we might just make it to the church on time," he said, and began humming gently to himself.

"Do you give your new young men any special help with their singing?"

"Most certainly! If you want a general rule: have them sing gently at all times. Their new voices are very delicate and easily hurt. Singing softly will help them make a nice sound and will also help them to hear the other voices around them. Some lads find it physically difficult to pitch a right note in the early stages of their voice-change and listening to others can be a great help. You'll find that new altos and tenors tend to sing flat, and that young basses tend to rasp out the octave or so of notes that they have available. Soft singing will tend to cure both these faults."

"Yes," commented Bob, "I can remember that when I first started singing bass I had only about eight notes I could use. It was a very frustrating time for me."

"That's right! Feel free to share your own memories of voice-change with lads who are going through it, for you'll be saying to them, in effect, 'I know what you're feeling, for I've experienced it, too.' Tell them that their range will increase very gradually. Make time to see them in pairs pretty regularly and always be encouraging. They'll love you for it and tend to stay with you to become valuable members of your men's section.

TEEN GIRLS

"What about girls?"

"Well, as I've said, their voices don't go through such a traumatic change. Instead they get better and better. And so you need to encourage them to remain with you also, right through their high school years."

"How can you do that?"

"Well, first and foremost, give them challenging music to sing. You won't get a high schooler coming to your practices if all you give her is 'kiddy music.' You'll find that, if you've taught her to read music when she was in second or third grade, she'll now be capable of singing almost anything you put in front of her and so use her capabilities to improve your whole choir program.

"You may find that she won't necessarily want to join your adult choir, for she'll think of them as being so old! Instead you might want to start a teens' choir, where both young men and young women can sing together. Here, at my church, I have the girls go right through from third grade to twelfth grade in the one choir, and they sing most ambitious music, as you've already seen. The girls' choir is well worth hearing. Six of them, as you know, also sing in the men and boys' choir, and that's a real challenge for them.

"Find out what opportunities and needs there are at your church for high schoolers, both girls and boys, and start a new program.

MIXING BOYS AND GIRLS IN ONE CHOIR

"Let me ask you about your mixing of boys and girls in your large choir," said Bob.

"Oh, I'm glad you mentioned that," said the director. "In my experience, as I've told you, it doesn't do to mix all your boys and girls together. Why?"

"Because the girls will grow faster and tend to overwhelm the boys."

"Right! And the boys will lose heart and leave."

"Why doesn't that happen with your choir? You've got six senior girls singing alongside twenty or more smaller boys. But your boys are very keen. What's different about your way of running this choir?"

"Well, first of all, the girls are not singing alongside the boys. They are singing alongside the teen men. The high schoolers in our choir form a separate peer group and they have little contact with the boys."

"Yes, but the girls sing the same vocal part as the boys."

"True, but they don't practice together."

"They practice together at your full rehearsal, and they sing together on Sundays," pressed Bob.

"True again. But they don't sit alongside the boys. They sit in the adult stalls—integrated with the teen men and the older men. This is where mixed seating comes in handy. The boys all sit together, so that they are perceived as one group. All the older singers are integrated, and so there is no direct competition between the girls and the boys.

"And there's one more thing," added the director as the car continued its way towards the church. "There are only six girls, but many more boys. If I increased the number of girls, then the element of competition with the boys would arise. But I keep the number of girls down to six, and this has proven to work very well. I commend it to you for it does give you a guaranteed soprano line for years instead of just months, which is generally the case when you have boys only."

BE SUPPORTIVE OF TEENS' PARENTS, TOO

"I suppose that the teens' parents will be grateful to you for what you are doing for their growing children."

"Yes, they most certainly are! But also be aware that some parents, mothers in particular, also find this a traumatic time. I said to one choir mother, when her son was going through the early stages of puberty, 'You'd be far sorrier if it didn't happen at all!' She said to me, 'Oh no I wouldn't! I want him to stay a little boy for the rest of his life!' So you need to be gentle and understanding with teenagers' parents as well, for you have their children for only a few hours a week, whereas the parents actually have to live with them!"

GIVE TEENS EXTRA RESPONSIBILITIES

The church came into view as the clock was striking the hour. "Hooray, we've just made it!" said the choirmaster as he drove into the parking lot once more. He looked at Bob as he turned off the ignition and prepared to go into the music building. "You will find that these young people respond very well to being offered some special job with your choir, such as assistant librarian. It will help them to see that they can go on fulfilling a useful role to the whole choir. They will appreciate the renewed personal interest that you show in them for, of course, you will be ready to give time to oversee what they are doing for you.

"This job is as much pastoral as it is musical," he said as he ran up the stairs to his office, closely followed by Bob. "That's another reason why I find it so incredibly fulfilling and exciting, and," he added as he tried to regain his breath, "healthy!"

44
MUSIC STAFF

In the director's office they found Nancy Willis, the associate director of music; Deane Parker, the librarian; and Rena Elvin, the music secretary; waiting for them.

"Sorry we're late," said the director, regaining his breath and introducing Bob to them, having forgotten that they'd already met him. "Let's get down to business." And for the next forty-five minutes they discussed every aspect of the music program for the next couple of months: who would play the organ for which anthem and who would conduct; when the director needed the music put out to start rehearsing for the Christmas concert; who would play special preludes before the monthly Evensongs; which choir adults would be asked to sing solo preludes before morning services; when the church piano needed to be tuned for an upcoming concert, and so on.

"What do you have for the meeting, Nancy?"

"Well, our two teen organists, Jesse and Kathy, should be invited to play preludes before services sometime next month; they're getting very good. I also want to talk with you about trying a new approach for rehearsing the adult choir."

"Okay, schedule the young organists, please, and tell me when it is so that I can make sure everyone knows about it. Let's talk about the adult choir after Rena's told us what's coming up."

Rena asked them to go through their calendars for the next few weeks to mark the publicity deadlines for special services and concerts. Deane asked how the budget stood, because the choirs needed some new folders.

Bob was interested in all that went on, not only because of the practical matters that were being discussed, but more on account of the happy relationships that flourished within the music staff. Clearly these regular meetings go a long way to foster smooth relationships among the music staff, he thought, and the more frequently they meet the less chance there is of misunderstandings arising.

The director spent the last five minutes of the meeting discussing a couple of pastoral issues regarding two singers, one adult and one child, whose families were going through a divorce, and Nancy mentioned that the wife of one of the adult singers was going into the hospital. "Let's send her some flowers," she suggested, "and also a get well card." "Great idea, Nancy," said the director. "Why don't we get the adult choir members to sign it at their practice tonight." "I'd be happy to take it to her tomorrow, and the flowers," said Rena, "for I live near the hospital." "I'll order the flowers this morning," offered Deane, and the director gave him some money from his discretionary fund. Wow! thought Bob. These people really do pull together. No wonder there's such a flourishing choir program here when all the members are cared for so lovingly.

Five minutes later Nancy and Deane left, leaving Rena and the director to wrestle with a pile of mail that had arrived during the last few days. "Why don't you play the organ again, Bob, or take a walk round the town. I'll be a couple of hours here, and then I'll take you home for lunch."

THANK-YOU PRESENTS

Bob took the hint and thought, as it was such a nice day again, he'd take the opportunity to do some shopping. He bought a bottle of wine and a thank-you card for the director, and a large box of homemade chocolates for his minister, as a thank you for enabling him to take this week off. The director's insistence on saying thank you at every opportunity has really come home to me this week, thought Bob as he walked back to the church carrying his presents in a plastic bag. I would never have thought of buying these presents if he hadn't shown me how important it is to show one's appreciation.

CHOIR LETTERS

He reached the music building as Rena Elvin was coming out to go to the main office. She was holding a couple of sheets of paper in her hand. "What have you got there?" he asked.

"Oh, this is a letter we're sending to all the members of the girls' choir and their families. We've had to make several changes in their schedule for the next few weeks and it's important that they know about them straight away."

"Couldn't the director just tell the girls at their next practice? Surely there's no need to go to the expense of mailing letters?"

Rena laughed and said, not unkindly, "Clearly you haven't run too many choirs yet, have you?"

"Why do you say that?"

"Because girls and boys, teenagers and, alas, grown men and women, all forget things like schedule changes as though you had never said a word to them. That's one of the greatest hazards of running a program like this—you have to tell people two or three times about what will be happening next week, or even the day after tomorrow. You have to put it in writing, so that they can see it from six feet away, and tell them to put it on their refrigerator door so that they'll see it at breakfast, lunch and dinner. It helps to put it on colored paper, so that they don't lose it, and you also have to write it on the chalkboard in the practice room, as well as pinning a notice to the outside door of the music building. In cases of extreme urgency, we even set up a telephone tree. We do that for all our choirs," added Rena, "for you never know when a crisis is going to happen. And even after we've taken all these steps, someone is bound to turn up on the wrong day and blame you!" And she laughed again.

"Golly!" said Bob. "I didn't realize people were so forgetful."

"Yes," replied Rena. "The average response to a circular letter is 10 percent, and so we go to great lengths to ensure that as many parents as possible really read these important choir letters. We've even had special envelopes printed to let parents know that it's choir mail rather than an appeal for money." And she gave him a cheery wave as she disappeared into the general office to photocopy and mail the girls' letter.

45

PUBLICITY

Bob bounded up the stairs to the director's office where he found him dealing with two small piles of papers. "What's going on here?" he asked.

"Rena and I have been getting out publicity for our first Choral Evensong of the season—it's in three weeks' time," he answered.

"Is that also something that a music director has to do?"

"It is, unless he's fortunate enough to have a director of publicity—which few of us have."

"What types of publicity do you use?"

LONG-TERM PUBLICITY

"First of all, there's long-term publicity," answered the director. "If you plan your whole season's program in advance you should send details of your concerts and recitals to the secretaries of all the musical organizations in the area."

"How do I find out who they are?" asked Bob, busily writing in his notebook.

"Your local library will have a list of them. You also need to send details to secretaries of organizations such as the local chapters of the American Guild of Organists and the American Choral Directors Association. Send them a short letter saying that the following musical events will be held at your church during the coming season, and you would be grateful if they would kindly include these details in the newsletters they send to their members. What sort of details will you send them?" he asked.

Bob thought for a moment, and then said, "Who is performing, what they are performing, when they are performing, where they are performing and how much it costs to get in."

"Excellent! You've forgotten one thing: whom they should call for further details! So include your own name and telephone number."

SHORTER-TERM PUBLICITY

"You then need to get a list of the names and addresses of your colleagues in the other churches in the town and area around you," continued the director. "Your minister will be helpful here. A month before each event you need to send a colored poster to your colleagues and ask them to display them in their choir rooms."

"Why colored? Oh yes! I've just seen Rena, who told me that if something is written on colored paper it's more likely to be looked at than if it's printed on ordinary white paper."

"Good! You can either get posters printed at a local shop or, better still, design your own on your wordprocessor—it's cheaper that way and you can print as many as you want whenever you need them.

"Two weeks before the event have your girls and boys, and adults too, if they will, go round the town to ask shops if they'll display them. Some schools may be willing to put them on their bulletin boards—you should send a note to teachers of music in local schools to ask if they will do this for you."

MUSIC SECRETARY

"This involves an awful lot of paperwork!" said Bob with a grimace.

"Hey!" said the director rather severely, "Are you going to fulfill your ministry as a musician with all your heart, soul and energy or are you not?"

"Sorry!" said Bob, sitting up straighter, "but I didn't realize that so many nonmusical functions were tied up with being a musician."

"Clergy experience a similar problem. They seem to spend a lot of their time raising money instead of preaching the gospel. It goes with the territory."

The director changed his position and said, more kindly, "You need to get yourself a music secretary, if possible, to help you in all these organizational matters. I couldn't manage without Rena—she's a jewel. Talk to your minister about it when you get back and see what can be done."

PRESS RELEASES

"You need to know how to write a press release so that your local newspaper will print it."

"Wouldn't it be easier to place an advertisement instead of writing a press release?"

"No! Advertisements in newspapers are extraordinarily expensive. You are looking for some free publicity, and the best way to get it is to write it yourself and send it to the news editors of all the papers in your area."

"What's so special about the way a press release is written? That's what reporters are for, isn't it, to rewrite what you send them?"

"My dear young man!" said the director with a smile, "Newspaper reporters are busier than choir parents. If their interest is not attracted within the first five seconds of reading what you have written they will throw it straight into the trash! No, you've got to capture their attention by (a) making what you have to offer sound interesting to a lot of their readers, and (b) writing in such a way that they won't have to change a thing."

"How do I do that?"

"Take a look at the press release you are holding."

FIRST CHURCH
101 Church Street,
Hometown, U.S.A. 08540   609-555-1110

Director of Music: John Belton

Press release—immediate   **September 15, 1994**

The men and boys' choir of First Church, Hometown, will be singing an hour of choral music by candle-light in First Church on Sunday afternoon, October 2nd, with compositions by American, English and Italian composers.

The choir, conducted by John Belton, director of music of First Church, and accompanied by associate director, Nancy Willis, will present this music during the service of Choral Evensong as sung in English cathedrals for the last 400 years.

Works to be performed include two anthems by American composer Gerald Near, a setting of evening canticles written for the choir of King's College, Cambridge, by the English composer Herbert Howells, and a setting of Psalm 100 by the Italian composer Giovanni Palestrina.

Before the service, which will be led by the chief minister of First Church, the Reverend Christopher Smith, there will be a short organ recital by Nancy Willis, who will play works by French composers Louis Vierne and Marcel Dupré.

The church will be lit by over one hundred candles for the service, which begins at 4:00 P.M. Admission is free.

For further details call First Church, Hometown, (609) 555-1110.

Contact person: John Belton. 609-555-1110

"That's simple, isn't it?" commented Bob.

"Yes, deceptively so. You need to notice several things:

1   It's written on church letterhead stationery.

2   You'll photocopy it onto colored paper.

3   The words 'Press release—immediate' mean that the news editor can use it straightaway rather than hold it back for a later release date.

4   There is no headline offered. Editors like to write their own.

5   It's written with double spacing and wide margins, for easy reading.

6   It's written in short, succinct paragraphs. Editors have no time to waste and so you must make it easy for them to delete a paragraph here and another one there. If they have only two inches of single column to spare and you provide enough material for five inches then, obviously, the editor will immediately delete three inches. So help him, otherwise he'll throw the whole thing away. If you get only the first and last paragraphs into the newspaper, you'll be doing well.

7   Always include the name of the contact person at the end so that the editor can call if he or she is really attracted by what you have to offer.

"You should send this in at least two weeks before the event. If you have a glossy 'Homes and Gardens' type magazine published in your county or state, you should call for their deadlines. They may need information up to three months in advance.

"Set the alarm on your word processor so that it alerts you when all these tasks should be carried out."

'WH' WORDS

The director stood up for a moment to stretch himself. "There are five 'WH' words which you should always include in all publicity material. I expect you noticed them in the release you're holding."

"What are 'WH' words?" asked Bob, as the director sat down again.

"You've used one of them already!" laughed the director. "Actually there are six—the last one is 'HW'! They are:

WHat is being performed,
WHen and WHere it is being performed,
WHo the performers are,
WHom to contact for further information, and
HoW much it costs."

"Oh, that's very helpful," said Bob, "thanks!"

PUBLICITY PHOTOGRAPHS

"Now, there's another thing which you should do to increase your chances of getting free publicity," added the director.

"What's that?"

"You should have a series of black and white glossy photographs taken of you and the choir so that you can send a different photo every time you have a press release."

"Why send different photographs each time?"

"Because once one photograph has been printed it's old news, and no newspaper is going to print old news!"

"That's obvious!"

"Yes, but it wasn't obvious until I said it," grinned the director. "Let me ask you a question," he continued. "Should you send a photograph of the whole choir, or of just two or three singers?"

"It would be nice to send a photograph of the whole choir, for they'll all be taking part in the service or concert."

"Yes—but is a photograph of a large group of people interesting to the general public? What they want to see, and what editors will publish, are photographs of very small groups of people, especially children.

"So find someone to take a lot of photographs of your kids, looking angelic if possible! You may also want the occasional adult, closeup photographs of yourself looking inspired, and some of your organist at the organ. Choose one picture to send with your press release and write on the back of it the names of those who are pictured, from left to right. If they are children, include their ages, too.

"What you need to do is to find a press reporter, or editor, who is a member of your church and ask if you can spend half an hour with her talking about these things. You'll learn a lot, and you'll also gain a friend who might be willing to help you promote your concerts."

"Great!" said Bob with a smile. "I'm really looking forward to creating press releases when I get back."

"I thought you didn't like paperwork!" said the director with a grin.

"Oh, that was before I knew how interesting it could be," answered Bob with a shrug of his shoulders. "Now tell me about this radio release."

RADIO RELEASES

"You need to be able to write conversational English for radio releases."

"I don't understand."

"There's a fundamental difference in the way you word your press release from the way you write your radio release. One is to be read, the other is to be spoken. Here," he continued, moving his swivel chair nearer to Bob, "compare these two releases and you'll see what I mean," and he handed him another sheet of colored paper.

✿

FIRST CHURCH
101 Church Street,
Hometown, USA. 08540   **609-555-1110**

Director of Music: John Belton

Repeat announcement 60 second announcement
Mon., Sept. 26 thru Sat., Oct. 1

If you like to hear choral music at its best, sung in a lovely setting by a fine choir, you should make a point of going to First Church, Hometown, next Sunday afternoon when they'll be presenting a program of choral music, sung by the choir of First Church, directed by John Belton.

The choir will perform music by American composer, Gerald Near; and also by the well-known English composer, Herbert Howells, and the sixteenth century Italian composer, <u>Giovanni</u> Palestrina, so there'll be something for everyone!

Pronounce:
Jo-vah-ny

First Church's associate director of music, Nancy Willis, will add to the musical fare by playing music by French composers. It will be an afternoon of international music-making!

What's more, the church will be lit by over one hundred candles. This is something you shouldn't miss!

The music begins at 4:00 P.M. next Sunday, but I'd get there early if you want a good seat. And don't forget: admission is free!

First Church is at the corner of Church Street and Second Avenue, and there's a parking lot right next door.

So, if you enjoy good choral music sung in a lovely church lit by candles, come to First Church, Hometown, next Sunday at 4:00 P.M.

For further details call First Church, Hometown: (609) 555-1110

Contact person: John Belton (609) 555-1110

"Oh!" said Bob, "I see what you mean. It's very different, isn't it?"

"Yes. And there are several things you should notice about this:

1   Several items remain the same: headed note paper, photocopied on color, double spacing, short paragraphs and contact person. The differences are:

2   Instead of having column inches to worry about, radio folk have time constraints to consider, so tell them how long it takes to read what you've written. They're more likely to read it if they know they've got a minute to spare.

3   They might read it several times during the week before the performance, so tell them what dates are appropriate.

4   Write in a half-column width so that you can write difficult words phonetically.

5   You'll notice that I've repeated some information—such as where the event will be held. That's okay, for listeners can't go back to the first paragraph themselves to check on the venue and time; these facts need repeating.

"Here again," added the director, "try to meet the disc jockeys of your local radio stations and chat to them about it to learn, at first hand, what they want from you.

VISIT YOUR LOCAL RADIO AND TV STATIONS

"Another very good thing to do is to get yourself interviewed on the morning radio show. That will generate a lot of interest. If you can supply a recording of the choir to go with the interview, you've got it made!

"Oh, I nearly forgot," he added, "when you present concerts thatneed tickets for admission, it's a very good thing to send three pairs of tickets, free, to your local radio station with the request that they send them to the first three people who call in. This costs you nothing, but it stimulates interest and ensures that you'll have six more people in your audience. Again, this is something your local radio people can tell you about.

"You may also be able to get your choir on TV, free of charge," continued the director, raising his eyebrows.

"How can I do that?" responded Bob, eagerly.

"Well, your local TV station will have annual money-raising efforts when they need folk to come in to answer the phones. Wouldn't it be great if the announcer were able to say, 'Tonight our phones are manned by members of the choir of First Church, Seattle, led by their choirmaster, Bob.' And they would show you on the screen throughout the phonathon, which would be free advertising for you and very helpful to them. You'd get to know some of the key people during that session, which would help you enormously with your future relationships with them."

"What a super idea!" enthused Bob. "I think some of my choir members would be excited to do it. We could have special T-shirts made for the occasion emblazoned with the name of our choir; we might even be able to sing a short song for them, if things go really well. I might compose one in honor of the TV station!" The director smiled approvingly at Bob's enthusiasm. Clearly, this young man would go far.

The director stood up and stretched himself again. It had been a long session and he was hungry. "Let's go home," he said, "I need some food," and, so saying, he ran down the stairs, two at a time, to his car.

My word, thought Bob, as he ran after him, this job does indeed keep you very healthy!

46
MUSICAL ORGANIZATIONS

He found that the director had already started his car and the passenger door was open, ready for him to jump in. "You do want to get home, don't you?" Bob remarked with a smile as the car sped out of the parking lot.

PREPARE YOURSELF PHYSICALLY AND MENTALLY TO GIVE OF YOUR BEST

"I need to go home to get an hour's sleep before our marathon practice session tonight. It's one of the most fulfilling, as well as being one of the most exhausting evenings of the week. We have all the boys for seventy-five minutes, then a choir supper for forty-five minutes, followed by the full men and boys' choir for an hour and a half, and we end with a ninety-minute practice with our forty-voice adult choir. This takes considerable physical and mental energy. Choirmasters always have to appear before their choirs radiating energy, goodwill, joy and enthusiasm, even if they are feeling unwell or tired.

"And so," he continued, as they drove through an attractive park, "in order to be sure that I can give the choirs my very best, I have to recharge my batteries. You might not need a nap like I do, but I suggest that you take things quietly before you have to expend a lot of energy.

PLAN YOUR PRACTICES

"You owe it to your singers to plan exactly what you need to get through for every rehearsal. Rehearsals have to be efficient as well as inspiring, and that doesn't happen by accident—it takes planning. And remember," he added as he slowed down again for some traffic lights, "that many of your singers will have come straight from school and from work. You must, in some way, animate them from your own reserves of energy and enthusiasm so that they can rise to what you demand of them."

SPECIALIZE IN ORGAN OR CHOIR?

The lights turned green and they continued their journey. As the road ahead was straight and clear, the director turned his head slightly to look at Bob and asked, "What do you want to specialize in when you begin your new job?"

"I'm really interested in becoming an organ recitalist as well as an inspiring choirmaster. There are so many fine organs in this country that I'd love to be invited to play, and it would be great to get paid at the same time!"

"You'll have to find out, by experience, just which of those two ambitions you will be able to follow."

"How do you mean?"

"To become a superb recitalist—one who is sought after all over the country, who chooses really interesting programs and presents them in a stimulating way, you'll have to spend many hours every day practicing."

"I did that when I was studying at school," responded Bob, confidentially.

"Yes. You thought you were pretty busy when you were a student," smiled the director, "but you'll soon find that your life will get even busier. If you spend several hours practicing every day you won't be able to give sufficient time to your choir programs and to the other issues that will arise when you become a fully integrated member of a church staff team."

The car stopped for yet another set of lights. "I had to make a conscious decision, when I began my work here, as to which facets of my musical life I would pursue. I felt that the work with my choirs came first, with composing and leading workshops second. I really give myself to my singers, both musically and pastorally, and compose and teach on my days off, which means that I have little or no time to practice the organ.

SOME PROFESSIONAL ORGANIZATIONS
FOR MUSICIANS TO JOIN

"You may find a similar choice awaiting you," he continued. "But what you should do immediately is to become a member of some of the leading professional organizations in this country. There's the American Guild of Organists (AGO), the Association of Anglican Musicians (AAM), the Association of Lutheran Church Musicians (ALCM), the Royal School of Church Music in America (RSCM/A), the Choristers Guild, the American Choral Directors Association (ACDA), and many more." (A list of addresses is supplied in Appendix B)

THE AMERICAN GUILD OF ORGANISTS

"What do these organizations do?"

"The AGO is a large organization, comprising several thousand organists throughout the United States. They publish a superb monthly magazine giving updates on what is happening in the organ world at home and abroad, and on what local AGO chapters are doing. You should join your own local chapter and support its activities—this will get you known by your peers very quickly. It also publishes helpful articles on practical organ and church music matters. It gives news of organists who have just been appointed to new churches. You should get your own name in there, quickly, once you've become a member, so that people know that you've arrived, and enclose a good photo of yourself, too. The magazine gives reviews of new music, new books, and new records, and it also advertises vacant organ posts. It holds annual conventions that you should attend to make friends and get yourself known. It is a must for every young organist who wants to make a name for him or herself in this country."

"I'll send in an application as soon as I return home!

THE ASSOCIATION OF ANGLICAN MUSICIANS

"What's the AAM?" Bob continued.

"This is an organization mainly for music directors of the larger Episcopal churches, but it is opening its doors to others so that its influence and usefulness will spread even more. You have to be nominated and seconded for membership; I'd be very happy to nominate you, Bob, for I believe that you would not only contribute to its life but also learn a great deal from involvement in such a lively and questing organization.

"They, too, publish a magazine with articles to help music directors, and their annual conferences, held at a different center each year, are superb. They attract some of the very finest music directors in the country, who come not only to lecture but also to listen. You'll find yourself rubbing shoulders with many of the great names in the field of church music when you begin attending AAM conventions."

"Wow! That sounds like a must, too," exclaimed Bob as the car neared the director's home.

THE ASSOCIATION OF LUTHERAN CHURCH MUSICIANS

"Speaking of denominations, the ALCM is a service and professional organization that works to strengthen the practice of worship and church music of all North American Lutherans. These are wonderfully helpful and supportive groups."

THE ROYAL SCHOOL OF CHURCH MUSIC IN AMERICA

"You've also mentioned the RSCM/A several times this week."

"Yes, it's through a long and intimate connection with the RSCM that I've learned most of what I now know of choirtraining. The RSCM helped me discover the importance of teaching children in small groups and to stimulate them by asking the right questions. It was the RSCM that showed me children can achieve far more than I had ever realized and that they can perform some of the greatest choral music in the world, if they are taught according to RSCM principles.

"They are a world-wide organization, and they publish a quarterly magazine, which gives news and helpful articles from leading church musicians from all over the world. When you get yourself and your church affiliated to the RSCM/A, you will be assured of every help from choirmasters who have had years of experience and who know, therefore, just what problems you may be facing.

"In addition, they publish a lot of splendid music for choirs of all sizes and levels of achievement, and it's available to members at a considerable discount!"

"Do they hold courses for choirmasters and organists?"

"Not in the United States—they do in many other countries. But one of the greatest benefits of membership is the opportunity for boys and girls of all ages to attend week-long summer courses led by the very finest choirmasters in this country. They also invite inspiring choirmasters from England to direct these courses, and the children come home so fired up that they become strong leaders in their home choirs for the next season."

THE CHORISTERS GUILD

"I've heard of the Choristers Guild."

"Yes, they are essentially a North American children's choir organization with a very large membership. They issue yet another glossy magazine full of know-how, and they also publish a lot of music, especially for children. You need to write to them to find out just how they can fulfill some of your needs. They have an enthusiastic following from many choirmasters of different denominations and are very efficiently run."

THE AMERICAN CHORAL DIRECTORS ASSOCIATION

The car pulled into the director's drive and they got out. "Tell me about the ACDA," asked Bob as they walked up to the front door.

"This, again, is a large and efficient organization that encourages the art of choral singing throughout the United States." The director opened the door and they went in. "Their annual conventions are attended by many of the finest American choirs. They give concerts to the delegates, and so you can quickly meet many leaders in that field." He led the way into his kitchen and opened the refrigerator door. "The choice of organizations for a church musician to join is very rich indeed. You'll have an interesting time discovering just what you need to join.

"Now then," he continued, "our choice for a snack lunch is brown toast with cheese and pickles, cheese and apples, or cheese and bananas. Which will you have?"

Bob considered for a moment, excited at the prospect of all the musical organizations that he could join. "A little of everything, I think!" he said with a smile.

47
TEN COMMANDMENTS FOR PRACTICING THE ORGAN

Two hours later, after a refreshing sleep and an equally refreshing cup of tea, the director and Bob were driving back to church in the warm afternoon sunshine. This time, because they were early, the director took Bob on a slightly longer route. "We were talking about a possible career for you as an organ recitalist, Bob," said the director as they drove through an attractive village, past a Presbyterian church that was over two hundered years old.

"Yes," responded Bob, "but I found the actual process of practicing very difficult when I was at school."

"What did they teach you there?"

"I was taught a lot of German and French organ music and some American, but I was never really given much direction in how to practice."

The director turned left onto a country road in stunned silence. He was truly dismayed by the lack of perceptive teaching that Bob had experienced. "Would you like me to run through a list of essentials that could transform your practicing life?" he offered.

"Oh, yes please!" responded Bob gratefully, getting out his notebook.

"Right, here goes:

1   "Set aside a specific time every day when you know you can practice without any interruptions. This may mean that you have to get to the church at 7:00 A.M., before anyone else is there.

2   "Work on an assortment of pieces during your practice time, to give yourself a varied fare and to sustain your own interest. Do a little of each piece every day."

He glanced at Bob, who was writing furiously in his notebook. "Should you practice on the organ loudly or softly?"

"Oh, I suppose, softly for much of the time, so as not to disturb folk who come into the church."

"Quite right. But there are two other reasons that affect you personally. If you practice loudly you very soon get tired because of the decibels assaulting your ear. And the second reason is that it's much easier to hear what you are doing if you play on single stops, say 8-foot flutes on manuals and also on pedals. And so my third point is:

3   "Practice quietly and really listen to what you are doing, until you need to practice stop changes.

4   "Work out your fingering and your pedaling in minute detail. Every note should have its own finger. This is a matter of economy of movement as well as of efficiency. All the greatest players know exactly what they are going to do at any one moment. The more time you spend on planning, the more focused will be your performance."

Bob interrupted to say, "That reminds me of a saying used by carpenters: 'measure twice and cut once.'"

"That's an excellent analogy," laughed the director as they passed a farmer's market with fresh vegetables displayed by the roadside.

5   "Practice slowly. This is probably the most difficult piece of advice to follow, for we all have the urge to play our pieces up to speed as soon as possible."

"Yes, I always do that," answered Bob, ruefully. "And I find, in the difficult places, there's at least one passage that I always play wrong. I can't understand it, for it happens every time, and I don't know why."

"I can tell you, if you want me to."

"Yes, please!"

"You always go wrong in those places because you always go wrong in those places!" He paused for a moment to see if Bob understood what he was saying. He didn't. "Don't you realize that when you come to those difficult bars you are saying to yourself, 'I always go wrong here,' and so you do! You are actually practicing going wrong instead of practicing going right. It's so simple!"

"I see! How can I start practicing going right?" asked Bob, helplessly.

"You do what I told you to do—you practice that section slowly."

"Is that all?"

"No! Let me ask you a question."

Here we go again, thought Bob. I've got to supply the right answer, and he won't stop until I do. But, by the end of the process I really will understand what he's driving at. He sat up a little straighter.

"What are you practicing, when you practice the organ—apart from the notes, of course?"

"Well," said Bob slowly, somewhat at a loss, "I suppose I'm practicing stop changes and page turns—I can't think of anything else."

"Yes, you're practicing all these mechanical things," answered the director, approaching a stop sign cautiously, "but what are you practicing regarding your state of mind?"

"My state of mind!" exclaimed Bob. "What's that got to do with it?"

The director stopped at the T-junction, looked both ways carefully and then made an easy turn to the left. He continued, "Your state of mind is just as important as the mechanical part of performing."

He changed gears and gradually increased his speed as he said, "Let's start from the other end. What state of mind do you want to be in when you eventually play this piece at a recital?"

"Oh, that's easy! I want to be totally confident in my ability to play it really well."

"Good! That's the right answer. You might have added, 'and I want to enjoy playing it so that my audience enjoys listening to it.' Musical performance is, as we discussed last Saturday, a matter of communication. But we'll talk about that a little later on."

The director made a right onto yet another country road. "And so how are you going to cultivate the confidence that you need when you play this piece at a recital?"

Bob was silent for a moment as he looked at the large houses that lined the road. "Oh!" he exclaimed suddenly, "I'm going to practice being confident while I learn the music! But how? When I practice, I always get worried."

"I've told you twice," responded the director firmly, "I won't tell you again."

Silence reigned as the car made its way along the quiet, tree-lined road. "Oh, of course!" exclaimed Bob, yet again, "I have to practice slowly."

"At last!" sighed the director as the town appeared on the horizon. "Slow, relaxed practice holds the key for 90 percent of your learning mode. When you practice really slowly, the notes are no longer difficult, especially if you have worked out your fingering beforehand. The difficulty comes, not from playing a note, but from getting to that note in time to play it." He paused to let his message sink in.

"When you practice slowly you have plenty of time to reach that note. You will feel confident about playing it, because you know you can. Conciously recognize that the next note will be right before you play it, and your self-confidence will grow by leaps and bounds."

"When can I begin to play the piece a little faster?"

"You must always play the piece at a speed consonant with knowing that the next note will be right before you play it. That's how it will be when you begin to learn the piece, and that's how it will be when you play it at your recital. It takes an enormous amount of self-control, for we all want to speed up before we are really ready to."

They'd reached a busy main road and had to wait until the traffic was clear before turning right. "By the way, ration yourself severely when practicing with a metronome. The whole essence of slow practice is to be able to play even more slowly when you are approaching a dangerous corner in the music, and you can't do that when a metronome is ticking away. It's just like driving a car: a cruise control is very useful, but not when you're approaching a yield sign!" A gap appeared in the traffic and the director made an easy turn. "Having got that message home, I hope, let's go on to some shorter helpful hints about practicing."

6   "Practice in different rhythms."

"For instance?"

"If your piece is written, for example, in 4/4 time with steady quarter notes, play them in pairs of dotted quarter/eighths. Then reverse the process and play them as eighths/dotted-quarters. Doing this really helps to get the notes into the fingers. I've heard one distinguished organist recommend that, for tricky passages, you should practice them backwards!

7   "Don't confine yourself to practicing on the organ. Some of the finest organists I know began their careers as pianists. Get to know your manual parts, hands separately at first, on the piano at home so that you can concentrate on one thing at a time."

"That's one of your favorite phrases, isn't it?" laughed Bob.

"Yes it is, because I proved it to be true! The same holds for the pedal parts on the organ. Practice without the manual parts, so that you can ensure getting to the next note well in advance of having to play it. Then you always know it will be correct.

8   "Ensure that your fingers and hand are beautifully shaped. A friend of mine in this town designs bridges and he told me that the strength of a bridge lies in its concave construction. Flat bridges need much more support, and bridges that bend downwards are set for col-

lapse. So it is with the shape of the hands and fingers. Watch your hands when you are practicing—if they look beautiful, and your wrists are relaxed and you are sitting easily, like a singer, supported by your diaphragm, the chances are that you are using all parts of your body to their best advantage." They approached some more traffic lights, which were just turning green, and the car made a gentle left onto Main Street.

9 "Which leads me to my last-but-one point," he said as he made an almost immediate right into Church Street. "Very early on in your learning process, begin to memorize the notes. Only when you can play the whole piece from memory can you really begin to get to know it!" The car made its way to its accustomed parking place and the director turned off the ignition. He turned to Bob and said, "Once you know the notes you are only halfway to knowing the piece."

"What do you mean?" asked Bob, returning his gaze.

"That's my last point:

10 "Get to know the music. What is the music saying? Why did the composer write it? Who was the composer?"

"I can look those things up in books," said Bob defensively.

"Yes, but do you?" pressed the director.

"Well, er, no."

"You are, alas, in very good company. There are many brilliant recitalists who play the notes, but very few who play the music. Very few convey, through the music, what it is that the composer wished to say." The director opened his window to let in some fresh air, and continued, "I remember hearing two recitalists, many years ago. The first was fantastic and I came away from his recital saying to myself, 'What a marvelous organist he is!' But when I heard the other recitalist playing Franck's Third Chorale I heard myself say, 'What a wonderful composer Franck was!'"

He turned to Bob and asked, "Which player am I commending?"

"The second, obviously, for he enabled Franck's music to come through unimpeded, and his technique and musicianship were directed solely to that end."

"Correct! That organist's name was Fernando Germani, whom I also mentioned to you last Saturday. I once heard him play Liszt's *Ad nos*—do you know it?"

"Yes. It's a long piece with a fiendishly difficult fugue at the end."

"Right! Whenever I heard other organists play it I endured the first ten minutes, which consists of a lot of Liszt at his most introspective, in order to get to the thrilling fugue. But when Germani played it, I found myself sitting on the edge of my chair all the way through and being moved and excited by every note he played; I didn't know why.

"He was staying in my home for his visit so, that evening, after the recital, I asked him what qualities he had brought into his performance had enabled him to communicate the message of the piece so directly to my inner being."

The director looked at Bob for a long five seconds and said, "His answer changed my whole approach to interpretation. It was like a conversion experience."

"What did he say?" asked Bob, with his pencil poised.

"He said, 'You know that this piece is a series of variations on a chorale from Meyerbeer's opera, *The Prophet?*' I said, 'No, I didn't.' He then spoke the sentence that sent a ray of light from heaven right into my heart. He said, 'Before I learned the organ piece, I learned the opera!'"

A minute's dead silence ensued as Bob wrote down Germani's words.

"In other words," continued the director, "he went to the source of Liszt's inspiration to discover what it was that he wished to say. Knowing that, he was able to communicate to his audience Liszt's innermost creative thoughts—and it showed."

"Wow!" exclaimed Bob reverentially, as he finished writing. "A number of composers write at the head of their works just what the piece is all about. Messiaen does, and so does Howells in his psalm preludes—and of course there's Reubke's 94th psalm, which is one of my recital pieces. But I've never looked at the psalm to see exactly what it is that he is conveying."

"Well, it's up to you, young man," said the director as he got out of the car. "You now know what you ought to do. Whether or not you do is your responsibility. Remember, you have only one life to live, so live it to the full!" They closed the car's doors and made their way into the music building for the beginning of a five-hour marathon of choir practices.

48
PLANNING REHEARSALS

How does this man do it? wondered Bob, as he followed the director into the practice room where several boys had already gathered. He just goes from one thing to another without turning a hair. I wish I had half his energy! He sat down in his accustomed corner ready to take notes during the ensuing practice, which he knew would be good. An air of expectancy filled the room as more boys took their places.

WEEKLY PLANNING
The director wrote on the chalkboard a list of all the music that would be rehearsed that evening; he'd already written it down on a clipboard, which he kept on the piano. Bob had noticed it earlier in the week; one page covered the entire week's rehearsals, with the music that all the choirs would rehearse, as well as spaces available for announcements at every practice and a space for noting excused absences. That man really does

plan everything in advance, he thought. That's the only way to run this sort of program—to prepare well ahead.

FIRST CHURCH, HOMETOWN	
Rehearsals beginning Monday...................1994	
Announcements	**Music to be rehearsed**
Monday: Boys Instruction with Mrs. Willis: Instruction with director: Teens Instruction with Jack Keen:	*Men and boys' choir*
Tuesday: Girls Instruction with director:	*Girl's choir*
Wednesday: Boys Instruction with director:	
Thursday: Full boys	*Adult choir*
Full choir	
Adult Choir	
Excused absences:	

49
FULL TREBLES' PRACTICE

SEATING IN THE PRACTICE ROOM

Bob saw that the head boys had arranged six movable choir desks into a large open oblong around the piano, so that all the boys could see the director and also see each other. There was also plenty of room for the director to get up from the piano and walk around to look at the boys during the rehearsal. He thought of his own practice room in Seattle where the chairs were all facing one way—towards the piano. That's fine for a choral society, thought Bob, but it bears no relation to the position the choir stands in on Sunday, for in the sanctuary they are on two sides, facing each other. I must rearrange my practice room and let the singers stand in positions similar to those they occupy on Sundays.

EXPERIENCED SINGERS STAND NEXT TO THE LESS EXPERIENCED

The boys came into the room in twos and threes, chatting happily, getting their music from their cubbies and going to their places behind the music desks. Bob noticed that each boy had his assigned place; the choristers were spread evenly around the desks; each had two or three boys next to him. Those will be junior and senior singing boys, thought Bob. Every chorister boy has his own small team of boys to look after during the practice. What a great idea! This gives them a measure of responsibility to help the less experienced singers. Bob thought of the director's dictum that the art of singing was "caught, not necessarily taught." The younger boys will certainly be able to catch a lot of the older boys' techniques during this practice, he thought, because they're standing so close to each other.

Bob also noticed that the probationers and novices were not present. They'd already had two rehearsals that week and certainly wouldn't have been able to attempt most of the music that was due to be rehearsed during the next seventy-five minutes.

The director, having written an alarmingly long list of music on the chalkboard, was going round the desks, chatting with the boys as they arranged their music in the right order. Some of the smaller boys were experiencing problems in finding all the music that they would be singing. "Haven't you got a copy of the Handel anthem, Scott?" the director asked a small boy. "No." "We're rather short of them, so why don't you share with Greg and he can show you where you are." This obviously pleased Scott, because Greg was a tall chorister whom he thought was terrific.

BEGINNING THE PRACTICE

The practice began in a similar manner to most of the others that Bob had attended. "Okay, people, let's begin," said the director in his clear, concise manner. There was instant silence. "Sing me a B-flat!" They did, without the pitch being given. The director checked the pitch on the piano and, as was his custom, walked round the desks looking each boy straight in the face as he sang a continuous Oo.

The boys know what to expect, they're ready for it and they enjoy it, thought Bob. He noticed that the director smiled encouragingly as he looked at each boy, and that this look was reciprocated. He's establishing a personal relationship with every singer at the beginning of the practice, Bob observed. They know that every individual is important to him and that he's glad they're there. That relationship will last right through the practice.

WARMUPS THAT MAKE SINGERS THINK

When it came time to sing scales, the director first had them sing one in unison, to a clear *Ah*, starting with E-flat major. He then divided them in half, with the firsts beginning and the seconds coming in two notes later. For the next scale the seconds began, followed by the firsts. And then, for the scale of F-sharp major he had each desk start in turn, beginning with the desk on his immediate left, followed two notes later by each succeeding desk so that the room was filled with the harmony of ever growing chords. What an amazing sound! thought Bob. This isn't easy—every boy has to think very hard in order to be able to sing the right note. What a great way to get singers to concentrate; they obviously enjoy it!

The director followed this with the scale of G major led by the second desk of four boys and followed by each other desk in succession, two notes later. The third desk led the scale of A-flat major.

He's not playing the piano at all, except for leading into the next pitch—why should he? for they don't need it. The boys standing behind the fourth music desk began the scale of A major, followed in their turn by the boys at the fifth desk leading the scale of B-flat major. Finally the director said, "B major, two octaves!" and pointed to the four boys standing behind the sixth desk on his immediate right. Every boy knew that he had to change from an *Ah* vowel to *Ee* at the octave, and to change back again halfway up. I've never heard anything like it, thought Bob. These boys could sing anything!

The director then said, "Arpeggios!" and played the chord of A major on the piano. "One octave up and two octaves down," he commanded. The boys opened their mouths deeply and sang the arpeggio to a clear *Ah*.

Ah _____

"When you approach the higher notes, should your mouth be open deeper or less deep?" asked the director. "More deep!" answered two boys simultaneously. "Quite right!" responded the director, "but one or two of you are pulling your lips back and you sound as though you are being strangled!" he added with a laugh. The boys tried the same arpeggio again and it was better, because all their mouths were the right shape and they were controlling their breath from their diaphragms.

"Up a half step" commanded the director again, as he left the piano and began to walk round the boys. They all sang the arpeggio of B major in the same effortless way, making a thrilling sound.

"Now," said the director, "up another half step, the firsts beginning and the seconds coming in only one note later." Bob listened as the boys sang the next arpeggio in two parts.

My goodness! he thought, these children really have to think while they are singing their warmup exercises. They can't sing like that without applying themselves fully to the challenges that the director gives them.

The boys sang ever higher and higher until they reached the arpeggio of E-flat. "We'll sing this in unison," said the director as he looked at all the boys, "one octave up and three octaves down!" And they did! It was an amazing sound even though not every boy was able to reach the lowest note—only the senior boys could do that comfortably, as they changed into their chest register. But they all felt that they were really ready for a good practice after their warmups, which had stimulated them as much as they had startled Bob!

The practice proceeded much as the other rehearsals had done on Monday and Wednesday with the more experienced boys: the director began with a verse from each of a few hymns, asking the singers to pitch the first note by themselves after looking at the music and then singing the tunes to various vowels, while the director accompanied very lightly on the piano. He then went through almost all the other music that he had listed on the chalkboard, spending more time on the anthems for next Sunday and less time for music to be sung later.

Every couple of minutes or so, when a musical problem arose, such as a wrong note being sung or a rhythmic inaccuracy, the director would go round the choir giving each boy a turn to see if he could solve it. Needless to say, the choristers were much better than anyone else, although there were a couple of times when a junior singing boy was able to sing a short passage better than a more senior boy. This pleased everybody and earned the boy a dot, which the head boy marked in the register.

Sometimes, when there was a particularly difficult passage to sing, the director said, "Choristers sing this," and they usually got it right. He then had the senior singing boys repeat the passage, followed by the junior singing boys. At other times he would let the junior singing boys have first try. He always keeps them on their toes, thought Bob. Everyone has to try hard all the time, for he might call on anyone to sing a solo; they all have to be ready.

HELPING LESS EXPERIENCED SINGERS

Throughout the practice the chorister boys were looking after the juniors next to them: showing them which piece of music they should be singing and pointing to the notes when the music became really difficult.

Half an hour before the end of the practice, Nancy Willis came in and watched for a few minutes while the director finished rehearsing an anthem. "Right," said the director, "whose turn is it to go with Mrs. Willis for the next fifteen minutes?" and two junior boys immediately raised their hands. "Okay, Douglas and Owen, you go first, and when you come back Matthew and Akeem can go."

That's great! thought Bob. The junior singing boys were struggling with some of the more difficult music, but they were learning a lot from the choristers standing next to them. Now that Nancy has come in especially to give them some individual training with their test cards they'll be able to sing music that is easier for them.

Bob was particularly interested by what happened at the end of the practice. The director had each boy put his music in a neat pile in front of him, said a heart-felt 'Well done,' and then handed over to Jay, the head boy.

Jay took over the director's place behind the piano and said, "Whose families are cooking choir dinner tonight?" Two boys put up their hands. "Okay, Alex, you can sing grace. He turned to the other boy and said, "You can sing grace next time Maxwell. Now then, who's going to tidy up after the meal?" Several boys put up their hands. "Okay, Jake and Sam can check that everything is clean afterwards. That will earn your three dots each."

The head boy stood a little taller and continued, "Now at the start of this new season I want everyone to understand that you must clear up your own space at the table when you've finished your meal. You don't leave a mess for Jake and Sam. What else will you do?" Another boy put up his hand. "Yes, Scott?" "We must stack our chairs neatly against the wall." "Quite right, well done!" Scott glowed with pleasure at this compliment from the head boy—he'd make jolly certain that he stacked his chair tonight!

"All right," continued the head boy, "who's going first?" Every boy immediately stood smartly to attention while Jay looked at each desk of boys. "You can go," he said, pointing to one set of boys, "and you...and you...." The boys went off happily, leaving their music neatly on their desks for the full practice that would follow the choir supper. The junior singing boys, who didn't stay for that practice, put their music away neatly in their cubbies on their way to the church hall where a team of choir parents had prepared a delicious chicken supper.

50
CHOIR MEALS

CONSCIOUSLY ENJOY LEADING PRACTICES

"That was a great practice!" enthused Bob predictably, as the director came over to join him. "You obviously enjoyed every minute of it."

"Well, if I don't enjoy the practices how can the boys enjoy them?" responded the director as they walked out of the music building towards the church hall. "The choirmaster must set the tone of his or her practices from the very start by being friendly, relaxed and yet firm. I consciously take delight in every moment of my practices and my singers immediately respond to my mood. If a practice goes badly it's almost always my fault. That's why I always rest before these long sessions, to ensure that I'm in tiptop form physically and mentally."

CHOIR SUPPERS

They walked into the church hall where they found a line of boys in front of the kitchen counter, joined by several teens as well as some of the choirmen. Bob recognized Dr. Jurgen George, chairman of the Choir Alumni Association, and Frank Stevens, chairman of the concerts' committee. After Alex had sung grace, the director introduced Bob to several of the other men, including Michael Rohrer, who had sung alto in the choir for many years and had, at one time, been senior warden. "Michael's got a Ph.D. in business administration," commented the director. "If you want anything doing around here, Michael is the person to ask."

"These choir suppers are a great idea," observed Bob to Michael Rohrer.

"Yes," agreed Michael as he was given a large helping of chicken and rice by Alex's mother and a plate of salad by the mother of Joe. "They give us the one opportunity in the week to enjoy each other's company on a social, rather than on a musical level." He gave two dollars to the head boy, who was at the cash register, and another two dollars for Bob.

"Hey!" said the director, who was bringing up the rear, "this should be my treat!"

"Not tonight, Mr. Director," said Michael with a smile as he led the way into the hall where two long tables had been set out by the sexton. "If a chap can fly all the way from Seattle just to see us, it's the least we can do to give him a good choir supper!"

CHOIR BREAKFASTS

"I see that you also have breakfasts for the girls' choir," commented Bob, as he sat between Michael and the director at the head of one of the tables that was filled with teens and choirmen engrossed in animated conversation.

"Yes," answered the director. "We felt it was important to give the girls an opportunity to relax socially with one another, and so their parents provide an orange drink and donut holes in-between the Sunday preservice rehearsal and the service itself."

"You can't compare a chicken dinner with a donut hole!" said Bob, with his mouth full of delicious salad.

"Quite right!" chimed in Michael. "But there just isn't the opportunity to give the girls a dinner like this during the week, and they understand that. But," he continued, "my daughter sings in the girls' choir and she thoroughly enjoys the five-minute snack that's provided for them whenever they sing on Sundays."

"The boys have also asked for an orange drink and donut holes on Sundays," laughed the director, "but we remind them that their treat comes on Thursdays, so it works out pretty well in the end."

"How do you cover your costs for meals?" asked Bob, helping himself to a drink of orange juice from a carton on the table.

"The two dollars we each pay covers the cost of the dinners, for the parents know how to shop in bulk," answered the director. "It's the best value for money this side of the Staten Island ferry," and he laughed. "In fact," continued Michael, "there's often a surplus, which the parents donate to the choir support fund."

"What about breakfasts?"

"We parents like to provide that for the girls," chipped in Michael. "It doesn't cost very much and it's nice to be able to meet my daughter's friends in a happy environment."

"If parents do have a financial problem providing breakfasts," interjected the director, "they let me know and I supply the cash from my discretionary fund."

END OF SEASON CHOIR DINNERS

"Of course, each choir is given a large dinner at the end of the season," continued Michael. "We have this hall filled twice over—once for the members of the men and boys' choir and once for the girls' choir, because they all bring their families, too."

"It's a great occasion," chimed in the director, "for all the parents bring food, and the men take care of the liquid refreshment."

"I suppose the choir support committee takes care of the organizing," remarked Bob, who was relishing another mouthful of roast chicken.

"Yes, they do," answered the director. "The clergy come, too, and I take the opportunity to say a few words of thanks to everyone."

"Only a few words?" interrupted Michael. "I timed your speech last year—it took twenty-five minutes!"

"Yes," laughed the director, "but once you start thanking people by name, you've got to be jolly careful not to miss anyone."

"How do you keep everyone quiet for twenty-five minutes?" asked Bob.

"That's a good question!" remarked Michael.

"The answer's even better!" said the director. "I walk slowly round the hall, in-between each table while I am talking, so that I am near everyone at least once during the speech and can look them straight in the face. I also encourage everyone to clap as often as possible, so that keeps them occupied."

"You're also very crafty," added Michael.

"Crafty?" asked the director, raising his eyebrows.

"Yes. You give your speech between the main course and the dessert, and so everyone has to sit still to let you get through it as quickly as possible!" and they all laughed.

"Speaking of dessert," said the director, getting up, "let's see what we have for today," and he went back to the kitchen, followed by Bob.

ORGANIZING MEALS

They found the two parents busily preparing plates of large brownies, with ice cream and chocolate sauce, as a steadily growing line of singers waited for their second course. "This must take a lot of organizing," remarked Bob to Alex's mother as she opened a second carton of ice cream.

"Not really," she remarked. "When you've done it once or twice you really know how to go about it efficiently."

"Yes," added Joe's mother, who was handing plates of dessert to a couple of teenagers. Bob learned later that they were Jesse and Kathy, the budding organists who would play preludes before services in a few weeks' time. "We arrange it so that an experienced family is paired with a less experienced one. That way we can learn quickly how best to do it."

"And we enjoy it," said Alex's mother, giving a surprised look at a diminutive boy, who had come for more dessert. "Have you got room for second helping, Tim?" "Oh, yes!" "Very well, but I think a half portion will be enough for tonight, otherwise you won't be able to sing for the next practice." Tim pulled a face, but smiled as he was given an extra squeeze of chocolate sauce.

A PASTORAL INSIGHT

At that moment the minister walked in and asked, "Is there anything left?"

"I think we can find you something," said Alex's mother as she brought out two pieces of chicken from the oven.

The director introduced Bob to the minister. "Yes, Bob," he said, "we met last Sunday at the parish picnic."

Whoops! thought the director, I'd forgotten—it seems such a long time ago.

"Are you enjoying your visit?" asked the minister.

"Yes, it's marvelous," answered Bob, his mouth covered, for the fourth time that week, with ice cream. "I'm learning so much and can't wait to get back to my church to try out some of the ideas I've picked up here."

"I'm glad," said the minister. "By the way," he added, turning to the director, "I wonder if you could spare five minutes tomorrow morning. I know it's your day off, but something has cropped up that we need to talk about."

"Yes, certainly," answered the director, fighting off a sinking feeling in the pit of his stomach. "Would nine o'clock suit you?"

"That would be fine," answered the minister, and he added, "I want to share some good news with you."

"I look forward to it," answered the director with a smile. He thought, Our minister really is a pastoral person, for he saw that his request for a meeting had unsettled me, and he immediately said something to make me feel better.

"I noticed what your minister said," remarked Bob a few minutes later, after they had finished their dessert and as he followed the director out of the hall.

The director stopped in his tracks. "You are a remarkably perceptive and sensitive young man. Clearly you will become a caring and pastoral minister of music. I envy all those who will be committed to your care."

51
HIGH STANDARDS

REGULAR MEETINGS WITH HEAD GIRLS AND BOYS

As they walked back to the music building they passed boys playing on the church lawn, getting rid of some of their considerable energy with a couple of Frisbees. "I've got a meeting in my office now with the head girls," said the director, as he dodged a well-aimed Frisbee making straight for him. "Come and see what we talk about."

"I thought you had the full practice now," remarked Bob, as he followed the director into the music building.

"I do," answered the director, running up the stairs, "but I squeeze in a ten-minute conference with my head girls and head boys at this time, alternating them every week. It's important to keep in touch with them regularly to hear what they say, for they're closer to the children than I am, and they know what's going on." He opened the door to his office where they found Jenny and Maya waiting for them.

For the next ten minutes Bob listened as the director discussed with his head girls a variety of topics, ranging from how well the girls' Singalong went the previous week, through how to encourage one girl who seemed to be half-hearted about the choir program this year, to the need to promote a couple of girls who had greatly improved after attending a singing course in the summer.

"When we meet in two weeks' time," said the director, standing up, "we must discuss the arrangements for the girls' weekend singing visit to Lincolnville. The choirmaster there will need a list of exactly who will be going, so that he can arrange hospitality in the homes of his choirgirls," and he led the way downstairs to the practice room.

FULL PRACTICE OF MEN AND BOYS WITH SIX SENIOR GIRLS. A RECAPITULATION OF CHOIRTRAINING TECHNIQUES

The room was already full of boys, teenagers and men, who were chatting animatedly to each other as they arranged their music in the order written on the chalkboard. "You see what I mean about this being a lively bunch of people," laughed the director. "It's like entering a lion's cage. I've got to make sure that I'm the one who's on top!"

He went to a cubby and brought down a set of music, which he handed to Bob. "Why don't you sing with us tonight, you'll enjoy it! You can stand next to Dr. George; he'll show you the ropes," and, so saying, he left Bob with his new host, while he went to the piano to get his own music in order.

IT TAKES TIME TO GROW A FINE CHOIR

"You've got a large choir here," said Bob conversationally as he tried to sort through the pile of music in front of him.

"Yes," replied Dr. George, "they're a very loyal group of singers. I've been in this choir for twenty years, and it's so good to have some men here who were boys in this choir when I first joined. A couple of them have their own children singing with us now."

HIGH STANDARDS OF SINGING AND
DISCIPLINE ATTRACT ENTHUSIASTIC SINGERS

"But you aim at high standards in all the choirs here," said Bob as he found the last piece of music he needed.

"They wouldn't come if the choirmaster didn't insist on us doing our best every week. We've come here to work..." The director began playing a slow arpeggio on the piano, and so Dr. George finished his sentence, "...and from the hard work comes immense satisfaction." An expectant silence reigned as everyone looked at the director.

WELCOME!

"Good evening!" he said in a friendly but firm manner. "Thank you for being here punctually. It's good to see everyone back again after the summer break." Turning to Bob he said, "And we give a special welcome to Bob who's come all the way from Seattle to be with us this week." A murmur of approval ran through the choir as they gave him a round of applause.

GIVE INSTRUCTIONS ONLY ONCE—LOOK AT YOUR SINGERS

"Right! Let's begin. Hymn 657." He waited for a few seconds and then played the first chord on the piano. I wonder why he didn't ask us to pitch the first note, thought Bob. The director walked away from the piano, leaving his hymnal behind, and stood in the middle of the choir, which surrounded him on three sides. "Sing the first chord in harmony to a gentle *Oo*," he commanded. He raised his arms, embraced everyone with an expectant glance, gave two preliminary beats and they all sang.

LISTEN TO EACH OTHER—
SOFT SINGING CURES A HOST OF FAULTS

The sound was lovely. Bob, who sang a gentle tenor, could hear Dr. George's fine bass voice on one side and a young alto on the other. "Listen to yourselves," said the director, looking at the choir as they continued to sustain the first chord. The sound grew softer and even more beautiful, and Bob became aware of the singers beyond Dr. George, and he could also hear some of those who were in front of him. Wow! he thought, I really feel part of a superb musical instrument. Now I know what it means to listen to the other singers.

THE CHOIR MUST ACHIEVE
WHAT YOU SET THEM TO ACHIEVE

The director stopped the choir and said, "Okay, sing the whole tune, very gently," and he brought them in again, as before. The choir immediately began to sing more vigorously, and Bob could hear a couple of strident young basses opposite him. The director immediately stopped the choir and said, "You didn't hear what I said. Do it!" Do what? thought Bob. Oh yes! he told us to sing very gently. This time the choir responded as the director wished, with all the voices blending together as everyone listened to those around them. The director didn't repeat himself, thought Bob. He expected everyone to hear what he said the first time, and he insisted that his wishes were carried out 100 percent.

MAKE CONTACT WITH EVERY SINGER,
ONE-ON-ONE, DURING THE PRACTICE.

Halfway through the tune the director told the choir to change the vowel to *Aw* and then to *Ee*, and finally to *Ah*. While the choir was still singing, he walked round to stand in front of a number of singers, smiling encouragingly at some, but urging others to drop their jaws more when singing *Ah*. He came over to stand in front of Bob, looked at him for a couple of seconds and said, "Nice sound!" before walking further on. Wow! thought Bob, that was a challenging moment! But he felt better for the director's encouragement and sang more confidently.

The director then got the choir to sing the words of a verse of the hymn, listening to each other again to ensure blend and tone. He's spent over five minutes on this simple music, noted Bob, but it's time well spent, for we all now feel part of a well-prepared team, having had to think of only one thing at a time. Now we can tackle more difficult music more easily.

VARY THE PACE OF YOUR REHEARSALS

For the next hour they rehearsed a lot of music. Bob noticed that the director allowed the choir to sing straight through several anthems without interruption, and he enjoyed the whole experience of singing. That's what we're here for, he thought. We're here to sing as well as to listen to the director. It's good that he's mixing several minutes of uninterrupted singing with more detailed work, when he rehearses only a few measures. The variety and change of pace keeps us on our toes.

DON'T WASTE SINGERS' TIME

Bob also noticed that every singer was kept fully occupied. The director didn't allow the other singers to wait for five minutes while he rehearsed the sopranos. Instead, when there was a soprano passage that needed attention, he soon had the tenors singing it at their own pitch before asking the sopranos to sing it once more on their own. The same thing happened for the altos and basses.

52

TEN COMMANDMENTS FOR LEADING SUCCESSFUL REHEARSALS

The director made a particular point of getting certain musical matters really right.

Notes. As everyone could read music, accuracy was not generally a problem. The only times when notes were not wholly secure came at turns of pages. Some singers turned a full measure before they reached the end of a page; they were the singers who were prepared for what was coming next. Those who turned late were not ready, and the director had to point this out to them and actually rehearse them in turning the page in time.

Bob noticed, with gratitude, that when there was a wrong note, the director didn't get cross with the singers, as some choirmasters might do. I sang a wrong note there, thought Bob, because I didn't know how to sing it correctly, not because I did it on purpose. I needed the director's help to enable me to put it right.

The director spotted why notes were wrong—either because a singer had misread an accidental, or because the leap from the previous note was awkward. The singers were allowed to try, once, to get it right on their own and, if they didn't, the interval was played on the piano, with the harmony underneath, so that the singers could hear how their note fitted into the tonal scheme as a whole. The whole passage was then sung by everyone to make sure that the note really was secure.

Concentration. On the other hand, when a couple of the boys sang a wrong note three times in a row the director did get annoyed. "You know perfectly well how to sing that correctly," he said brusquely. The room became very still, for the director could be pretty fierce when he needed to be. "You're wasting everyone's time by not concentrating. Do it right!" And they did!

Golly! thought Bob. Two things happened there. The director knew that the boys could correct their own mistakes if they tried harder, because he'd taught them to read music so well, and he insisted that they improve their concentration. How often have I seen children, as well as some adults, day-dreaming in the choirstalls when they should have been singing. The choirmaster must be constantly vigilant and insist on the highest standards of concentration at every practice. They'll realize, one day, just what he's given them.

Rhythm. The director insisted that dotted rhythms were not sung as lazy triplets, but really crisply. On the other hand, some singers tended to hurry eighth notes. When this happened, the director told them what they were doing wrong and modeled it for them. He then got the whole choir to sing a page to *Lah* on repeated, staccato eighth notes—singing two detached notes for quarters, and four repeated eighths for half notes, and so on. This gave everyone a sense of how fast eighth notes should be sung, and it also helped them to sing together really well.

On another occasion, when they were rehearsing a Palestrina motet, the director got the choir to sing a couple of pages very staccato, to a very short *Ta*. This is an amazing experience, thought Bob. It completely alters the sound because we sing every note for about a thirty-second-note duration, and then wait in silence until the next note is due. Everyone has to concentrate even harder. This works wonders for our sense of unanimity and also for the quality of their accuracy. Those two exercises were fun, thought Bob.

The director also asked the choir to alter the written length of certain notes, especially final notes of phrases, which he invariably shortened, sometimes by an eighth, sometimes by a quarter, depending upon the speed of the music. Bob remembered doing this with his chamber choir two days' earlier. That does make ends of phrases more graceful, thought Bob, and it also gives us sufficient time to breathe in order to start the next phrase together. The director invariably told the sopranos to shorten the last note of a phrase when it was followed immediately by a new phrase sung by the men. In other words, the end of one phrase did not clash with the beginning of the next.

"I learned that from Sir David Willcocks," said the director. "He came to conduct us a few years ago and we sang an anthem for double choir. One choir sang the first four measures, followed by the second choir singing the next, and so on. He told us to pretend that the anthem had to be sung by only one choir, and to take sufficient time for breaths in between phrases. And so," he concluded, "I apply that to music written in two or more parts. When one voice finishes a phrase and the other one takes over we must always shorten the last note of the first phrase so that the second phrase can start cleanly."

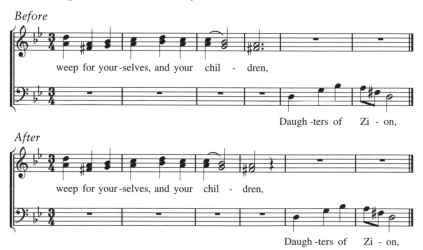

214

Intonation. Bob was glad to note that the director didn't say, when the choir sang out of tune, "You sang out of tune!" That would have been no help to them; they wouldn't have known if they were flat or sharp, who was out of tune, or where they began to sing out of tune. Instead, the director told the singers specifically what the fault was and how they could rectify it.

He sometimes had them sustain the out-of-tune note while the piano played it in sub-octaves; they could then hear it clearly. And he got them to sing the note before that, so that the approach to the awkward note could be rethought. When it was right, he had the whole choir sing the passage again so that the difficult note could be sung in context.

The director had a very keen ear, and could detect immediately when certain voices sang out of tune. When the choir tended to sing sharp he got them to sing more softly, which invariably cured the fault. When there was some flat singing, he was able to spot which note was the culprit and articulate how the fault could be rectified. Bob noticed, with dismay, that he himself tended to slack off when there were a number of repeated notes, and he consequently sang them a little flat. The director pointed this out in several passages and made the singers think of the repeated notes as being entirely new and fresh. "Imagine that you're singing it for the first time, not the tenth time," he said, "and lift each note a fraction. Raise your eyebrows, and it will happen!"

There were also certain intervals that tended to flatten. The director drew their attention to major thirds, perfect fifths, and leading tones that should be sharpened very slightly. The tenors and altos seemed to have more than their fair share of thirds and fifths, and the sopranos had a number of leading tones. "Basses," said the director firmly, "you must pitch your notes more accurately. Several of you scoop up to the notes, especially in your lower register. How can the rest of us sing in tune," he continued, "if you don't give us a really accurate bass line?" And he immediately followed this up by rehearsing the basses to ensure that his wishes were carried out. "You must visualize the note before you sing it," commanded the director, "It's no good singing it and then amending your pitch!" And he rehearsed the whole choir in singing a chord together, so that everyone was involved and benefited from what he had just said.

That's great! thought Bob. He doesn't just give us good advice, but he always follows it up with practice. Choirtraining is a practical matter, not one of good intentions!

Unanimity and clarity of diction. Vowels had to match, and initial and final consonants had to be absolutely together. Bob realized that his west coast accent had to be modified to match the sounds the director demanded. He also noticed that he was careless about pronouncing consonants, until the director's firm demands made him try harder. Final consonants of words sung before a breath had to be sung absolutely together. This took a lot of doing, but the director told them exactly where the final consonant should be. "Sing the *d* of *God* exactly at the beginning of the fourth beat, and make sure you sing the *d* on the pitch of the note."

The director also pointed out a number of occasions when the singers ran their words into one another. "Hey, people!" he said. "You're singing 'anthuh richee ath sen temtee away,' instead of 'and the rich he hath sent empty away.' Make sure you sing all the consonants—the *d* on *and*, the aitches on *he hath*, and put a *p* in the middle of *empty*."

The choir sang the passage again. "That was better. Now be careful to put the *t* on *sent* at the end of that word and not at the beginning of *empty*. We were getting 'senn tempty.'" The director modeled it for them, making the very slightest break between the two words, and also singing *empty* with a light *i* vowel at the end, instead of a drawn-out *ee*. They sang it once more and it was right.

The director also used a word with which they were not familiar. "We need a schwa on the word *savior*," he said. Several of the other singers looked puzzled, and so the director explained. "A schwa is the indeterminate vowel sound of many unstressed syllables, such as the *a* in *about*, which you say as 'uhbowt.' And so," he continued, "on the word *savior*, sing it '*sey*-vi-uh, instead of 'say-vee-*orr*.' Try it!" They did, and it worked. "The basic principle," concluded the director, "is that you should sing words with the same emphasis as you say them—when you are speaking clearly, of course!" he added with a grin.

Color. Bob was fascinated by the director's insistence that they sing in color. Sing in color? thought Bob, what does he mean by that?

"At the beginning of Parry's 'I Was Glad,'" said the director, "make the word *glad* sound really happy. You are all looking so serious when you sing it; you can't possibly convey the sense of the word *glad* if you look so miserable!" and they all laughed. "Now, smile!" he ordered, as he led them into the beginning of the anthem again. They sang it once more and it was better. "Now," interrupted the director, "notice that the word *glad* is repeated. When you repeat a word, should it be more emphatic or less?" Several of the boys put up their hands. "Yes, Joe?" "More emphatic!" "Quite right, well done. 'I was glad, GLAD when they said unto me.' Do it!" They sang it again, and the effect was thrilling.

Near the end of the anthem the director spent a minute getting them to sing the word *pray* in color. "When you sing 'O pray for the peace of Jerusalem,'" he said, "I would like you to sing it in such a way that the congregation is forced to its knees!"

Wow! thought Bob. If we can sing it like that, the message really will reach everyone: choir and congregation alike.

The choir sang it again and it sounded good. "You're nearly there," encouraged the director. "Make a slight crescendo on the word *O*, and trill the *r* on the word *pray*." They tried it, and it worked.

"Which is the most important syllable of that phrase?" There was a moment's silence, and one of the tenors said, "'ru' of Jerusalem." "Thank you, Brad. Quite right! So you know what to do—underline that syllable and make a gentle crescendo towards it, and a diminuendo after it." They sang it for a third time and they knew it was in color, for they could feel the spirit of the words coming through in a lively manner. Even though they hadn't rehearsed the remainder of the anthem in detail, they continued to sing in color.

Golly! thought Bob yet again. The director had only to rehearse a few measures in great detail for his promptings to be applied automatically to the next few pages. What a great time saver. That's choirtraining at its most creative!

Breathing. The director insisted that everyone breathe at certain places and not in others. This enabled the choir to sing in long, creative and expressive phrases. Again, Bob noticed that he was not paying as much attention to his own breathing as he should have been. There were so many other things to think about. But because the director insisted that breaths should be taken in one place and not in another, he marked his copy lightly with a pencil and concentrated even more.

The director nearly always told the choir to breathe at punctuation marks. If there wasn't a comma or period, then the music invariably had to be sung in one breath. He was meticulous, when rehearsing Stanford's "*Magnificat in B-flat*," to get the choir to breathe where the meaning of the words demanded it.

I hadn't realized that the words governed the interpretation of the music so strongly, thought Bob as he marked in his copy the director's wishes.

He was particularly interested in what happened when they rehearsed Mozart's "Ave Verum Corpus." "We are singing this at two services," the director announced. "At the first service we shall sing it in English, and at the second we shall sing it in Latin, so please mark your copies with different breathings for each version."

That illustrates very clearly the principle of working out where breaths should be taken, thought Bob again.

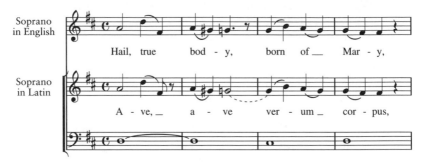

Expression. How easy it is not to notice the expression marks, thought Bob as he sang a passage rather loudly even though it was clearly marked piano. This drew an immediate glance from the director that said, in effect, "You should know better than that; do something about it!" He did.

The director was also meticulous in the matter of balance between the voice-parts. The melody was generally sung by the treble voices, but when another voice sang it, the director made sure that all the other voices could hear the melody being sung. In other words, everyone else had to sing more softly to allow the melody to be heard easily.

The director spent a lot of time polishing the choir's abilities to sing crescendos and diminuendos really smoothly. Bob realized that many choirs get too loud too soon, and too soft too soon. They also altered their tone. "Maintain exactly the same sound on this sustained chord," said the director. "You'll see that the composer calls for a crescendo for the first two measures, and a steady diminuendo for the last four and a half." They were rehearsing the final *amen* of Balfour Gardiner's "Evening Hymn."

"And so," continued the director, "make the culmination of the crescendo coincide with the first beat of the third bar, not the last beat of the second measure." They sang it three times before the director was satisfied.

"The final diminuendo needs even more care." He went to the chalk-board and drew a gentle concave curve sloping downwards to the right.

"Sing me the final four and a half measures, starting forte, and diminuendo steadily as I point the last eighteen beats on this curve." The choir tried it and were remarkably successful, because they stayed louder longer. Golly, thought Bob, having a visual aid when we're singing a diminuendo really helps! The director pointed out that they had made a diminuendo for three of the measures, but then stayed at a steady piano for the final six beats. "Go on getting softer, right through to the very end. In fact," added the director, "diminuendo to total silence!" They tried it once more, and it worked. What a wonderful effect that is, thought Bob. It was worthwhile spending several minutes to get it really right.

When the choir was rehearsing a Magnificat by Howells, the director said, "You need to know two things about his music. First, whenever there's a long note, you almost invariably crescendo right through it, even if the composer has marked no change in dynamics. The same can be said of almost all romantic music. And second, you can ignore almost all the tied eighths which he puts after long notes."

God. _____ (d)

"Why is that?" asked one of the young basses. "Because Howells wrote them in order to be sure that the choir pronounced the final consonant at the very end of the long note, instead of before it had been sung for its full length," answered the director with a smile. "I was a pupil of Howells, so you're getting it from the horse's mouth!"

Believe it! "You're singing Mozart's 'Ave Verum Corpus' beautifully," he said. "But it doesn't grab me. Think what the words mean: 'Hail, true body, born of Mary.' Here you are actually singing to Jesus—you're not singing to me, and you're not singing to the congregation. Visualize yourself actually doing that—especially later in the anthem when you sing about him hanging on the cross."

The director paused for a moment, and then asked, "When we are singing our anthems and hymns in church, to whom are we singing?" Dr. George raised his head and said in a quiet voice, "We're singing to God. God is the audience, not the congregation."

"Thank you, Jurgen," said the director, equally quietly. A stillness had descended upon the choir during the last few minutes. The director waited for a full five seconds, letting everyone feel the mood of the moment, and then he brought them in to begin the anthem again. It was a truly spiritual experience.

The order of rehearsing music. The director rehearsed next Sunday's music in great detail. This took fully half the practice. He allowed the choir to sing several pages uninterrupted, repeating just a few measures to get a point right. I'm glad he keeps changing the pace of the practice, thought Bob. That way we don't get bored and we must be ready for what he wants next.

Halfway through the practice, the director and several of the men had notices to give out. The singers took the opportunity to relax for a couple of minutes, because the pace had been continuous and their level of concentration high.

The rehearsal then resumed, but the director told the choir that they would spend the rest of the time singing through the music that they would be performing during the next few weeks. Even though the atmosphere was a little more relaxed, because they were not rehearsing in such detail and they were getting through twice as much music as they had for the first half of the practice, the director still insisted that all the notes were correct and sung in tune even if they were not wholly tidy.

This part of the rehearsal gave them the opportunity to sing a lot of music, some of which they knew and some they didn't. The new music caused few problems because of the high level of sight-singing. I must teach all my choir members to sight-sing, vowed Bob to himself. It makes the leading of practices so easy!

The final piece, a coronation anthem by Handel, was one which everyone enjoyed, and so the practice ended, as it had begun, on a good note.

53
MEN'S REHEARSALS

SMALL GROUP PRACTICE FOR THE MEN

At least he thought that the practice had ended, when all the sopranos left the room, but he discovered that the men and the male teenagers stayed behind. What's going on? he wondered.

"Okay, gentlemen," said the director. "Let's spend fifteen minutes looking through a couple of new anthems we shall be singing next month."

What a great idea! thought Bob joining the others as they gathered more closely around the piano. There must be a lot of choirs whose menfolk would appreciate a short, regular practice with the director. So many tenors and basses I've met become rather discouraged due to lack of numbers. Having the director's personal attention in a small group once a week could do wonders for morale!

He really enjoyed those fifteen minutes. The whole atmosphere of the practice room became more relaxed. The social interchange between the young men and their older counterparts was delightful. These young singers really feel accepted by their elders, observed Bob, and they're learning a lot from the men's example.

The director was also noticeably more relaxed and exchanged some jokes with his singers as they read through anthems by Mathias and Brahms. One of the men was helpful regarding pronunciation of German, and the director made full use of his expertise as they sang the second anthem slowly, first to vowels, to help them get the notes right, and then in short sections, to work on the pronunciation.

COACHING FOR SOLOISTS

After the practice, one of the men stayed behind for a further five minutes to run through a solo with the director. He was singing it in two weeks' time as part of the prelude before the morning service. Bob noticed that the director asked the soloist how fast he wanted the music played. That's interesting, thought Bob. The roles are reversed here, the director is doing what the singer wants, and not vice versa.

However, there were a couple of places in the music where the director made some helpful suggestions, such as varying the lengths of the phrases by planning the breath marks at punctuation. "The message of the words has to come through clearly, Steve," he said. "The composer drew his inspiration from the words—so let the words inspire you, and through you, the congregation."

The director also encouraged Steve to sing even more expressively. "There's only one thing more beautiful than a well-controlled crescendo," he said with a laugh, "and that's a well-controlled diminuendo!"

"I wonder if you could put it down a step for me," he asked.

"Thanks for giving me notice, Steve!" replied the director with a wry smile. "I'd be happy to! Let's run it through with the organ after next Sunday's service." And with that the practice really came to an end.

54
MIXED ADULT CHOIR REHEARSAL

"That was quite a session!" said Bob.

"Yes, it was," replied the director, clearing his music from the piano as Nancy Willis came towards him with a pile of music in her hands. "But now Nancy is going to lead the adult choir rehearsal, which starts in ten minutes!" Already several women and men were coming through the practice room door and getting music from their cubbies while Nancy erased what the director had written on the chalkboard and began making her own list.

WORKING WITH SOLOISTS

"I noticed that you deferred to Steve for much of your rehearsal with him," commented Bob as they walked away from the piano.

"Yes! I did that because he really knows what he's doing. That's something you should remember."

"What?"

"The more professionally competent your singer is, the more you should fit in with his or her interpretation of their solo. That's especially true when you hire soloists for concerts. I was surprised, recently, to hear a story of a cathedral director of music who was rehearsing an oratorio. He said to his distinguished soprano soloist, 'Madam X, you aren't watching me!' She replied, 'Dr. Y, it is you who should be watching me!' And she was right!"

WHY SINGERS COME EVERY WEEK

The director took a quick cup of chocolate from his ubiquitous thermos flask and began talking with the singers as they came through the door. Bob noticed that several of the men who sang in the men and boys' choir also sang in the mixed adult choir. He saw Dr. Jurgen George and also Frank Stevens. They must be awfully committed, he thought, to sing in both choirs. That means three hours of rehearsal tonight and two services every Sunday! But he understood why they were so dedicated—the director had told him several times the reason that singers came to practices even if the weather was bad: they come because the director makes it worth their while to come. They know that they are going to work hard, learn something and achieve a lot every time they come through that door. And they know that the director will show his appreciation of what they are doing, through words of thanks and through sharing his friendship with them all.

SHARING MUSICAL LEADERSHIP

By this time, the practice room was full again and Bob noticed that Nancy Willis, unlike the director, had a young assistant playing the piano for her. She was talking to him as she arranged her own music.

It was nearly time to begin and the director joined him in the corner of the room to watch the practice. "Who's the pianist?" Bob asked.

"That's Victor Rodney. He's a student from a nearby music school who sings in the adult choir," answered the director. "He finds it very helpful to be drawn into such active participation in our program because he learns a lot that way. He's thinking of becoming a church musician."

"Why don't you lead this practice?"

"Well, my predecessor used to, but found that he had so little energy left after leading two other major rehearsals on the same evening that he asked his associate to take charge. Nancy, who joined us two years ago, is very good, as you'll see." He continued, "She's a trained singer as well as a brilliant organist. She sometimes invites me to rehearse an anthem with the adult choir, or to accompany a more complicated work, which she conducts. We take turns; she accompanies the men and boys' choir on Sundays—it's a delightfully constructive way to operate, if one is as fortunate as I am to have the services of such a gifted colleague."

A DIFFERENT APPROACH TO BEGINNING A PRACTICE

While they had been chatting, Nancy had also been talking with several of her choir members, who clearly relished her outgoing personality. But as the church clock began to strike the hour she moved to her music desk, looked around the room as everyone was busily talking and said, "The Lord be with you!" Instantly came the response, "And also with you," followed by silence.

Wow! thought Bob. That's another way to get people quiet before a practice! Nancy led her singers with a prayer, after which everyone said a firm *Amen*, and looked at her expectantly.

WARMUPS

Bob was fascinated to see that Nancy's approach to choirtraining was very different from the director's. Her warmups were designed to encourage the singers to use their diaphragm creatively.

First she said, "Stretch your arms way out in front of you while you clasp your hands." They all did this, enjoying the feeling of relaxation that it gave them. They unclasped their hands when Nancy said, "Now, rotate your shoulders three times, clockwise." After they did, she added, "And three times counterclockwise."

Next she got the singers to put their hands on their diaphragms and breathe in deeply to the count of a slow three. She insisted that everyone feel that their tummys were coming out "like a balloon filling with air" and that their shoulders were not raised. "Now hiss out to the count of ten," she said, and began counting while the room was filled with the gentle hissing of all the singers as they watched their conductor.

"Put your hand over your heads and do it again, for not everyone's diaphragm is working properly." They did it again and found it easier to be conscious of how they were expelling the air, as they gradually pulled their tummys in.

"Ts'ts'ts'ts'TSSS" modeled Nancy, with her hand on her own diaphragm. The choir copied her, but some of them were controlling the air by tightening their throats. "No!" she said immediately, "always keep your throats relaxed and open, and control your singing from down here. Do it again." And they did, and it was better.

Then they began some singing exercises, with Nancy modeling each new one for them, and then subsequently going up a half step, without any help from the piano.

Mee, mey, mah, moh, moo.   Mee, mey, mah, moh,

moo.   Mee, mey, mah, moh, moo.

Vee, vey, vah, voh, voo.　　*similar*

Ah, ———— ah, ah, ah, ah, ah. ————————

Ee, ————

Eh, ————

Ah, ————

Aw, ————

"Make sure you sing from the front of your mouth, not the back of your throat," said Nancy to one or two singers.

The men always sang an octave below the women, and the exercises were sung rhythmically but only moderately loudly. "Control the staccato notes by the muscles in your diaphragm, not by your throat," commanded Nancy, again.

"Always be sure to breathe in well and to imagine the first note before you sing it," she added, as one or two singers made untidy entrances.

She walked round the room while they were singing, looking every singer in the face so as to encourage them to do their very best.

My word! thought Bob, She really makes contact with all these singers. Even though most of them are amateurs, they really know how to stand, how to breathe and how to produce their voices.

"Sigh out to *Oo*," said Nancy, and they all made a two-octave scooping descent from a high falsetto note to as low a note as they could reach. They were really warmed up!

55
How to Introduce
New Ways

ENCOURAGING CHOIR MEMBERS
TO THINK FOR THEMSELVES

When she had finished the exercises, Nancy Willis stood in the middle of the choir room and said to her choir, "Well, now then, friends, the director and I have been talking, and I think that I've been too kind to you during my first two years here!" She threw a look at the director, who raised an eyebrow, and then continued, "I believe that I don't get you to think as much as you ought to!"

There were a few furrowed brows among some long-established members of the choir and puzzled looks from others.

"When we come to a practice, everyone should not only work very hard indeed, but also do a lot of independent creative thinking."

"What do you mean, Nancy?" asked one of the senior basses, whose wife, Naomi, sang alto in front of him.

"What I mean, Andrew, is that so far you've all been responding wonderfully to everything I've asked you to do—but only because I've told you everything I wanted from you and not asked you to think for yourselves what you ought to be doing."

"This sounds a little too complicated for me," remarked Naomi, and her husband nodded his agreement.

"I mean that you've sung softly when I've asked you to sing softly, or loudly when the song needed to be loud. I didn't ask you to look at the music to see what the composer's wishes were. In other words, I did your thinking for you, and didn't encourage you to look creatively at the music—to take responsibility yourselves for deciding just how the music should be sung."

"What are you proposing to do about it!" asked Andrew somewhat defensively.

"We'll try an experiment for this practice—to see if you like this new approach. We'll save the last five minutes of the rehearsal to discuss it." She embraced everyone with a lovely smile and said, "Who's willing to go along with me, just this once, and see what happens?" There were quiet grunts of acquiescence from some of the older members but more audible cries of yes from the younger singers. "If it doesn't work," continued Nancy, "we won't do it again, but I think you will enjoy it!

"Now," she said brightly, "turn to 'O Come, Ye Servants of the Lord' by Christopher Tye. The boys were rehearsing this last Monday, and so we'll need to collect the copies afterwards to give them back. We're singing it in three weeks."

The choir quickly found their music and looked at Nancy expectantly, wondering what she would do next. "I've asked Victor not to play the first chord for you yet," she continued. "Look at the music, and try to visualize what your first note sounds like. No!" she added hastily as several singers began to moan a few notes, "Don't make a sound until I ask you. You've all sung the chord of G major before—see if you can remember what it sounds like."

There was silence for a few seconds, and then Nancy said, "Right, I'm going to ask you all to risk singing the first word to the note that you have chosen, and we'll do it all together, and sustain it to hear what it sounds like! One-two-ready-breathe!" And the choir sang O to a very peculiar chord!

"Go on singing your note," encouraged Nancy as she walked round the room listening to each singer in turn. "Some of you are very nearly right!" After a few seconds she stopped them with a wave of her hand, turned to Victor, who was sitting at the piano with a broad grin on his face, and said, "Vick, play the first chord for us!" He did, and half the singers suddenly realized that they had been singing a note very close to the correct one. "Who was absolutely right?" asked Nancy, and several hands shot up accompanied by happy smiles. "Yes, you were right, Gaskill," she said smiling at a tenor on her right, "and so were you, Shirley," with an equally happy smile at a soprano standing in front of him. She turned to the whole choir and asked, encouragingly, "Who was nearly right?" A number of hands were raised, including those of Andrew and Naomi. "Well done!" beamed Nancy at them, "I'm proud of you!" Naomi and Andrew tried hard to look modest, but didn't entirely succeed.

DON'T PLAY THE PIANO UNLESS YOU HAVE TO!

"Well," continued Nancy, "having heard the chord played once, we're going to try to practice the whole anthem, unaccompanied, without Victor playing the piano again for at least five minutes!

"Ready to begin!" she commanded, raising her arms and embracing the whole choir with an encouraging smile, "Sing the first chord only, and listen to it. One-two-ready-breathe." Most singers sang the chord correctly, but a few singers, who were not yet ready to think actively for themselves, were out by several notes, for they had been expecting Victor to play the chord for them as he usually did. "Everyone sustain that chord and listen to the note that you're singing. If it doesn't fit with the rest of the choir, alter it until it does."

It took fully ten seconds before the chord was sung accurately; Nancy found that she had to go to a couple of singers who, clearly, were not used to listening to themselves and were singing too low. To get them to sing higher, she raised the palms of her upturned hands to them coupled with an encouraging look. It worked!

HOW TO ATTAIN BLEND QUICKLY

"Well done!" said Nancy, still looking remarkably cheerful. "Now that's got the first note right." She looked round the room and continued,

"But did you make a lovely sound?" The shaking heads that met her gaze indicated that they had not. "Right," she continued. "We'll sing that chord again, and you will decide how to make it sound beautiful. How do you think you're going to do that?" she asked. There was a pause and then Becky, another soprano, suggested, "Perhaps we might listen to what we are actually doing?"

"That's a great idea, Becky!" enthused Nancy, as though that thought had never occurred to her. "Let's see if Becky's idea works." This time Nancy brought the choir in very gently to encourage them to sing softly. After five seconds almost every voice was blending beautifully, except for a too-loud bass. Nancy went gently right up to the bass and put her finger to her lips indicating that he might want to sing a little more softly. This took a little longer that she expected and the bass ran out of breath. The instant he stopped singing she said, "Oh, what a lovely sound you are all making! Do it again!"

The bass, by this time, had got the message and sang more quietly. Nancy glanced at him to show that she appreciated what he was doing and said, "Yes, you are all making a really lovely sound. Now let's sing the first page of the anthem to the vowel *Oo* still making that beautiful blending sound."

THE CHOIRMASTER MUST BELIEVE IN WHAT SHE IS DOING

While all this had been happening, Bob and the director had been looking on with great interest, for Nancy had been showing a lot of tact as well as giving very clear instructions. She was so gentle with them all that no one was threatened, and when singers approached the level of thinking for themselves and listening to themselves that she had asked for, she responded with a gratified smile and a word of encouragement. Clearly, this was new to them all and they were finding it a really enjoyable experience, for their own thinking was altering the way they were singing. The choir was getting better every minute because everyone had the mind to pursue excellence, and all Nancy had to do was to ask the right question, such as, "Now you see that we sing the first page twice, because of the repeat mark in the last measure. I think you'll find that the editor has suggested that we sing it differently the second time through."

This remark was greeted with puzzled looks from several singers who were not used to looking at expression marks. "Look at the very first measure," she said, "and it will tell you what to do." She waited for a few seconds while one or two of the more experienced singers indicated to their younger colleagues what they should be looking for. Most of the worried frowns disappeared.

LOOK AT THE CHOIR WHEN CONDUCTING

"Right," said Nancy, "we'll sing the first page twice, exactly as the editor has suggested." And for the next minute she conducted the choir from memory, looking into the faces of every singer as she made it crystal clear by her gestures that the first time through was soft, and the repeat was loud.

"Wasn't that good!" she enthused. "And did I tell you how to do it?"

"No," said Andrew, "we did it ourselves." And then he added with a smile, "I don't think we need you at all, Nancy, for we sang it far better when every one of us was doing the thinking instead of our old way, when you did the thinking for us!" Everyone laughed at this, for they knew that he was giving Nancy a well-deserved compliment, for it was she who had encouraged them to think and the experiment was working very well.

HOW TO BRING THE MUSIC TO LIFE

The practice continued in the same vein. Instead of telling the choir where they should breathe, Nancy asked them where they thought breaths should be taken. Generally they decided to breathe at punctuation marks, but occasionally there was a difference of opinion. "Should we breathe after the second word—O *come*,?" asked Gaskill, the tenor. "There's certainly a comma there," answered Nancy, "but I wonder if it would stop the flow of the music if we breathed so soon after beginning. What do you think?"

"I think we should sing the first four measures in one breath," responded Gaskill, "and make a crescendo up to the important word, *praise*, and diminuendo after it. 'O come, ye servants of the Lord, and *praise*, his holy Name.'"

"That sounds terrific, Gaskill. Let's do it!" They did, and it sounded great.

Having established the principle, Nancy pursued this one thought for the remainder of the anthem—asking the choir which was the most important syllable of each phrase and encouraging them to crescendo towards it. They all found that this brought the meaning of the words to life, not only because each phrase was now beautifully shaped, but also because the choir was actually thinking about the words that they were singing.

They found that they could even crescendo at different levels. There was a gentle one when they sang the first page softly, and then a more vigorous one when they repeated it loudly. They discovered that they couldn't crescendo if they started the repeat too loudly, and so they decided to change the expression mark from *forte* to *mezzo forte*, which achieved the editor's objective and gave them enough room for rise and fall in dynamic level.

GOOD CHOIRS PAY ATTENTION TO SMALL DETAILS

The next thing Nancy asked them to think about was if they were really pronouncing all the letters in each word. "Can you hear the *d* in the phrase 'and praise his holy Name'?" she asked. "Let's have one side of the choir singing it while the other half listens. Tell me if you can hear them singing that *d*," she asked with a smile. This element of competition between the sides worked very well, resulting in broad grins from the better side, and stronger resolution from the other so that, in the end, both sides achieved what Nancy had been seeking.

To everyone's delight, having focused their attention on the need to pronounce the *d* in one word, the standard of enunciation improved for much of the anthem without anything further having to be said.

DEFINITION OF A GOOD CHOIR!

Nancy looked with appreciation at her singers after the choir had a sung a page really well. "Do you know," she said with a smile, "that the director has defined a good choir as one that you can listen to without pain!" Everyone laughed. "But," she continued, "a superb choir is a choir that one would pay good money to listen to, and you are fast approaching this high standard!" There were smiles all round at this compliment, and everyone stood just a little bit straighter, determined to do even better next time.

GIVE THE SINGERS TIME TO THINK

After rehearsing another page, Nancy asked the choir to go back to the beginning of the anthem. She gave them sufficient time to look at the note they had just been singing and compare it with the note they were about to sing, so that they could get it right without a chord being given on the piano.

"Do you realize," said Nancy, lowering the tension a few degrees, "that we haven't asked Victor to give us a chord for over ten minutes!" Victor played up to this by closing his eyes and giving a loud snore, which brought a laugh from everyone.

THE MORE YOU EXPECT YOUR CHOIR TO THINK, THE BETTER THEY WILL GET

Bob turned to the director and whispered, "It's amazing! The whole character of the practice rose by several degrees when Nancy showed the choir what fun it was to get everyone to think for themselves."

"Of course it did!" answered the director. "A choirmaster needs to treat singers as intelligent adults, but know exactly how far she can push the choir at any one time. They must succeed in the challenges she sets them so that next time they'll come back for more and reach greater heights."

"She's not getting through too much music tonight, is she?"

"You can answer your own implied question," whispered the director as Nancy continued the practice.

What implied question? thought Bob. After a few minutes watching Nancy progress with her choir, he realized that the initial pace, which had been slow, was gradually increasing in speed and effectiveness as the choir became more attuned to her wavelength. Ah! thought Bob, once she's got the choir really thinking for themselves, she will begin to achieve more in a far shorter time than she did by the old way. What's more, they'll remember what they have decided to do when it comes to singing the music on Sunday."

56
POINTS TO PRACTICE

Bob noticed that Nancy concentrated on a few major points while she was rehearsing her choir:

PRACTICE SLOWLY

When they were learning a new anthem, she got the choir to sing it through slowly, with a light accompaniment on the piano. It's just like learning a new piece on the organ, thought Bob. You have to practice it slowly before you can play it up to speed. This way the difficult bits seem easier, for everyone has time to think.

SING EXPRESSIVELY

Nancy encouraged the choir to sing expressively. "The composer didn't put expression marks for every note," she said. "Just think what the words mean, and you'll want to crescendo to the important ones."

There's a parallel there, too, thought Bob. When I put fingering on my organ music, I don't write them over every note—only on the important ones. It's the same with choral music: the composer only puts expression in at important places. But Nancy is saying that every note should be a part of a phrase that is either getting louder or getting softer. Singing expressively certainly makes the music and the meaning of the words come alive.

SING COLORFULLY

Nancy followed the director's example in getting the choir to sing words colorfully. "Instead of singing, 'There is a green hill far away,'" said Nancy, "try singing 'There is a blue hill far away.'" They tried it and everyone noticed that the word *blue* was sung in a subtly different manner from the word *green*. "Now try '...a red hill.'" Every singer entered into the spirit of the moment and found that they were bringing the different colors to life in a wholly new way.

"Now let's go one stage further," said Nancy. "Sing, 'There is a green hill near at hand.'" They did. "Now go back to the original words," commanded Nancy. The choir found, to their surprise, that they sang the word *far* in a way that really gave a feeling of distance. They couldn't explain it, but they certainly all felt it.

Golly! thought Bob. This is really exciting. It's like registering my organ music—deciding if a solo should be played on a flute or on a trumpet. If I play with varying colors on the organ, how much more should a choir sing with different colors when it has such wonderful words to bring to life!

KNOW HOW MUCH YOUR CHOIR CAN ACHIEVE
Bob was interested to see that Nancy stressed some of the other "Ten Commandment" points that the director had followed in his own practice an hour earlier. She knows exactly how far to go with each point, thought Bob. She is stretching everyone just a little beyond what they think they can achieve, so that they get excited by what they are able to do, not discouraged by what they cannot. This way they'll get better and better every week. Wow!

ANNOUNCEMENTS—CHOIR PARTY
Halfway through the practice Nancy allowed time for some announcements. "Joanna is in the hospital," she said, "but she is doing well after her operation. We've sent her some flowers and I've brought a get-well card to send to her. I'm sure we'd all like to sign it."

A young soprano put up her hand. "Yes, Judy?" "Ted and I would be happy to offer our home for a lunch party after church in two weeks' time." Appreciative murmurs greeted this announcement. "Yes," added a bass standing behind Judy, "we'd like the men to bring a variety of liquid refreshment and the women some food." "We've put a sign-up sheet on the notice board," said Judy, giving a smile to her husband. "One column for those who will bring salad, another for those who will bring a main course, and the last for desserts. Please try to get an equal number of names in each column."

"Thank you, Judy and Ted," said Nancy with a smile. "Let's have a show of hands to give us an idea of how many will be coming. One hand for yourself and another for your spouse or friend." Most people raised their hands. Clearly it was going to be a good party. Bob wished he could be there for it. I must arrange a party for my choir as soon as I get back home, he resolved.

LISTEN TO DISSENTING OPINIONS WITH UNDERSTANDING
At the end of the practice, the five-minute discussion on the new way of leading a practice received a lot of praise from almost everyone. A few singers remained unconvinced, but they knew that Nancy had listened to their opinions carefully, and that was all they really needed. The general consensus was, "Let's do it again next week!"

"We really enjoyed that!" said Naomi to Nancy as they put their music away in their cubbies. "It's raised my whole level of consciousness about the singing process." "Yes," chimed in her husband, "I didn't realize I knew so much about music. I'm taking home a couple of anthems to practice for next week." "He's never done that before!" whispered Naomi to Nancy as she followed Andrew out of the door, "You've really got him hooked tonight!"

The other singers were also chatting happily to each other as they put their music away. The director came over to Nancy and said, "Well done! That was a thrilling practice."

"Thank you!" responded Nancy gratefully. "Most of it went very well indeed, but there were a couple of times when I lapsed into the old ways and did their thinking for them, and there were times when I couldn't see how to get a point across without actually giving them the answer."

"That's okay, Nancy. You have so many gifts of your own to offer your choir! You need to work out your own way of working with them, incorporating not only their gifts and their knowledge, but also your own considerable expertise. It's taken me a lifetime to get where I am at present, and I hope I'm continuing to improve!" And with that he turned to speak to some of the other choir members who were still visiting with one another. It had been a most happy as well as a productive evening.

57
INTEGRATING MUSIC INTO A CHURCH PROGRAM

"Are you joining us for pizza, director?" asked Frank Stevens, as he put his music away neatly in his cubby.

"Yes, I'll be along shortly," responded the director, "but I've got to discuss a couple of matters with Nancy. Why don't you take Bob along with you—you can tell him about your concerts' committee."

"Great idea!" said Frank heartily. "Come on, Bob, we can get the pizza ordered before the others arrive." And so saying he led Bob out to his own car.

CHURCH POLICY REGARDING A LIVE MUSIC PROGRAM

"I've never experienced so much activity in a music program," said Bob as Frank drove out of the church car lot. "You seem to have so many people involved in such a lot of activities."

"Yes, we're very fortunate here. The church officials want a live music program and they give us a lot of support, both moral and financial. We couldn't do it unless it was clearly laid down as church policy."

"How did that happen?"

A HEALTHY CHURCH SUPPORTS ACTIVE PROGRAMS

"It's built up gradually over the years. The ministers realized that if the church has a lively choir program it is immediately beneficial to the church as a whole."

"How do you mean?" ask Bob as they waited for the lights to change on Church Street.

"Some ministers feel, alas, that a big choir program is a threat to themselves and they put a stop to it." The lights turned green and Frank made a right following a line of cars making its way slowly down Main Street, past brightly lit shops. "They can't see that an active music program helps to bring life to all parts of the church's ministry. The choir children bring their parents along, who become active members of the congregation; the adult singers put their children into the church school program. Singers, both children and adults, often bring their friends to join them in the choirs. We draw other people into our congregation through the concerts we arrange and, as you will have seen, several of the choir people are leaders in the parish."

"Yes, I met the junior warden yesterday. He is a choir parent."

"Five members of the church council are past or present choir parents and another one sings in our adult choir," added Frank. "Another choir parent chaired last year's Christmas bazaar, and yet another is chairing the church's new building program."

TEAMWORK AND PERSONAL RELATIONSHIPS

"But how can a large music program coexist alongside the other programs this church arranges?"

"It's all to do with personal relationships," answered Frank as he made a left into another large street. "The minister encourages collegiality among his staff. I expect the director has told you about their weekly meetings when everyone is able to talk about his or her program and listen to what else is going on."

"Yes, he's meeting with the minister tomorrow," answered Bob. "I can see that regular meetings help to oil the wheels of collegiality, as you put it."

"One of the reasons that the church hired our director was because he had proved to be a team player. You can't run any organization, be it a church or a soccer team, unless the players are willing to work together—to honor one another, and to help one another. When a player scores a goal, the whole team wins, not just the player who scored the goal, for everyone played his or her own part in helping that goal to be reached.

SINGERS SPEND MORE TIME AT CHURCH
THAN ALMOST ANYONE ELSE

"You see," continued Frank, "a church choir program demands more commitment from its members than most other church programs."

"How do you mean?" asked Bob.

"It's obvious! When children join the choir their parents almost always have to bring them to church—that means one or two double journeys to church for weekly practices and also once on Sundays. It's a similar situation for adult singers.

"Michael Rohrer told me that the director of music has more influence on the children and some of their families than the minister."

"Why?"

"Because the director works with them so closely for two, three or even more hours a week. They know him better than anyone else at the church.

"And so," continued Frank, "once a family has accepted such a strong commitment to the church in the matter of time and effort, it's only a small step to ask them to commit even more. Look at me," he said with a laugh, "I sing in two of the choirs as well as chairing the concerts' committee, and I've got a full-time job that takes me through three states every week. But I come here because I love it, and find that I'm supported so strongly, not only by the director, but also by my fellow singers, their families, and the clergy."

"Wow!" said Bob, predictably.

MUSIC BUDGET

"And there's more to it than that," continued Frank as they neared the pizza restaurant, which was lit with a garish neon sign glowing "Monty's Pizzaria."

"Like what?"

"The church authorities have seen that a successful music program actually helps to build up the church as a whole, not only in numbers of people who fill the choirstalls Sunday by Sunday, but also with their friends and relations who sit in the congregation and who, equally obviously, contribute to the church budget."

"Yes," interrupted Bob, as Frank drove into the restaurant parking lot, "you're fortunate to have quite a large music budget here; not many of us are so lucky."

"The music budget is more than taken care of through the number of families who are actively involved in our music programs and by others who come to the church because of the quality of its music," answered Frank as he found an empty parking space. "If this church decided to cut out the music program entirely, it would lose not only a lot of loyal workers who are involved in many other activities, but it would find that its income would drop way below what it costs to maintain such a program."

They got out of the car and walked up to the brightly lit restaurant entrance. "And so," continued Frank, as he opened the door to Monty's, "the church council has made it a policy to support a lively music program—and this cannot be altered by any individual unless a contrary motion is raised and debated fully by the whole parish."

He found a couple of empty tables and began to rearrange them to make one big table. "The church is committed to us, and we are committed to it; we are all stronger because of it," he concluded as he set ten chairs in their place. "It's like the joining of these two tables," he added with a laugh, "you can have a church where everyone gets on with his or her own program, sitting at different tables and not communicating; or you can join together as one big family, recognizing that diversity is a sign of strength and order, and not weakness and disorder," and so saying he sat down and smiled hopefully at a waitress who was walking towards them.

58
ORGANIZING A CONCERT SERIES

The waitress greeted Frank with a big smile, and said, "How many will it be tonight, Frank?"

"About ten, Cindy. We'd better have three large pizzas—one with pepperoni, one with sausage and mushrooms, and one with peppers and garlic. Two pitchers of beer and a large bottle of 7-Up. The director will want his usual glass of burgundy; he should be here soon."

He turned to Bob and asked, "What will you have, Bob?"

"I think I need a burgundy, too, please!"

Cindy wrote down their order, gave them both another smile, and said, "The pizzas will be ready in fifteen minutes, but I'll be right back with your drinks," and she hurried off.

FIND A MUSICAL NEED AND FILL IT

"Tell me about your concert series, Frank, because I want to organize one in my new church."

"The first thing you need to do is to discover what your community lacks in the way of concerts and how far you can go to supply that need."

"How so?"

"Well, is there a choral society in your part of the city?"

"Yes! They give annual performances of *Messiah* and a couple of other concerts during the season, with a large orchestra to accompany them."

"So you don't want to compete with them, for they've already cornered that part of the musical market. You have to find something that no one else does and do it really well. What about organ recitals?"

"Well, the cathedral has a magnificent organ and a fine recital series, so I can't compete with that."

"True," mused Frank as Cindy brought Bob's burgundy to the table, along with a pitcher of beer and a supply of glasses.

"On the other hand," said Bob, as he took a sip of wine, "I know there are some fine instrumentalists at my church. I might arrange a series of concerts for instruments and organ."

"That sounds great," said Frank. "Ah," he added, "here comes Deane. He's on our concerts' committee. Let's see what he can suggest."

Deane sat down next to Bob and filled a glass with beer as Frank put their problem to him.

"We've found that presenting a concert once a month, on a Sunday afternoon, attracts a good audience," said Deane. "We light the church with candles and keep the program under ninety minutes."

"Why do you do that?" asked Bob.

"Because people like to be at home on Sunday evenings, and if we can assure them that they can come to a concert at church and also spend the evening at home with their families, they're more likely to become regular attenders, especially if we offer them a varied fare of music," he added.

PUBLICITY BROCHURE

"What are you presenting this season?" asked Bob.

"Here's our brochure," said Frank, pulling a brightly colored pamphlet out of his pocket. "We're rather proud of this. It's been designed by Roberta, who sings in our choir. And here she comes, right on cue," he laughed as the attractive soprano took her place opposite Deane. "Roberta's in the advertising business," continued Frank, "and we make full use of her expertise."

"But you pay me for it!" said Roberta with a grin.

"Yes, but you don't charge us the full rate. That's one of the wonderful things about belonging to a lively church—you find that there are a lot of people who are only too willing to lend their talents to help you, if you show that you mean business."

Bob looked at the brochure and saw that there was a concert every month from October through May, ranging from a program given by the director's chamber choir with Nancy Willis playing organ solos, through chamber concerts for piano and other instruments, a Christmas concert given by the combined church choirs, some medieval music on authentic instruments, and even an organ battle featuring the church organ and an internationally known computer organ.

"Wow!" he exclaimed. "There's something here for everyone."

"Yes," responded Frank, "we think it will go well. A lot of people have worked very hard to make it a success."

SMALL COMMITTEES ACHIEVE MORE

"You must have a large committee to run a program like this," said Bob, conversationally.

"Ah, that's just what we don't have," said Deane, with a smile. "We've found that the more people you have on a committee, the less efficient it becomes."

"How big is your committee, then?"

"There are only nine of us," answered Frank.

"That means that you, Deane, and Roberta must be on it for starters," said Bob confidently.

"Wrong!" said Roberta. "There's no need for me to be on the committee. I can get on with designing the brochure without having to attend interminable committee meetings. All I need to know is what concerts have been arranged and I do the rest."

"Roberta came to one meeting," said Frank. "We needed to see what ideas she had regarding the design for the brochure, what it would cost, and also the date for delivery. Once we'd given our official approval we didn't see her again.

PUBLICITY

"Our publicity officer can't stand committee meetings either," he added. "We give her the basic material and the phone numbers of the artists, and she works on the publicity from her home. She's got an enormous list of folk to send mail to, which includes all the church members as well as the folk on mailing lists from other music societies in the neighborhood. She's a really efficient person, and so she knows exactly when she should send details to the press and radio people. We couldn't do without her."

RECORDING

"We also couldn't do without David Major," said Deane.

"Who's David Major?" asked Bob, somewhat overwhelmed by all that was coming his way.

"David records all our concerts for us, with the permission of the performers, of course," answered Deane. "He sends recordings of concerts to our local radio stations as well as to National Public Radio. A couple of our concerts were broadcast nationwide last season. He really helped to put us on the map!"

VOLUNTEERS

"You see," continued Frank, as two more choir members joined them—you need a small committee made up of people who will work really hard. You can always ask for volunteers to help with other tasks." He turned to the new arrivals, "Bob, I don't think you've met Ted and Judy Brewer."

"Oh yes," said Bob, "you were singing with the adult choir tonight, weren't you?"

"Yes," said Ted, pouring a couple of glasses of 7-Up for his wife and himself, "and Frank makes us work hard for his concert series, too."

"We take tickets at the door, stuff envelopes with publicity material for all the members of our church," said Judy, "and generally help when things need to be done. We really enjoy it."

"And they help me with moving chairs and setting up the stage for some of our concerts," added Deane. "It's a big family effort, because Frank and the music directors are always there with their sleeves rolled up when there's work to be done."

FINANCE

"How do you finance your concerts?" asked Bob.

"Well, we had to start with a float of several thousand dollars from the church council, who were very careful to ensure that their money would not be lost," answered Frank. "That meant that we had to work closely with the minister and formulate very careful plans for our first season.

"Because we are a church, and therefore tax exempt, we cannot charge admission to the church building."

"How do you get around that?"

"We ask for a donation at the door, with special rates for students and senior citizens. The donation can be treated as a tax exempt deduction. If someone cannot afford to offer a donation we are happy to admit them to the concert free, for it is a place of worship."

"We give a cut rate to those who subscribe to the series," said Deane. "We offer eight concerts for the price of six. That encourages people to become subscribers, which helps us at the beginning of the season when we have to meet bills for the printing of the brochure and the publicity mailing."

"We also encourage folk to help us financially by printing the names of those who give us $100 or more. These are our patrons.

"Of course," he added, "if you are organizing a really big program you will want patrons who give considerably more than that. You'll also want to investigate the possibilities of grants from public bodies and large corporations, and also get advertising for your programs from local shops and businesses.

"If you choose a well-informed treasurer, she will know the right people in your area to go to for advice about such things. Your minister is, as always, the first person with whom you should discuss this, for your concert series must eventually become financially self-supporting.

MAKEUP OF THE COMMITTEE

"And so, tell me exactly who is on your committee," asked Bob for the second time.

Frank leaned forward and began to count on his fingers. "There's myself as chairman; there's a secretary, who not only takes minutes but also carries out a lot of the decisions that the committee makes. There's a treasurer, whom I've already mentioned. Hers is a vital role, for all our accounts have to be submitted to the church council at the end of each season, and they have to be in good order."

"There's also Nancy Willis and myself," said a cheery voice—it was the director who'd just come in. "The concerts come within our responsibilities as heads of the church's music program."

"And there's a wonderful choir parent who has strong connections with some of the leading instrumentalists in the area," chimed in Nancy as she sat next to Deane. "And Deane has recently joined us to be in charge of staging our concerts."

"We have an official representative from the church council who's equally wonderful," added Frank. "She's always full of good ideas and challenges us to think big! Last season she suggested that our major concert should be in aid of a local charity. She got together with their committee and they helped us to arrange the whole thing. We've never had such a big audience, and the charity raised over $7,000, after we'd cleared all our expenses.

"And finally, we have the minister," added Frank, "as he is ultimately responsible for everything that happens in the church."

"You seem to have a wonderful group," commented Bob.

"Yes, we do," answered Frank, "and I aim to keep all our committee meetings down to ninety minutes. It's amazing what you can do when you set a time limit on discussions!"

59
FINANCING NEW MUSIC

They paused as Cindy and another waitress brought three large pizzas to their table. "Thank you, Elaine," said Roberta. "Those look delicious," and she passed the plates around the table as Dr. George joined them. "You're just in time, Jurgen. What'll you have?"

"One slice of sausage and mushroom, please," answered Dr. George. "I'm cooking a meal for some friends when I get home tonight, so I can't stay long."

Bob looked at Dr. George's lean frame and wondered where he put it all, for he'd already had two helpings of choir supper earlier in the evening. Bob turned to Deane, who was enjoying his second slice of pizza, and asked, "How can you afford to buy new music for the choirs? I noticed that there were several brand-new anthems in the choir cubbies tonight. Does the church pay for them?"

"It's not easy," answered Deane with his mouth full of peppers and garlic. "Until a few years ago, the church budget allowed us to buy new music pretty regularly, but that isn't the case now. Hopefully, your music budget will cover these expenses."

"Well, how do you go about finding the money to buy new music?" persisted Bob.

"I can answer that," said the director, helping himself to another slice of pizza. His diet was clearly on hold for the evening. "We find that parents, whose children have been through the choir program, are happy to memorialize their offsprings' time with us by buying a set of music for the choir. It could be an anthem or even a collection of anthems. We put a printed label on the inside cover of the music stating that this music has been given by the family of Jane Doe as a thankoffering for her time in the choir.

"And whenever we sing that anthem," continued the director, "I let Jane's parents know so that they can come to church and hear her music being sung."

"That sounds a wonderful thing to do," commented Bob.

"Yes, and the word is spreading, for we are getting more and more offers of help to buy music, not only from parents of singers, but also from other couples as a thankoffering for their years of marriage."

"And you must remember the bequests we received last year," added Nancy Willis.

"Oh yes!" said the director. "Two strong supporters of the music program died last year and their relatives asked that donations should be given to the church's music program in their memory. We received so much money," he continued, "that we were able to buy seventy copies of a book of one hundred anthems that had just been published. We are singing well over half of them this season, and so the memories of these two wonderful folk are being kept very much alive in our midst."

"Golly!" said Bob, at a loss for words.

"It's important to keep all our sheet music in good repair," said Deane. "I spend a lot of my time putting stiff covers onto copies of our anthems. It costs quite a lot to do that, but in the long run, it saves us money, for we can use them for many years before they wear out."

"I see now why you have sub-librarians to help you," said Bob.

"Yes," said Deane with a satisfied smile as he finished his third slice of pizza, "we couldn't manage without the willing help of our young people. The more we ask of them, the more they seem willing to give."

"Speaking of giving," said the director, standing up, "it's time to contribute to the cost of tonight's feast. I need to get home. How much do I owe for Bob and me?" he asked Robert, who had assumed the mantle of treasurer for the evening.

"Nothing at all," answered Robert with a smile. "It's our treat tonight, not only for Bob, but also for you, because," he continued, embracing his colleagues with a merry grin, "last week was your birthday. Let's all join in with a rousing chorus of 'Happy Birthday'!" The choir members rose and sang a spontaneously harmonized version of the birthday song, which ended with Judy singing a top C, much to the delight of the other customers, as well as to Cindy and Elaine, who had begun to clear the table of the few remaining crumbs from the post-practice feast.

"That was a terrific day," said Bob with a sigh as he and the director made their way to the car. "I wish I didn't have to leave tomorrow."

"There'll be plenty of time for us to talk before you go," answered the director as he unlocked his car. "But first we'll both need a good night's sleep. Let's go home!"

60
BODY LANGUAGE

They drove along in companionable silence for a while, enjoying the darkness of the country roads as the car's headlights cleaved a shining path before them. "We've got to be on the lookout for deer in these parts," said the director. "They're liable to spring out in front of the car without any warning. I know of several people whose cars have been totaled because the drivers tried to avoid them and hit a tree instead."

"And I thought driving in the city was dangerous!" said Bob, stretching himself.

"You're tired, aren't you?" said the director, glancing at his passenger.

"Yes! How can you tell?"

"That's obvious. You just enjoyed a good stretch. It was just as apparent that you didn't want to leave the party at Monty's tonight. I looked at your feet!"

"What have feet got to do with it?" asked Bob, sitting up straight and getting out his notebook.

"When I was an associate professor at a music college in England, one of my colleagues was a Mrs. Barlow, who was responsible for coaching singers for the college opera. She taught them how to express the meaning of their songs through movement. Her specialty was body language."

"What do you mean by that?"

"She could tell, just by looking at you, what you were thinking! It could have been a rather threatening situation if she hadn't been such a delightfully kind and understanding person."

"How could she tell what you were thinking just by looking at you?"

"Because the body has its own language just as much as the tongue has. When you stretched just now you were telling me that you were tired. That was obvious to both of us. But Mrs. Barlow showed me that there are many other signs the body gives, which, if you can read them correctly, give an equally clear message."

"This is fascinating," said Bob, sitting up straighter and turning towards the director, insofar as his seat belt allowed him to.

"There! You're showing me right now that you are interested in what I'm saying," said the director with a laugh. "You're turning towards me and you're sitting up straighter. This gives me a very clear message."

"Tell me more," said Bob.

"Well, Mrs. Barlow had learned all about body language from a French professor who, I believe, was the first man to classify and codify this subject. Many of my theory pupils, who were singing students at the college, told me how helpful Mrs. Barlow had been to them. I asked her if she would address my choirtraining class and explain to them how to stand better before their choirs and how to convey their musical intentions through more expressive conducting. She agreed and gave us a wonderful lecture, which I will never forget."

"I'm listening!" said Bob, eagerly turning a page in his notebook.

"She told us that the body was divided into three parts: the cerebral or thinking part—our head; the emotional or the part that shows how we feel—our torso; and the volitional or the part that shows where we want to go—our legs."

"How obvious," commented Bob, busily writing in his notebook.

"Of course it is! Everything I tell you is obvious, don't you remember?"

"Oh yes! But it's not obvious until you actually say it. Please carry on!"

"Mrs. Barlow then went on to say that each of the three major sections of the body can be subdivided into the same three parts, and they can be further subdivided, and so on."

"Let me see if I can begin to work this out," interrupted Bob. "The forehead, or brain, is the cerebral. The part from the eyebrows through the mouth is the emotional, and the chin is the volitional."

"Absolutely right! But the important thing is to know how to interpret this knowledge."

"How do you mean?"

"Let me give you an example. If you are really on my wavelength, really concentrating on what I'm saying, will your forehead be pointing towards me or away from me?"

Bob thought for a moment and then said, "My brain box will be pointing towards you, as it is right now!" and he laughed.

"Right! Now tell me why it is important for a conductor to look at his musicians."

There was a further pause and then Bob said, "Because you show your emotions with your eyebrows, with your eyes, and with your mouth."

"Right again! Conductors who have their noses buried in their scores cannot possibly convey their wishes to those they are conducting. Do you remember what I told you about my teacher, Boris Ord?"

"Yes! You said that his great secret was his eyes, the way that he looked at his choir when he conducted them."

"Right! He used only minimal movements of a finger on each hand on the top of the choirdesks to beat time. He didn't wave his arms about as most of us do these days—he commanded his choir through the expression in his eyes. My word!" continued the director nostalgically, "His singers really had to concentrate in those days. That's why they were so good."

"Tell me more," asked Bob, hoping that what he was writing was legible, for they were still driving along dark country roads.

"Well, you can work a lot of it out for yourself. But consider subdividing the arm. The hands are clearly volitional; they tell you what the tempo is and one's fingers point out directions. Do you think that any part of the arm is cerebral?" he asked.

"It should be the top part of the arm, from what you've told me," said Bob, shrugging his shoulders, "but I don't know."

"What did you say?" asked the director, with a smile.

"I said, I didn't know," he answered with a slight frown.

"What did you do when you said that you didn't know?"

Bob thought for a moment and then said, "Oh, I shrugged my shoulders! My shoulders communicated by gesture what I'd just said in words. Wow!"

"But," continued the director, "if I want to convey emotion when conducting, which part of my arm do I use?"

Bob thought for a moment and then said, "Your elbow. I noticed this several times when you were conducting your chamber choir. Now I know why you did it—golly!"

"It's the same with one's legs," said the director with a smile. "If someone put a hand on your knee, what would they be telling you?"

"They'd be making a pass at me!" laughed Bob.

"Right! Putting their hand on your foot wouldn't convey the same message."

"Speaking of feet, you said that you knew from looking at my feet that I didn't want to leave tonight's party."

"That will be obvious to you as soon as I say it," said the director. "Mrs. Barlow used to say that feet never lie. The feet are the volitional subsection of the volitional part of the body, so they give a strong message about where one wants to go. Your feet, under normal circumstances, always point to the person or the thing in whom you are interested. And the fascinating thing is that one is not aware that one is giving this message—it's a purely subconscious gesture."

"My feet aren't pointing to you right now," observed Bob, "even though I am interested in what you're telling me."

"Remember that I said 'under normal circumstances.' Sitting side by side in a car does not give you complete freedom of movement, and so I have to look for other indications in your body language to see if you are really interested in what I'm saying. And," continued the director, "you're giving them to me very clearly."

"I know," laughed Bob. "I'm sitting up straight, I'm turning towards you, and I'm also writing down in my notebook what you say."

"Right again! You can tell if choir members are really paying attention to you by the way they sit. If they're sitting up straight and turning towards you, you've got their whole attention. But if they are slumped in their seats, their thoughts are elsewhere.

"Body language not only expresses what we feel, but it also, in some measure, conditions what we feel."

"What do you mean by that?"

"Well, I've just said that if you are really communicating with members of your choir, they will sit up straight for you automatically. But if they are not paying attention, then you need to get their bodies into an attention-giving posture. This will help them to feel more like paying attention."

"Oh!" exclaimed Bob. "That's why we tell children to sit up straight. It's to help them to concentrate better. Wow! this is great!"

"Yes, it is fascinating, isn't it! That hour spent with Mrs. Barlow helped to change my life."

"But you still haven't told me how you knew, from looking at my feet, that I didn't want to leave the party tonight."

"Well, that's obvious isn't it?"

"Not yet!"

"One foot was pointing towards me, and the other one was pointing directly at Frank Stevens. Clearly you were very interested in what we were saying—and it was your feet as well as the way that you were leaning towards us, that told me!"

There was a long silence as Bob digested this information. He then asked, "Where would my feet have been pointing if I'd wanted to leave?"

"Where do you think they'd have been pointing?"

"At the door?"

"Right!"

"Wow!"

"I know it's hard to believe," commented the director as the car approached his home town. "But spend a little time observing people during the next few days and you'll find that what I've told you is correct. Notice whether a person crosses his legs towards you or away from you; whether his torso is towards you or away. Actions speak louder than words, if you know where to look. And, nine times out of ten, a person's body will tell you what he is thinking."

"What about the tenth time?"

"A person may cross his legs away from you, even though he's interested in what you are saying, purely because he needs to change his physical position. You have to weigh up the external factors that may influence the position of a person's body. But, after a little practice, you will get to know far more about people than they know about you!"

They drove on in companionable silence for a while as they neared the director's home. Bob was sitting up straight, looking at the road ahead, and both hands were holding his notebook, which was on his knees. The director cast a sideways glance at him and smiled. "I can tell that we are in total accord," he remarked.

"How?" asked Bob, with a sideways glance in his direction.

"Because our bodies are in a mirror image. You are sitting up straight, just as I am; you are looking at the road ahead, as I am; and you are holding your notebook in a similar manner to my hands on the steering wheel. You'll find that to be true, time and time again. When two people agree, the position of their bodies will match."

"Wow!" said Bob, putting his notebook away as the director moved one hand towards his garage door opener.

"You're doing it again!" said the director with a laugh. "I changed my position, and you changed yours."

Bob laughed a little uncomfortably, for he was beginning to realize that the director could perceive his innermost thoughts. He folded his arms across his chest.

"Sorry about that, Bob" commented the director as his car made a left into his short driveway. "I know I've made you feel a little uncomfortable by what I've just said."

"How do you know that?" asked Bob, hiding his hands under his armpits.

"You'll discover one day if you keep your eyes open. I promise not to do it to you again." He got out of the car and closed his door quietly. Bob also got out of the door and closed his door equally quietly. The director chuckled to himself, but didn't say anything as they went into the house together. He knew that they were on the same wavelength.

♪ FRIDAY ♪

61
Personal Relationships

At 7:30 the next morning the director knocked gently on Bob's bedroom door. "Would you like a cup of tea to wake you up, Bob?" he asked as he looked at a lump hidden beneath the bedclothes. An answering grunt assured him that this would indeed be acceptable. "Well, here it is," said the director, placing a steaming mug on the bedside table. "We're leaving here at 8:45, which means you've got just over an hour to get up, pack, and eat your breakfast," and he left, closing the door, not too silently, behind him.

An hour later, after stripping his bed, folding his blankets, putting the sheets in the bathroom with his towels, and cleaning the wash basin, Bob appeared in the kitchen, looking remarkably fresh. He carried his suitcase in one hand and his briefcase in the other.

"How about an egg to start your day?" asked the director.

"Great! Four minutes, please."

"It's been in for three already—help yourself to toast. I'll join you for a cup of coffee." Bob was glad that he'd missed seeing the director eat his bowl of cereal, yogurt, and juice. There's a limit to what I can stand first thing in the morning, he thought, taking his egg out of the boiling water as two slices of toast sprang up from the toaster.

"What time is your plane?" asked the director as he poured freshly brewed coffee into two mugs on the kitchen counter.

"Twelve noon," came the answer.

"Well, we'd better plan getting to the airport an hour before. We can manage that easily enough, for I'm seeing the minister at 9:00 A.M., and then we'll be free to go."

"Before we leave," said Bob, reaching into his briefcase, "I'd like to give you this bottle of wine as a small thank you for everything you've done for me this week."

"Well, that's very kind of you," said the director, strangely moved. "It's been really terrific to have you here. I've enjoyed every minute of your visit and only wish you could stay longer." And he gave his guest a big hug.

MUSIC DIRECTOR'S ADVISORY COMMITTEE

Ten minutes later they were bowling along in the director's car towards the church.

"Do you find your minister supportive?" asked Bob as he looked once more at the passing scenery of trees and fields.

"You know I do! I've been very fortunate with my clergy for most of my life. The previous minister here—the one who appointed me—showed his support, when I first came, by creating a special committee of leading parishioners whose task it was to advise and help me during my first couple of years here."

"That could have been very threatening for you," observed Bob.

"Yes, it could," agreed the director. "I'd not been used to the American way of doing things, and I did feel threatened until the committee first met with me."

"What did they say?"

"They asked me what they could do to help me. I told them that there were a number of things I wanted to do."

A WELL-DRESSED CHOIR TENDS TO BE A GOOD CHOIR

"Such as what?"

"Such as insisting that the boys and girls wear good clothes and dark shoes for Sunday services. Being new to the job meant that I had to have strong backing for any changes I wanted to make, and this was the first one."

"Did they back you?"

"All the way! Children and adults should make a special effort when coming to church, so that their standard of dress matches their standard of singing. You can't be a good team member unless there is an element of discipline, and clothes are an outward and visible sign of that."

"What else did you want to do?"

"They were supportive when I wanted to increase the number of practices for our children; they were supportive when I asked for an increased budget; and they were supportive when I wanted the practice room remodeled. They were a wonderful group of people, and they are still among my strongest supporters here as well as being my greatest friends."

STARTING A MUSIC DIRECTOR'S ADVISORY COMMITTEE

"Do you think I should have such an advisory group in my new church?"

"You know the answer to that yourself, my dear Bob! I suggest that you talk it over with your minister and tell him that you want to do your very best in his church, but, in order to do that, you need the active and sympathetic support of a few of the leading members of the congregation.

"I had three wardens, a senior choirman, and a couple of choir parents, one of whom was the associate minister whose son was in the choir. All of them had the minister's confidence and they quickly gained mine. We met every three months for a year or two, to discuss how things were going and how they could help me to improve what I was doing. Their advice, as well as their support, made all the difference to what I was able to achieve. I commend the idea to you wholeheartedly."

CLERGY-CHOIRMASTER RELATIONSHIPS

"How do you maintain good relationships with your present minister?" asked Bob as they approached the outskirts of the town.

"In addition to our weekly staff meetings, I meet with him, one-on-one, regularly, and keep him fully informed about any problems that arise. My problems are his problems. If I am experiencing a difficulty with a choir member it is up to him to help us resolve our differences, for both of us are members of his church. We are his pastoral responsibility.

GOALS

"When our present minister first came," continued the director, "he asked me to put in writing what my goals were. After a little thought I came up with three."

"What were they?"

"One. To enhance the worship of the church through music. This includes not only music for congregation and choir, but also the promotion of concerts.

"Two. To seek the highest standards of singing in all choirs, especially through the education of singers with regard to improving their ability to read music.

"Three. To work closely with the minister at all times, both professionally and personally.

"He took one look at my goals and wrote the word *approved* at the bottom, and signed it. Neither of us has seen the need to change a word of what we agreed upon in those early days of our ministry together.

MAINTAINING GOOD PERSONAL RELATIONSHIPS

"On the other hand," continued the director as the church came into view, "I've also found that it is not helpful to communicate controversial matters in writing."

"Why is that?"

"Because the written word is so much stronger than the spoken word. If the minister were to send me a note saying that he wanted next Sunday's anthem changed, that would give me no opportunity to ask him why, or enable me to put my own point of view to him. It's much better to discuss it face-to-face and each be prepared to hear what the other is saying.

"It's also very important that I don't say anything behind his back that I wouldn't say to his face. He shows the same courtesy to me and to all his staff. He's a marvelously pastoral man, as you will have noticed, and we respect each other. I am very fortunate indeed and wish that all my colleagues were similarly blessed."

The director drove to his accustomed place in the church parking lot as the clock struck the hour. "Right on time," he said. "Why don't you play the organ once more while I'm meeting with the minister. I'll come get you when we've finished." And so saying they went their separate ways.

62
ORGAN ACCOMPANIMENTS—
HYMNS

When Bob entered the church he found Nancy Willis already there, practicing for the Sunday services.

"Hello, Bob," she said, with a smile, "have you come to play the organ?"

"I had, but I won't interrupt you because you're obviously hard at work."

"Yes, there's a lot of music to prepare for the next few weeks and I have to get on top of it all," she said, indicating a small pile of anthems on the organ bench.

HYMN PLAYING

"I wonder if you could spare five minutes to tell me how you approach accompaniments. We weren't given much help with that when I was a student."

"You're not alone in that," said Nancy with a grimace. "Many music schools think that organists will spend their lives playing Bach and Messiaen, whereas the truth is that we spend much of our time playing hymns and anthems."

"What can you tell me about playing hymns," said Bob.

"Well, the first two things I can tell you is not to do what almost every organist does."

"What are those two things?"

PLAYOVERS

"Don't waste the time of the congregation by playing over an entire verse of a hymn before they start to sing. There's no reason to do that, unless the tune is unfamiliar. A playover of half a verse gives them sufficient time to find their place in the hymnal as well as to remind them of how the tune goes."

"How fast should I play the introduction?"

"You should play it at the speed you expect it to be sung; no slower and certainly no faster."

"What stops should I use?"

"You should play with stops appropriate to the meaning of the words. Look," she said, thumbing through the hymnal, "Would you play over 'Praise, My Soul, the King of Heaven' on flutes? No, of course you wouldn't. Similarly you wouldn't play 'Once in Royal David's City' on Swell reeds."

"Oh!" exclaimed Bob, "that's very similar to the point you and the director were making last night about getting the choir to sing their words in color. The organ must be played in the appropriate color, too!"

"Well done!" laughed Nancy. "You'll have a lot of fun finding exactly the right stops for your introductions. What you do will set the mood for the whole hymn. The hymns are the folk-theology of the people, and so they are a vital part of a congregation's worship.

"You could also try soloing out one phrase in the treble register, and the next phrase on a different stop in the tenor register. The introduction should be a musical experience for the congregation, not a waste of time." Nancy paused for a moment and then asked, "Can you improvise?"

"Yes, a little."

"One's ability to improvise improves with practice. You might like to try practicing improvised introductions to some hymns. Choose only those hymns which are well-known and create an eight- or sixteen-measure introduction that will inspire the congregation to start singing. One hint, though."

"What's that?"

"Don't finish your improvisation in the tonic, but in the dominant key. This will lead naturally to the first tonic chord of the hymn."

"Great! What is the second thing I shouldn't do that many organists do?"

COLOR EACH STANZA DIFFERENTLY

"You shouldn't lead the whole hymn on an unrelentingly loud organ sound. Many organists play entire hymns with Swell reeds coupled to Great-to-mixtures. They have no idea how painful it is to try to battle against that sort of sound, especially when the organ is a large one."

"But I thought that the organ had to lead the congregation, and that can only be done with a strong sound," said Bob, very surprised.

"Yes, the organ should lead the congregation, but it should not drown it. There are many ways of leading other than by force. The most gracious way is to lead by kindness."

"What do you mean by that?"

"I mean that you can lead by color and not volume; you can lead by strong rhythmic playing and not by unrelenting decibels.

"If your church is a large church, then you may well have to begin the first verse with a fairly full sound, just to get the congregation going. But once they have started, you should quickly, but subtly, quieten the organ until you are sustaining them, rather than dragging them forcibly."

"When should I do that?"

"You could begin halfway through the first line of words. Take off the Great mixtures, and gradually close the swell box. If your choir is giving a strong vocal lead, there's no need for you to carry the entire responsibility for the congregational singing yourself.

"Similarly," continued Nancy, "if you are playing for a small congregation, you should scale down your volume considerably. The director and I find it very helpful to listen to the effect of what we are doing. One of us goes to the other end of the church during services when the other is playing and really listens to what is going on. You'd be surprised how different the organ sounds away from the console."

"That's a great idea," responded Bob, enthusiastically.

"There's one more thing. Don't play the entire hymn on one set of stops."

"You've said that already," said Bob.

"No, I haven't," said Nancy kindly. "What I mean is that you should change the color of your registration for each verse of the hymn. As every verse gives a different message, so that message should be reflected by the colors you choose. The difference should be so subtle that the congregation isn't really aware of it. Don't alter the volume significantly for that really will unsettle your congregation. They should feel only that the organ is helping them to express in a lively and meaningful way the message of the text they are singing.

"This means," concluded Nancy, "that you should know the hymn tune so well that you can follow the words of every verse and not look exclusively at the music. You can help the congregation to breathe at punctuation marks and to carry over ends of lines where there is no punctuation."

"Thanks," said Bob, "those ideas will really help me out."

63
ORGAN ACCOMPANIMENTS—
ANTHEMS

THINK ORCHESTRALLY

Bob looked at the pile of anthems on the organ bench. "Could you give me some basic principles for accompanying anthems, please. No one has ever shown me how to accompany well."

"Certainly, Bob," replied Nancy, choosing one of the anthems from the pile beside her. "The director and I work closely together on exactly what he wants from me when he's conducting.

"Basically, the organ should provide changes of color and not too violent changes of volume, unless the composer requires it."

"What does that mean in practice?"

"It means that you do a lot of accompanying on the Swell, where you can change color easily and alter the volume subtly by use of the swell box."

"But you also play on the Great, too, don't you?"

"Yes. The basic stop when playing on the Great should be an 8' flute. This gives a little more body to the sound without overpowering the choir. If you want a brighter sound, add a 4' Principal and then a 2'. This, when coupled to Swell reeds, is generally loud enough for most choir accompaniments."

Nancy paused for a moment, and then added, "You know that English composers up to the 1950s were not keen on high mixtures."

"No, I didn't know that."

"The organs that Stanford, Elgar, Vaughan Williams, and Howells had in mind when writing their beautiful music were all based on full 8' tone, with lots of subtle use of the swell box. The so-called baroque revival didn't reach England until after 1951 when the organ in the Royal Festival Hall in London was built. That opened up a whole new way of thinking for the younger generation of composers. And so, when you are accompanying music of the pre-1950 romantic school, be careful not to make the sounds too bright."

"Don't you ever use the full Great?"

"Only very rarely. The most effective time to use a full Great organ sound in a loud anthem is when the choir isn't singing."

"How do you mean?"

"In many anthems the choir is given a number of measures rest. It's in these places that the organ can play a little louder to help carry the volume of sound along. If you are accompanying the choir on the Swell organ, for example, and the choir is given a few measures rest, then you should consider playing the organ music in these measures on the Great, otherwise the musical flow will tend to sag."

"What about soloing out various parts of an accompaniment?"

"That's a very good question. Playing a few measures on a solo stop, be it a clarinet or some mutation combination, adds much color and interest to your accompaniment. The accompaniment should always be interesting, expressive, colorful and constantly changing, unless you are playing music from the classical period or before.

"Bach's music, for example, should generally be played on one set of stops—using a bright combination for happy fast music, and 8' or 8' and 4' stops for slower, more reflective music.

"There are some particularly interesting things I've learned from the director about accompanying," continued Nancy.

"What are they?" asked Bob, turning yet another page in his notebook.

"Frequently accompaniments have interesting musical lines in the left hand. Now if both hands are playing on one manual, the left-hand part tends, generally, not to be heard so clearly as the notes in the right hand. The director showed me how effective it is, when the right hand is on the Swell, to play such left-hand parts on a soft Great, coupled through to the Swell. This is particularly true of romantic music such as music of the Stanford-Howells genre.

"The director told me that the accompaniments of this romantic music were conceived in a quasi-orchestral style. And as one of his professors was a pupil of Stanford I listened to what he says!"

"How do you mean?"

"If you listen to any orchestral music of the 19th century, you'll hear the composer changing the sound very frequently. He brings in a flute for a few measures, and then the clarinet, and then the oboe. Sometimes he has just the strings playing, and, at other times, only the woodwinds. Orchestral music of that period is continually changing color and texture.

"One should approach organ accompaniments in the same vein. One should aim at changing stops, subtly, every four or eight measures, either by adding a 4' flute to a soft Swell sound, or an oboe stop to give a little more edge to the sound. This matter of changing stops is especially true when a composer indicates a change of dynamic. Going from *piano* to *mezzo forte* doesn't mean just opening the swell box, it means adding a stop or two, or going on to the Great from the Swell."

"This is fascinating," said Bob, enthusiastically. "You are opening up a whole new world for me."

"Thank you," said Nancy with a smile. "And there's one more thing," she added.

"What's that?"

"Don't overuse celestes when you are accompanying. The celestes are effective in inverse proportion to the amount you use them. It's exactly the same with your 32' stops. Some organists use them far too much. In other words, if you use your celestes infrequently, say, for the final few measures of a soft anthem, their effect is very beautiful. If you have them out for the whole of a devotional song, as some organists do, then their effect quickly becomes cloying. It's like eating a whole box of candy. The first bite is delicious, but the last bite makes you want to throw up!"

"Who wants to throw up?" asked a cheery voice from the bottom of the organ loft stairs.

"No one does," laughed Bob, as the director's head appeared at the top of the spiral staircase. "Nancy's been very kind by giving me some helpful hints about accompanying during the last five minutes."

"During the last half hour," corrected the director with a smile.

"Good gracious!" exclaimed Bob, "The time just flew by as Nancy was talking with me. I had no idea it was so late." He turned to his mentor and said, "Thank you so much for giving me such wonderful insights into the art of accompanying. I've really learned a lot from you this morning."

"It's my pleasure, Bob," said Nancy getting off the organ bench. "We all learn from each other in this business, and you'll be able to pass on to your students what you've received this week." She gave him a big hug and said, "Have a safe journey home and let us know how you get on."

When Bob and the director reached the bottom of the organ loft stairs Nancy called down to them. "Have a piece of candy from the 'swell-box'!" And, so saying, she threw a couple of lemon drops, which they just managed to catch.

"Thanks, Nancy!" said Bob with a grin. "As soon as I get home I'll get my own 'swell-box' and fill it with candies and other good things."

"But only eat one at a time, or you'll throw up!"

"Yes, I will be sparing in my use of the celestes," answered Bob, enigmatically.

What was all that about? wondered the director, as they left the church. What have celestes got to do with candy?

64
PASTORAL CONCERNS—STAFF

CHOIR IS PART OF A CHURCH'S OUTREACH PROGRAM

"How did your meeting go with the minister?" asked Bob they got into the director's car.

"Very well indeed. He told me that we've just received a bequest for the outreach ministry of the church and, as he feels that our choir program is part of outreach ministry, some of that money will be coming to us."

"Golly!" said Bob, as the car made its way along Church Street, "It has never occurred to me that a music program could come under the heading of outreach."

"How do you think we attract so many girls and boys, their parents, and adult singers and their families to this church. A lively music ministry is certainly a most effective form of outreach.

"Don't you remember that I told you, earlier this week, that the reason our associate minister became ordained was because he sang in a church choir when he was a boy? Two of our choir parents became ordained during my time here, and two more are currently seeking ordination. Fully one third of all clergy sang in church choirs when they were children. And that's only the tip of the iceberg."

He reached in his pocket as they waited at the lights into Main Street. "Here's a letter I received only this morning from a choir parent. Read it."

Bob took the letter from the director's hand as the lights changed to green.

> Words are inadequate to describe our gratitude for all that you are doing for our sons: the music education, the discipline, the deepening of their faith and sense of joy. Your music has filled our home and our hearts. Thank you!

"That's terrific," said Bob, handing back the letter to the director. "I'm sure you'll keep that letter for a long time."

"I most certainly will, Bob. And, if you do your job well and also care for those committed to your charge as well as caring about the music they sing, you, too, will receive letters like this. It makes it all so wonderfully worthwhile."

WORK AT FOSTERING GOOD RELATIONSHIPS

"I hope that I shall enjoy such good relationships with the members of my new church as you do with yours," remarked Bob as the car made its way along Main Street.

"Good relationships don't just happen," answered the director, "They're like all worthwhile things. You have to work at them to enable them to flourish."

"How do you work at good relations with your clergy?" asked Bob, "apart, of course, from meeting with them regularly."

"It's important to recognize that we are all different," said the director as they began to leave the town behind them. "It's also important to realize that we are, in many respects, the same."

"How do you mean?" asked Bob, bringing out his well-worn notebook.

STAFF AWAY TIMES

"The church staff recently enjoyed a twenty-four-hour retreat. We go every year and it works wonders for our sense of community; we not only work together, planning the course for next season, but we also play silly games that bring all sorts of barriers crashing down. I commend this idea to you.

MYERS-BRIGGS

"However," continued the director, "during this particular time we took the Myers-Briggs psychological tests, and the results were amazing. I confess that I was a little skeptical about them at first, but, as the day continued, and the consultants whom we had hired helped us through the process, I got more and more excited."

"Why?"

"Because we found out who we all were, deep down. I discovered who I was and found that I could be accepted exactly as I am, and not as I ought to be. My weaknesses were as much a part of my personality as my strengths. The same went for everyone else, and this bound us together in mutual understanding in a wholly constructive way.

"For example," he continued, as they drove past a delightful lake, "only a few of us were extroverts. I was amazed! Some of us were highly organized people while others preferred leaving things to the last minute. I suddenly realized that everyone didn't have to be like me in order to be a valuable member of the church staff!" and he laughed.

"And so you found that you could accept each other in a new way," observed Bob.

"Yes, indeed. We also learned some valuable lessons about ourselves."

"Such as what?"

"Such as, extroverts don't really trust introverts, because we don't know what they're thinking. It was important for all of us to learn that truth, for we felt better about our attitude to each other once it had been brought out into the open.

"On the other hand, we extroverts were told that we don't always realize what our enthusiasm is doing to others. We sometimes need to look into our driving mirror to see whom we've just run over!"

WELCOME DIFFERENCES

"That must make you more careful in your relationships with others," said Bob as the director made a right on to a pretty country road.

"That was one of the main values of our time together. We recognized that we all had weaknesses. Some of these were clearly defined for us and, recognizing them, we could start doing something to rectify them."

"And so you now know where you stand in regard to your colleagues, and they know the same about you. That must be very helpful."

"It is. To know that my minister is, in many respects, different from me, enables us both to value those differences and to complement each other's weaknesses with our strengths. Of course, this has to be done tactfully by both of us. But if we are aware that we each value and respect the other, it goes a very long way to help us pull in the same direction.

"But you should be very careful if you find that your minister is similar to you in many respects, for that would tend to make one of you redundant. A constructive relationship generally flourishes between people who can fill a lack in their partner's life. Welcome the differences that become apparent as you and your minister get to know one another."

SIMILARITIES IN CLERGY/MUSICIAN VOCATIONS

They approached a set of lights, which was against them, and waited until they changed before the director made a left onto a main highway.

"One of the major similarities between the musician and his minister comes about through the nature of our vocations."

"How do you mean?"

"Both of us preside over mysteries. The minister celebrates the Eucharist, which can only be discerned spiritually. Similarly, the musician presides over music, which cannot be seen, but can be experienced emotionally.

"Both of us tend to respond subjectively to situations. We feel things more tenderly than others because of the nature of our calling, and so we can easily get hurt by harsh words or deeds.

"And both of us need praise. If no one at our weekly staff meeting mentions how well the music went last Sunday, I feel that my work is not really appreciated. But," added the director, as he overtook a truck only doing fifty, "I then ask myself why I hadn't said a word of appreciation to the minister for his fine sermon!"

He got into the slow lane hastily as another truck bore down upon them doing sixty-five. "Nothing is so healing to personal relationships as words of genuine praise and appreciation."

"Yes," said Bob, glad that the director wasn't in too much of a hurry that morning, for the traffic was pretty busy on the highway, "I remember you telling me that you begin each staff meeting with five minutes of appreciative words of each other."

"Yes, and we're finding that we're tending to say appreciative things to each other more frequently outside meetings as well. And this all came about because of the retreat," said the director, contentedly as he followed a car which was doing a steady fifty-seven.

65
Pastoral Concerns—Clergy

HANDLING CONFLICT

"But you do need to realize that conflict will arise between you and your minister, and you should know how to handle it."

"Tell me."

"Conflict can be a thoroughly creative process, if it is handled sensitively by the two parties involved. One might say that almost nothing worthwhile was ever created unless it came out of conflict. And so, when a difference of outlook does arise between you and your minister, you should ask him if he could spare a few minutes to see you in his office."

"Why in his office instead of yours?"

"Because he will be in his own territory, and will, therefore, be more inclined to give you a sympathetic hearing than if he had to enter yours."

"Wow! I hadn't thought of that."

"Let me ask you a question. Should you say, when you meet him, that he has a problem?"

"Oh, no! That would put him on the defensive immediately!"

"Right! How about, 'We have a problem'?"

"That's not much better, is it, for it still implies that it's his fault."

"Well done! What should you say to him?"

"I have a problem and need your help, please!"

"Absolutely right. Tell him what the problem is without, in any way, implicating him, and also tell him how you feel about it. And then let him talk to you and listen for any particularly helpful things he may suggest. Repeat these back to him in your own words, so that he knows that you've heard what he's been saying. That will go a long way to healing any breach that may have occurred between you."

DISCUSS YOUR PROBLEM OVER A MEAL

Bob wrote busily in his notebook as the car sped on its way towards the turnpike. The director added, "It's particularly helpful if you could ask him out to lunch, should you have a really difficult problem on your mind."

"Should I ask him to my home for the meal?"

"Certainly not! It should be on neutral territory, such as a local restaurant, where you can talk uninterrupted."

"Should I mention the problem before the meal?"

"Again, no! Enjoy your meal together. Take pleasure in talking about a whole range of subjects so that you get to know one another better. This will ease your communication when the problem is brought up over dessert and coffee. Raise the subject gently so as to maintain the courteous relationship that you enjoyed during the beginning of the meal. Preface your remarks with a word of genuine appreciation for something he has done to help you in the past. This will make it easier for both of you to enable him to help you again. And make sure you end the meal on a note of unity. Talk about some other issues of mutual interest. This will help both of you in your efforts to seek a long-term solution to your problem."

The director waited for a minute as Bob filled yet another page in his notebook, and then asked, "What will you do immediately when you return to your office after lunch?"

Bob thought for a moment, and then said, "I'll write the minister a note, thanking him for the pleasure of his company and also for the help he gave me with my problem."

"Well done," said the director with a smile. The sign for the turnpike entrance came into view, and the director began to slow down. "There's one more thing you can do to help heal breaches in personal relationships."

"What's that?"

"You can pray for the person with whom you have a problem. At the very least, that will help to transform your feelings towards them, for you cannot pray for someone unless you have at least a spark of love towards them. And at most, you might find that God steps in and transforms the whole situation for both of you. That's happened to me several times. I commend it to you."

"Wow!" said Bob as the director took a ticket from the toll booth and drove onto the turnpike.

MAINTAINING GOOD RELATIONSHIPS
WITH YOUR COLLEAGUES

"There are two more things I can share about maintaining staff relationships," said the director as he picked up speed.

"What are they?"

"You need to get to know all the other members of the church staff well. Show them as much courtesy as you do to your minister. For example," he continued, "when you went away for vacations during your student days, did you send a card to your colleagues at church?"

"Oh yes! I always did that. I addressed it to 'All my colleagues at St. Mary's Church.'"

"Well, if I may say so, that isn't very helpful."

"Oh!" said Bob, feeling crushed, "I thought they would appreciate it."

"I'm sure they did. But how much better it would have been if you had sent a card to every member of the staff individually!"

"Oh!" said Bob again. "I hadn't thought of that."

"Few people do." They drove on for a few moments in silence, and then the director said, "I make a practice of working out, before I go on vacation, exactly to whom I want to send cards. That way I'm sure not to miss anyone. I used to print address labels for everyone, but now I print their names and addresses on envelopes, so that I can write a really full message of greeting on each card."

"Sending cards is always a risky business, for they don't always get delivered on time," said Bob, glad to be contributing to the discussion creatively.

"That's another reason I send cards in envelopes. If possible, I discover the home addresses of my colleagues. They're really glad to receive a card from me, especially if I take the trouble to write something is of interest to them, and not just 'Having a wonderful time, wish you were here'!

LEANING!

"There's one more thing I should mention about being an active member of a collegial staff."

"What is it?"

"It's something I learned from the minister who appointed me here. He told me that, if I wanted anything really strongly, I should lean on it."

"What did he mean by that?"

"I had no idea, until I saw him putting this technique into practice on me!"

"What did he do?"

"Well, at a staff meeting early in the season he said, 'I would like the congregation to sing the "Benedictus" to Anglican chant during Advent.' I said, 'I really don't think the congregation would be happy about that. Anglican chant is very difficult to sing well.' He shrugged his shoulders and changed the subject.

"The following month he said, 'I think it would be a good idea if the congregation sang the "Benedictus" to Anglican chant during Advent.' I was surprised at this, for I thought that we'd agreed it wouldn't work. I said, 'It would be a rather untidy thing to do, and I don't think everyone would sing too enthusiastically.' He shrugged his shoulders again and went on to other business."

"What happened next?" asked Bob, who was clearly intrigued by this story.

"Well, two weeks later, the minister said during our staff meeting, 'I would like the congregation to sing the "Benedictus" to Anglican chant during Advent.'"

"What did you say?"

"I said, 'okay'! I knew when I was licked and I was grateful to him for showing me how to go about getting something that I really wanted. That's how I got 32' electronic pedal stops on my fine tracker organ. It took me three years of very gentle leaning, mentioning it, casually, several times over a period of two years and then gradually increasing the tempo."

"Wow! That's great," exclaimed Bob. "Thank you for sharing that with me."

66
PASTORAL CONCERNS—PARENTS

CONFLICTS WITH CHOIR PARENTS
They passed a sign that said Airport 10 Miles. "We'll soon be there," said the director, "and we're in very good time."

"Tell me about how you deal with conflicts with choir parents," said Bob. "I imagine that you must have some problems in this area from time to time."

"Yes," answered the director. "Whenever you succeed in doing anything, you are certain to have some people who object to what you are achieving. It's almost a badge of honor to have a few people who disagree with you, for it shows that you are making progress. But that wasn't your question. You were asking about problems that arise with folk who have been among your strongest supporters."

"Right!"

"Well, I've learned a lot about that side of things here, and I'm particularly grateful to one parent who showed me just how best to handle this problem."

DON'T ACT HASTILY
"What happened?"

"Well, this choir father came to see me after one service and we had a strong disagreement as to how I was treating his son. I knew I was handling the situation badly, but I just didn't know how I could do better.

"However I did do something right during those uncomfortable five minutes."

"What was that?"

"I said, 'Let's meet tomorrow when we've both had a chance to calm down.'

"He called me first thing the next morning to ask if he could come to see me. I said yes, and immediately called the superintendent of our church school to ask her to pray for me. Her prayers were heard!

"Half an hour later, this man walked into my office, looking very stern, and sat down in a chair. I dreaded what he was about to say."

HOW TO ENSURE THAT YOU ARE HEARD
"What did he say?"

"Well, he spent fully five minutes telling me how much he and his wife appreciated all that I had done for their son during his time in the choir.

How much the other parents valued my ministry and how much they all enjoyed the music we sang at our services. I was amazed."

"He certainly got your attention," observed Bob.

"That was the whole point of the exercise. He needed to know that I was hearing what he was saying. If he'd started by telling me what I was doing wrong, I wouldn't have heard him, for I'd be on the defensive. However, he was a wise man and knew best how to get his point of view across."

"So what did he do next?"

"Well, after telling me for five minutes what I'd been doing right he then told me what I was doing wrong. And I heard what he said!"

"What did you do?"

"I sat quietly and listened, without interruption, to everything he wanted to get off his chest. That's another major point to remember whenever you're in a conflict situation."

"What is?"

"Always let the other person speak first, and don't interrupt. They're much more likely to listen to you after they've run down, so to speak, than if you try to challenge them. That would put them on the defensive, and that would not be helpful.

"Anyway, to get back to the story: after he'd said everything that he needed, it was my turn. What did I do?" asked the director unexpectedly.

"You took the lead he'd given to you. You told him how much his support had meant to you during his son's time in the choir; how talented his son was, and how you valued the friendship of his whole family."

"Right! I needed to get him to hear what I wanted to say, and I had learned, very quickly, the way to achieve that. Once I'd got his attention, by showing my genuine appreciation of what his family had given us, it was my turn to say, 'May I give you my side of the story?'"

"And he listened."

"He did, and he recognized that my perception of the situation had something to commend it, as well as his side of the story. We were able to explore common ground and, after half an hour, we shook hands as adults who respected each other.

"I cannot tell you how much I learned from that experience," he added. "It has helped me more than I can say."

DON'T WRITE A LETTER!

They drove on for a little while in silence as Bob digested what he had just learned. Then the director said, "There are bound to be times when you will have a disagreement with your choir parents. How do you think you should handle it?"

"You've encouraged me to write letters as often as possible—especially to say 'thank you,'" answered Bob. "I suppose the best thing would be to write a letter—giving it a lot of thought, to show exactly why I am right and they are wrong."

"Alas, my dear Bob, you are gravely mistaken on both counts," said the director, glad that he'd raised the subject. "You should never argue or even put your considered point of view in writing, when there is disagreement."

"Why?"

"Because at best your letter will be thrown away only half read, and at worst you could find it published on the front page of the local newspaper! In either case, you will only make that parent more angry with you. That is not the object of this exercise. Similarly, you should never argue over the telephone."

"Why?" asked Bob, again.

"Because each person is on his or her home ground, be it office or home; and it is easier to say hurtful things into a machine than it is to a person's face. One of you is almost certain to end the conversation by banging down the receiver, and so the situation becomes worse rather than better.

"And the second reason why you are mistaken," continued the director, "is that you need to think through what your objective is with your encounter with this parent. It's not to prove yourself right, but..."

"Oh, I know!" exclaimed Bob, "it's to sow peace and healing."

"Very well put indeed! Yes, your object is to make that parent feel better and, if possible, bring about an agreement. You remember what I said when we were talking about conflict with your minister? It's the same with parents. Never put contentious matter in writing—it's far too strong. What should you do?"

Bob thought for a moment and said, "I should write a brief letter in which I show gratitude for past support and friendship and then ask if we can meet, face-to-face, to discuss the matter."

"Excellent! You've now got the right idea. Always try, however hard it may seem, to be constructive and to believe that good will come out of your meeting. There are two more things you should do. What are they?"

Bob thought again and then, taking a deep breath, said, "I should tell my minister what is going on, before the meeting takes place, and I should pray for that parent."

"Well done, indeed!" and they drove on again in companionable silence as the director made a right onto the airport exit.

PASTORAL COUNSELING

After paying the toll the director said, "You know that your job will entail more than just musical duties, don't you?"

"Oh yes! You've already told me that I shall be an unofficial sexton as well as a stuffer of envelopes," Bob said with a laugh.

"No, I mean more than that," said the director seriously. "You will also have an increasingly strong pastoral responsibility for your singers and their families."

"But I don't know anything about pastoral counseling," protested Bob.

"You only need to know enough, at this stage in your career, to get by. All serious counseling should be passed on to your clergy, for they are trained in that art."

"What should I do when someone comes to me with a pastoral problem?"

"Well, the first thing you should be prepared for, as a young, single male, is that some unattached females in your congregation will make a beeline for you. But know that churches tend to attract some people with big problems—that's one reason the church is there. If an unattached female asks to see you confidentially, make sure to tell your minister first, for he might know something about her and step in to take her off your hands. If this person does come into your office, make sure you leave the door open and ask the church secretary to call you every fifteen minutes so that you can have a pretext for bringing the interview to a close quickly."

"Golly!" said Bob, as the entrance to the airport parking lot came into view, "They didn't tell us anything about that in school."

The director took a ticket from the machine and quickly found a parking space. "Let's get your luggage checked in and then we can have a cup of coffee," he said.

"But not everybody who comes to see me with a problem will be unbalanced," remarked Bob as they walked towards the departure building.

"Quite right. Most of them will be well-adjusted folk who need to get something off their chest."

"How should I deal with them, then?"

"All you need to do is to show that you are listening to what they are saying."

"Shouldn't I try to help them solve their problems?" asked Bob as they entered the building and walked towards the checkin counter.

"Not unless the problem directly affects you, such as rearranging a practice to accommodate a child's schedule. No, all you need to do is to make sure that your visitor knows that he or she is being heard sympathetically."

They found a line of people waiting to check in their luggage. "How do I go about doing that?" asked Bob as he put his suitcase on the ground.

"You need to use your knowledge of body language and turn your whole self to look at your visitor as she is talking. You need to nod your head when she makes a point, and have a sympathetic, understanding look on your face.

"But you need to do one more thing," added the director.

"What's that?" asked Bob as they inched nearer the front of the line.

"You need, every so often, to repeat back to her what she has just said to you. But you need to say it in different words. That way she'll really know that she is being heard."

"How do you mean?"

"If she says, 'No one understands me these days,' you could reply, 'You're feeling lonely, aren't you?'"

"Oh, I see!" exclaimed Bob as they neared the head of the line. "That's so helpful."

"And you could ask her, at the end of your meeting, if she has your permission to mention her problem to the minister. If she says yes, then your task is done."

"Suppose she says no?"

"Be on your guard against setting up another appointment, for you mustn't let yourself become personally involved in other people's problems. Say that you are always ready to talk with her again, but don't fix a time. You must go straight to your minister and tell him what has happened, and ask for his advice. There is a major difference between getting involved with people and getting entangled with their problems. So I say again, be on your guard."

67
CONTRACT

Bob picked up his suitcase thoughtfully and checked it in at the counter. The plane was on time, and they had an hour to fill before he left. "Let's go and have some coffee," said the director. They strolled towards the restaurant where they had enjoyed dinner seven days before.

"While we are on serious subjects," said the director as he helped himself to a sticky bun, "have you got a contract at your new church yet?"

"No, I haven't," answered Bob, following the director's lead and helping himself to a Danish.

"Well, that's something you need to get fixed straight away. It's in your own interest, as well as the church's, to lay out very clearly what they expect of you. That way no misunderstandings will arise should you be asked to undertake extra duties."

"What things should be covered in my contract?" asked Bob as they went through the checkout counter and found themselves a table.

The director sat down and began counting on his fingers: "Salary, pension, health benefits, musical duties, fees for extra services, secretarial help and office expenses, assistant organist/choirmaster, days off, annual vacation times and also time off after Christmas and Easter, arrangements regarding outside engagements such as giving recitals, provision for having private pupils, further education grants, and an annual review of salary."

"Phew!" exclaimed Bob, "That's quite a list." They took a sip of coffee and Bob asked, "What is a further education grant?"

"It's in your church's interest to keep you, professionally, fully up-to-date. Therefore they should be able to offer you some financial help when you attend an AGO, AAM, or some other conference. We've talked about these organizations before. Attending conferences is one of the best ways to get yourself known in the musical world; it's a great way to make new friends, and it also gives you the opportunity to expand your own thinking. I always come back from these conferences really fired up and ready to explore new paths."

PENSION AND LIFE INSURANCE

"You also mentioned pension," remarked Bob. "I don't think I need to worry too much about that at this stage, do I?"

"You most certainly do!" exclaimed the director, so strongly that the coffee cups rattled.

Uh-oh! thought Bob, I've clearly said the wrong thing again.

"You cannot begin putting money into your pension fund too early. Your church should have a pension plan for its employees organized by some central ecclesiastical body. Talk to your minister about that."

Bob made a note of this and underlined it, for it was an important point.

"You also need to find some extra pension plan over and above that which your church offers you," added the director. "I commend to you a plan organized by the AGO. Write to them and ask them about it."

"Thank you, I will."

"You also need to look into the matter of life insurance. Should you get married one day, your family should be provided for if anything happens to you. Again, your minister and his financial staff should be able to help you think about this creatively."

The director leaned forward and tapped Bob's notebook. "One thing you must think about very early is to make the first moves to buy your own apartment or house. To own one's home is one of the major expenses of our lives—and it is one of the most important. Renting property is money down the drain. So start thinking about buying now!"

PASTORAL RESPONSIBILITY AND
TERMINATION OF EMPLOYMENT

He looked at Bob for a moment and then added, "It would be helpful if mention could be made, in your contract, of your pastoral responsibilities to your choir members and their families. I think your minister would be glad if you showed that you were interested in them as people rather than just singers."

The director took a large bite out of his sticky bun, and said, as best he could through a mouthful of raspberry preserve, "There should also be agreed guidelines in your contract regarding termination of employment. Your own sense of security needs to be addressed, for you cannot adequately fulfill your vocation there if you are constantly looking over your shoulder, wondering if you'll still have a job next month."

Bob turned another page in his notebook as the director concluded, "Talk to your local AGO dean about all these matters—you'll find that person very helpful."

"Thanks! I'll call as soon as I get back."

68
CONDUCTING ORCHESTRAS

Bob got up from the table, leaving his half-eaten Danish behind. "Excuse me for a minute," he said, enigmatically. "I've got to make a call."

"Okay," said the director, thinking he knew what Bob meant. He didn't! Bob wanted to mail the thank-you card he'd bought a few days earlier, to make sure it arrived at the director's house the next morning. He wouldn't forget that the director had stressed the importance of saying "thank you" at every opportunity. And I'll write him a long letter when I get back home, he thought, as he made a purchase at a novelty store. I want him to know just how much I appreciate all he's given to me this week. What he's said and done will transform my life. He hurried back to his host, hiding his purchase in a pocket.

"I've got two fresh cups of coffee," said the director with a smile. "We've still got half an hour before you need to leave. Is there anything else I can share with you?"

"Yes, there is," said Bob, taking a drink from his steaming cup. "I've never conducted an orchestra, and I wondered if there is anything I need to know. My predecessor used to hire some instrumentalists to accompany her choir from time to time, and I'd like to do the same."

"My word!" exclaimed the director, "I'm glad you mentioned orchestras, for they are a specialized subject."

"I thought that there wouldn't be much difference between conducting a choir and conducting an orchestra," said Bob, opening his notebook again.

"There's all the difference in the world—and you need to learn some essential skills before you conduct your first rehearsal."

"I'm listening!"

"Let me make a list of things you should know and skills you need to acquire:

1 "You need to practice conducting time with your right hand and bringing in instrumentalists with your left. Your left hand should also indicate changes of expression. Not many choral conductors can use their arms independently because they don't practice this skill. If you practice in front of a mirror you should find it very helpful. It's rather like being able to pat the top of your head with one hand and rub your tummy with the other. It doesn't come easily, but it is a knack you need to develop if you are going to become a worthy orchestral conductor.

2   "Buy a baton from your local music shop and practice wielding it. Some professional conductors don't use batons, but a baton is much easier for orchestral players to see, and so I recommend that you use one. The whole idea of conducting with a baton is to extend, effectively, the length of your arm. Some conductors hold their baton and still conduct from their hand. You need to practice conducting from the tip of the baton, for this is what orchestral players can see best.

3   "Conducting an orchestra calls for the ability to conduct the beat very precisely; your down beat must be clearly down, and your up, unmistakably up. Your left beat should be precisely left, and your right, right! Don't do what some amateur conductors do; they beat with a kind of bounce, so that you can't tell where the beat really is!

4   "Practice, with your left hand, bringing in a flute here and the timpani there, while you are conducting a steady beat with your other hand. And practice, also, looking at the instrumentalist you are bringing in. You need to glance at that particular player, or group of players, one measure before they are due to play. They will be looking at you, and so you just need to catch their eye to say, in effect, 'Stand by, it's your turn next!'

"I cannot stress too much that you need to practice conducting. You wouldn't think of playing a postlude without practicing it, would you?"

"No!"

"Then how much more should you practice how to conduct before you actually come to the performance. A conductor, in effect, is 'playing the orchestra' as much as the organist is playing the organ. Both require meticulous practice.

5   "Mark your full score in the manner I mentioned a few days ago. Choose one color for the woodwind, another for the brass, a third for the timpani, a fourth for the strings and another for the choir. Mark every entry so clearly that you can see it from six feet away."

"Remind me why I should do that," said Bob, busily writing in the last few pages of his notebook.

"Because you must know the score so well that you only have to refer to it when conducting. Practice playing from the full score on the piano. Know about the transposing instruments, so that you can say to the horns, 'Your written F should be sounding a B-flat, not a B-natural.' You should only glance at it every few measures, to remind yourself what is happening next. You must, on no account, read your score, for that will mean that you have no eye contact with your performers."

"Why is eye contact so important?" asked Bob looking the director straight in the face.

"Ask me that question again while you are looking at your book," said the director unexpectedly, "and tell me what you feel."

Bob did as he was asked, and then looked at the director again as he said, "I didn't feel I was making contact with you." He paused for a moment, for the director was looking over his shoulder at some customers who were coming into the restaurant. When the director turned back again, Bob courteously repeated his answer.

"Why did you tell me that twice?" asked the director.

"Because your attention was elsewhere the first time." There was a pause as the director continued looking at Bob. "Oh!" he said, "Now I understand why it's so important to look at the performers I am conducting. Thank you for the practical lesson!"

"That's what I'm here for. But let's get on, because time is flying."

"You were saying that I should mark the entries in colored crayon. Should I mark every entry?"

"No, only the important ones. For instance, a measure when everyone is playing together for the first time, a solo entry, or an entry after half a dozen or so measures rest. This is particularly important for brass and percussion players who usually have many measures rest before playing."

"I thought that orchestral players counted their measures, and so they don't really need to be brought in."

"True. If you are an inadequate conductor, your professional players will usually play well in spite of your ineptness. You don't want that, do you?"

"No, I don't. How can I go about being adept instead of inept?"

"By learning your score so well that you know every note and have the physical dexterity to conduct with independent hands. I've mentioned that before, but it does no harm to repeat it. Nothing is so guaranteed to impress orchestral players, and singers too, as to say, 'Violins, someone played an F-natural in that measure instead of an F-sharp!' You will earn ten marks out of ten with your players, for they will be keeping a record as to how you are doing! If you only say, 'Someone played a wrong note in that measure,' you will earn only five out of ten."

"How can I learn a score that well?"

"That brings me to my next point:

6 "Buy a recording of the work you will conduct. Listen to it over and over again, and practice conducting from the full score as you listen to it. Practice bringing in the instrumentalists where they need your help. Practice raising your head to look at them. Practice time-changes so that the players furthest away from you can tell instantly that you are changing from 4/4 time to 6/8, or whatever.

7 "Your job as a conductor is to enable your players to perform as one instrument. Unlike singers, they should all have sufficient professional skill to play for you 100 percent correctly. All you have to do is to be the facilitator to enable this to happen.

"You may have to ask them to play a passage a little softer, so that your choir can be heard, or this passage more rhythmically, or this passage better together. You may have to ask them, when their playing is untidy, 'Am I giving you a clear enough beat?' If the answer is no, then it is up to you to conduct more precisely. If, on the other hand, the answer is yes, then you need to say, 'Let's rehearse these measures again to ensure that we are really together.' You may have to say, 'Cellos, you were a little late coming in there. Let's go back to measure so-and-so and try it again.' They will respect you if you can define clearly what the problem is and then give them the opportunity to put it right. On no account should you get cross with them, for that is a sure sign of weakness when dealing with professionals. If they are not delivering what you ask of them, what should you do?"

Bob thought for a moment and then said, "I have no idea."

"That's an honest answer! You should consult with your concertmaster (the leader of the first violins). Step off your podium and ask her, quietly, what she would recommend. You will find the advice you are given to be worth following.

8   "How can you ensure that the orchestra starts absolutely with you?" continued the director, taking a sip of lukewarm coffee.

"That's easy," replied Bob, confidently. "You should conduct an empty bar, similar to the one-two-ready-breathe technique one uses for a choir."

"I'm glad you said that, Bob, for it is exactly what you should never do with a professional orchestra!" Bob looked crestfallen at this mild rebuke. "No, don't look like that, Bob," said the director encouragingly. "I said what I said rather strongly in order to save you from making a professional faux pas. Only amateur conductors give an empty bar—because they have no idea how to start."

"Well, how can I bring in the orchestra without conducting an empty measure?"

"You have to stand erect, and know deep down inside yourself exactly how fast the music should be played. You should know it so well that you can actually hear it inside yourself. You raise your conducting arm, look at the instrumentalists who begin the piece, wait for a few seconds and then you will feel the tempo of the beat immediately before they come in. It's similar to the one-two-ready-breathe technique that you use for your choirs, except, for orchestras, you begin with 'long pause—breathe (exactly one beat before the music begins)—start!' This, too, needs a lot of practice. Stand in front of a mirror and see if what you are doing works.

"On the other hand, added the director, "there will be occasions when a soloist will be singing or playing a few measures by himself when you need not conduct. What should you do then?"

"You've just told me—I shouldn't conduct!"

"Well, how are the orchestral players going to know the number of measures the solo part occupies?"

"Oh, I hadn't thought of that!"

"Precisely! You will have to mark the beginning of every measure by a firm downbeat, rather like the ticking of a slow pendulum. This way your players will still be able to count the number of measures going by.

9   "And always remember," added the director, "to look at your players, especially for the first few measures. Don't bury your head in your

score, for that's a sure sign of uncertainty on your part, which, as a conductor, you must never allow."

10   "We've mentioned, when talking about singing technique, that a singer should always be relaxed. Any tension in the body will tend to bad vocal production. It's exactly the same with a conductor. If you feel any stiffness or undue strain in your body, you are not in full control of the situation. You have to epitomize, in your whole person, the message of the music, and any awkwardness in you will inhibit this message. When the players look at you, they should be able to see the mood of the music they are playing, because you are visualizing it all the time."

The director paused for a moment to take a final sip of coffee from his cold cup. "What haven't I mentioned so far with regard to making contact with your performers?"

"Well," said Bob thoughtfully, "you've mentioned giving a clear beat with your right hand and expressive gestures with your left. You've mentioned knowing the score very well indeed, and you've also mentioned, more than once, the importance of looking at your players."

"Yes, it's an extension of the last point, which we've discussed before several times."

"Oh!" said Bob, "You mean the expression in your eyes, don't you."

"Yes, I do. I cannot overstress the importance of making eye contact, not only to give warning to players that they are about to come in, but also to show them the how the music should be played."

"I'll remember that," said Bob firmly, looking the director straight between his eyes.

69
MORE ON CONDUCTING ORCHESTRAS

An announcement came through the loudspeaker system. "The departure of the flight to Seattle has been postponed for thirty minutes. We apologize for this delay."

"I hope that won't make you late for your interview with the bridal couple," said Bob anxiously.

"You've got a good memory, young man! That shows that you will be a reliable director of music. It doesn't do to forget engagements.

"But, thank you," he added, "I'll make it in good time if there are no further delays." He stood up and said, "I need another cup of coffee. Can I get one for you, Bob?"

"Yes please, and another Danish. All this writing has made me hungry!"

The director returned a few minutes later with a tray of food and drink. "It's a good thing that your flight is delayed," he remarked as he put the steaming cups and the laden plates on the table, "for we've not finished talking about orchestral matters yet."

"Haven't we?" asked Bob in amazement. "I thought that you've covered pretty well everything I needed to know to avoid making a fool of myself the first time I face an orchestra."

"No. There's more to come." He took a bite from his own Danish (the diet could wait until tomorrow!) and continued:

11   "You will find, almost certainly, when you bring your orchestra in for the first time that they will all play behind your beat."

"Why is that?"

"I've no idea," responded the director with a laugh. "It's just a habit many orchestral players have, and their conductors let them get away with it. What should you do if they do come in late?"

"I should conduct even more vigorously to get them to play with my beat instead of after it," said Bob confidently.

"My dear young man," said the director with a sigh, "you haven't been listening to what I've been saying. You must never get into a conflict situation with your orchestra. Beating more vigorously, as you put it, immediately says to them, 'You're not doing it my way, therefore I'm going to try harder until you do.' If you think along those lines they'll let you try harder and harder throughout the whole rehearsal, and you'll end up a physical wreck, because there are more of them than there are of you."

"What should I do?" asked Bob nervously.

"You should define the problem and then get them to do what you ask of them."

"How do you mean?"

"You should stop them after a couple of measures and say, 'No, you're not playing with me, you are playing after my beat. I need you to play exactly with my beat because that is how the choir will be singing. Let's try it again.' And you do it once more, and again if necessary, until they are playing exactly with you."

12   The director paused for a second mouthful of Danish, and then said, "Some orchestras will test you, rather like schoolboys test a new teacher. If you show, from the very beginning of the rehearsal, that you know exactly what you want and will not be satisfied until you get it, they will honor your professional competence and play all the better for you. You must show that you are as least as professional as they are and yet show them respect at the same time. If you respect them, they will respect you."

The director took a long drink from his steaming mug of coffee while Bob wrote busily in his notebook. "Do you play any instrument apart from the organ and piano?"

"No, I don't."

13 "Well, you need to know at least the basics of string playing and wind playing. The wind are fairly easy, for their playing can be likened to a choir singing. They need to be able to breathe and to play their phrases expressively in one breath. If you think of them as professional singers, you won't go far wrong.

"On the other hand," continued the director, "you really should get some basic practical instruction in string playing. You need to know what problems string players have to deal with. They don't have to breathe, but they do have to use their bows well. You need to know the difference in effect between an up-bow and a down-bow. You need to know the practical meaning of some string terms, such as *arco, pizzicato,* and so on.

"I strongly suggest that you take a few lessons from a professional violinist as soon as you can. You will find that you'll make a pretty awful sound, but what you will learn will stand you in good stead when you conduct your orchestra. You need to talk their language. You need to learn, practically, how to tune your instrument, and what it means to play on one string as opposed to another. You need to look up all the Italian words on your score, and put a translation alongside. For example, do you know what *sul G* means as opposed to *muta in G?*"

"I've no idea," answered Bob somewhat helplessly.

"Well, I won't tell you! I only brought up that example to encourage you to take note of what I'm suggesting and to do something about it when you begin your new job.

14 "It's always a good idea to hold a separate rehearsal for your orchestra before they play for your choir dress rehearsal. That is," added the director hastily, "unless you are performing a well-known work such as *Messiah.*

15 "When the time comes for the rehearsal to begin, you should turn to your concertmaster and ask him if the orchestra would like to tune up. He will take charge for the next minute or so, and then they will be ready for you. After the rehearsal has been going for forty-five minutes, or so, the orchestra may like to retune their instruments. Ask you concertmaster about this, too.

16 "You know how to call for silence, don't you?" asked the director.

"Yes! I tap the rostrum a couple of times with my baton."

"Well done! Make sure that your choir knows this, so that they stop talking immediately, for the orchestra will certainly respond to your call for silence, especially if you do it with an expectant look on your face. Remember always to radiate confidence!

17 "Is your choir going to be punctual for their rehearsal with the orchestra?" asked the director.

"They'd better be!" responded Bob with a grin.

"Yes, but there'll always be one or two people who are late. The orchestra, on the other hand, will always be there on time, and the timpani players will get there early, for they will need to set up their instruments. You need to give your choir a firm pep talk the week before your dress rehearsal. Tell them to get there fully fifteen minutes before the rehearsal is due to start, because, if they are late, they are costing you a lot of money in players' fees."

"I expect the orchestra won't mind staying on for five minutes or so after the rehearsal is due to end, if we are late in starting," commented Bob.

"Wrong, wrong, very wrong!" said the director firmly. "That leads me to my next point:

18   If you are working with professionals, your orchestral players will be hired by an agency or a contractor who knows about these things. This person will lay out for you, very clearly, exactly how long the players have been engaged for. If you find that you have five minutes' more music to rehearse when their time is up, it is very unlikely indeed that they will give you those few minutes free of charge. They will either get up and walk out at the end of their contracted time, or else their agent will come to you and tell you that the extra five minutes will cost you an extra fee, which will not be small!"

"Wow!" exclaimed Bob. "I had no idea that orchestral players could be like that."

"Not all of them are, but if you hire fully professional adults from your local symphony orchestra, they will play it by the rules, and there will be no leeway allowed. Students from a music school could be more amenable—but don't count on it! You see, now, why it is important to run an efficient, punctual rehearsal?"

"Yes, I jolly well do," answered Bob with a touch of perspiration.

"And there's one more thing about abiding by union rules."

"What's that?"

19   "Orchestral players will demand a break after an hour's rehearsal. You must observe this meticulously. Your agent will tell you exactly what is required, so be sure to follow the agent's instructions."

"I surely will," replied Bob, feeling not a little intimidated.

"I'm laying all this on you rather strongly," said the director kindly, "because conducting an orchestra is a serious business. If you are really well-prepared, then it will give you one of the most exciting musical experiences of your life. If you do it badly, then you will not enjoy a good sleep that night!"

The director finished his Danish and said, "But there are several things you can do to help your players feel good about playing for you."

"Tell me what they are," said Bob eagerly.

20   "When they are ready to begin your rehearsal, you should say a word of welcome to them: 'We are delighted to have with us the ladies and gentlemen of the so-and-so orchestra whose playing will transform our concert and give enormous pleasure to us and to our audience.' Your choir will then give them a round of applause, and you should shake your concertmaster's hand. That will get you off to a good start.

"On no account should you say to your orchestra, 'I'm only a church organist and not experienced in conducting orchestras, and so I shall be relying on your kindness to help me through.' This will tell them that you don't really know what you're doing. They'll play well enough for you, but they will not follow any of your musical directions, such as playing more softly here or more closely with your beat. You've told them that they are better than you are, and so they'll just go ahead and prove you to be right!"

"Wow!" said Bob, feeling repressed again.

21   "But what you should do, for their break, is to provide them with a comfortable room to themselves where coffee, fruit juice, and cookies are ready for them. You should do the same for the performance. Treat them as you would honored guests, for they are special, and they will respond to your thoughtfulness. And remember to tell them where the rest rooms are!

22   "Their room should also be locked when they are not there. They will need a place where they can put their coats and instrument cases. If you are rehearsing on a Saturday for a performance on a Sunday, the percussionists may want to store their instruments overnight. Make provision for this."

The director looked at his watch. "We've got five minutes more before you have to leave. I've nearly finished."

"And I've only got one page left in my notebook," said Bob with a smile. "It's all working out very well, isn't it?"

"Yes it is! Next point:

23   "Discuss with your orchestral agent whether or not you should provide music stands for your players. Some like to bring their own, but many are grateful if the stands are there, ready for them.

24   "Make sure that there is sufficient light in your church for players to see their music clearly. Many churches have inadequate lighting. If this is the case with your church, you will have to hire someone to fix special lighting for you, or ask the players to bring stand lights. Make sure that the lights don't shine in the eyes of the audience, though!

25   "You will almost certainly have to hire the orchestral parts from an agency. Invariably these come covered in pencil marks. I suggest that you don't clean them up before you get them to your players, for most of the marks will be helpful. Some players will appreciate having the music beforehand so that they can practice it, especially if it is an unknown work or if your performers are music students. Your agent will tell you about this. Make sure that your librarian collects the orchestral parts from the players' stands immediately after the concert is over, otherwise some of them could easily disappear into players' instrument cases, by accident. And by 'immediately,' I mean, the instant the players begin walking off the platform!

26   "I've not mentioned the importance of the entry of your choir before the concert begins," added the director.

"Yes," responded Bob. "They should line up in the church hall or in some other convenient place, standing in the positions that they will occupy on the platform."

"Right! It's very helpful to have a master of ceremonies to do this for you," added the director, "a senior singer who can command good order. He, or she, should make sure that everyone knows where they ought to be; how to walk in and how to walk out. And then the end singer of each row in turn, starting with the back row, should lead the way to the platform."

"Should they sit down when they get there?"

"No! They should wait, standing very still with their hands at their sides, holding their music in their right (or left) hand—so that they all look the same. They should stand motionless until the concertmaster has taken his bow, and then the soloists and yourself have taken your bows. At that point you indicate to the choir that they should find their place in the music, and you are ready to begin.

27 "And finally, at the end of the performance, you must observe the customary etiquette when the audience applauds."

"What's that?"

"You acknowledge the applause first, briefly. Then you indicate that the soloists should take their bow. Then you shake the hand of the concertmaster and indicate that the orchestra should stand for their share of the applause. And finally, you wave a gracious hand at your choir, so that they may share in the audience's appreciation. Tell your choir, beforehand, to smile happily during the applause, and not to be putting their music away or conversing with their neighbor. You then follow the soloists off stage. Wait for a few moments and then return, going through the same performance of applause acknowledgment. Don't overdo it—smile and show genuine appreciation not only of the audience's applause but also of your performers' efforts. End on a happy party note."

70

CODA

"And speaking of ending on a happy party note," said Bob as he wrote his final few words on to the bottom of the last page in his notebook, "it's time I made my way to the plane."

They stood up and walked, companionably, towards the gate.

"I can't begin to tell you how much I've enjoyed having you stay with me this week," said the director. "It's been such a delight to talk with you about all the things that matter to me most."

"I feel just the same," said Bob affectionately, for he had grown fond of this man who had shared so much of himself during the last seven days.

"I think that, if I were to sum up everything I've said in one word it would be the word 'love.'

"How do you mean?" asked Bob for the last time.

"If you really love your singers as much as you love yourself, especially those who, at first sight, are unlovable; if you love the music you inspire them to perform because it brings all who hear it to the gate of heaven itself; if you love your church, and all who serve her, because it is the body of Christ on earth; and if you love your Lord because he loved you even before you were created in your mother's womb, then blessed will you be. St. Paul really knew what he was saying when he wrote to the Christians in Corinth that 'the greatest of these is love.' It's a wholly practical matter that you can apply every day to bring the gift of life to all you do."

"Thank you so much for sharing that," responded Bob, his heart strangely warmed by what the director had just said. "Let me show you a token of my love right now." He brought out of his pocket a red rose that he had bought an hour before, and pinned it on to the director's lapel. They embraced warmly and silently. No words were needed.

Bob picked up his briefcase and walked steadfastly through the departure gate without looking back.

The director watched him go until he was out of sight. That young man will go far, he thought, and I don't mean just to Seattle!

APPENDIX A *The Role of the Christian Church Musician*
   John Bertalot

from a predinner address given to the American Guild of Organists'
Region IV Convention, Charlotte, N.C., July 18, 1985

As I look at you all sitting here, hoping I'm not going to talk too long before dinner is served, I'm reminded of a story of the Bishop of Manchester, who was leading a service in his cathedral in England shortly after the new prayer book had been published. He was having trouble making himself heard over the loudspeaker system and said, mezzo forte, "There's something wrong with this microphone," to which his congregation dutifully responded, "And also with you!"

The title of this talk implies two things: one, that there are Christian musicians who are not church musicians; and two, that there are church musicians who aren't Christians!

When I was an associate professor at the Royal Northern College of Music in Manchester, England, before I came to Princeton in 1983, I used to attend the annual degree ceremony in the college concert hall. The Duchess of Kent presided. Every year she presented honorary degrees to half a dozen distinguished musicians of international reputation before she gave degrees to the graduating students.

One particular year she included England's outstanding mezzo-soprano, to whom fell the task of making a speech of thanks to the Duchess on behalf of her colleagues. Her presence and her speech were as gracious as her lovely singing voice. She said that, as her voice and musicianship were a gift from God, she could claim no credit for them. What she could claim credit for was using those gifts.

Her Christian witness in those secular surroundings made a deep and lasting impression. Jesus' parable of the talents came readily to mind: "Well done, thou good and faithful servant..."

By the way, the term *Christian* has a precise meaning, rather as the English term *gentleman;* had an exact meaning. Both have tended to become generalized in the public mind to mean someone who is a good citizen. Being a Christian means far more than that.

Our position as church musicians is often opposite that which our Victorian forebears sought for their children, for, we are often hidden behind curtains or placed in organ lofts; we are heard but not seen. This geographic position in the building may sometimes influence our standing in the church itself.

When I was organist of St. Matthew's Church, Northampton, England, the church for which Britten wrote *Rejoice in the Lamb* and where Alec Wyton began his career, as well as Michael Nicholas and Stephen Cleobury, I had to sit at a console that was halfway between choir and congregation: the organist belonged to neither—it was a lonely position.

It would seem easier, in some ways, not to be a Christian in a church music program, for a Christian must allow himself to become involved in the things that the church stands for and which the church does, and thus he allows himself to be hurt. A church musician who keeps his home life separate from his church life seems to be setting up a contradiction and a conflict within himself that must result in damage to himself. Jesus said, "A kingdom divided against itself must fall." When this does happen there will be no one around to bind up his wounds, for he has cut himself off from those who are there to help him. But there are two sorts of wounds: one, which is intended to kill, and the other, which is intended to heal. One comes from the sword of the enemy, and the other from the knife of the surgeon, but both spill blood.

Last year we lost a wonderful choir family from Trinity Church, Princeton, when the father, whom I shall call Jim, was appointed to a university post in California. He and his two children, a girl and a boy, sang in our choirs, and his wife was active in many of our choir support programs.

Jim told me that, some months after they had arrived in their new home, he took the children to Choral Evensong in their nearby cathedral. When the choir began to sing Stanford's *Magnificat in C,* which we often sing at Princeton, both children burst into tears. Their wound was a spiritual one: they remembered what it was like to worship God "with heart and voice." As the hymn says: "My soul bear thou thy part, Triumph in God above, And with a well-tuned heart Sing thou the songs of love." Or, as St. Paul says: "I will sing with spirit and with understanding also." This is the motto of the Royal School of Church Music.

This is not to say that "heaven" or "spiritual reality" can only be found in singing Stanford in C. (Although it does mean that, when Stanford is sung from the heart, it is being used for the purpose for which it was created: as a vehicle to enable us to worship God.) No, we worship not only through singing Stanford, or Howells, or Palestrina, or choruses with guitar, that is, corporate worship, but we also need private prayers if our Christian 'profession' [what we profess] is to be balanced.

Jesus worshipped God in synagogue and temple, but he also spent long hours in prayer alone. And it was usually after his times alone with his Father that he made the big decisions regarding his ministry, such as the choosing of his disciples and his submission to being betrayed by Judas. If the Christianity that we profess is limited to leading music in our church's worship, it is as unbalanced as the religion of those who ask, "Why do I have to go to church to be a Christian? I can worship God just as well in the privacy of my garden." Our profession of faith needs to be balanced so that it can show itself in action. As the hymn says: "Let our ordered lives confess the beauty of thy Name." Or the Choristers' Prayer: "Grant that what we sing with our lips we may believe in our hearts; And what we believe in our hearts we may show forth in our lives."

A beautiful example of faith in action came my way last week during the Royal School of Church Music course that I directed in Charleston,

South Carolina, which culminated in our singing the opening service for this Convention:

Three of us adults were having lunch in the cafeteria of the college where we were staying. One of our boy choristers came to our table carrying his tray; he was only nine, and he asked if he could join us.

He sat down, closed his eyes and silently mouthed his grace. We didn't say anything, but, for all of us, it was as though heaven had been opened for a brief moment. That, for me, was the high point of our whole course, eclipsing even the opening service of our convention.

This act, apparently, cost him nothing, for his prayer was a prayer of innocence. For an adult to have done this, even though that grace would have been said, supposedly, in the presence of those who profess and call themselves Christians, there would have been a cost; a drop of blood would have been spilt.

And how true it is that, like Peter, we would say, "I'll never deny you"—the grand gesture. But who was it that caused him to deny his Master?—a slip of a servant girl! In theory, the last drop of blood may seem easy to shed for one's faith, but, in practice, how difficult it is to shed one's first drop! That hurts.

Do we have a faith, individually and corporately, that we value enough and find sufficiently true in daily experience to make the shedding of a little blood a small price to pay for the joy that it gives us to be Christians? Are we prepared, as the Bible says, "to give a reason for the faith that lies within us"? Can we even define what we believe to be the gospel? Not what we think the gospel ought to be, but the gospel that can be backed up, as the saying goes, by chapter and verse? Are we aware that there is much more Christianity to be discovered and experienced than that corner of the good news in which our own denomination may specialize?

Stuart Blanch, when he was enthroned as Archbishop of York, gave a wonderful illustration of this in a memorable sermon that was delivered to his clergy and people in the packed Minster. He said:

> The Christian faith is like a man going for a walk in the
> country who sees at his feet a beautiful sprig of heather,
> which he stoops down to pick. When he stands up again,
> he finds that, as far as his eye can see, in every direction,
> the whole countryside is filled with heather!

What a wonderful encouragement that was to some of his clergy and people who may, perhaps, have lost heart.

Sometimes we need to get away from familiar surroundings for a while in order to be able to rediscover those things which have, through familiarity, become jaded and undervalued. As the poet says, "What know they of England/who only England know?"

To return to the matter of hurting: A church is, in some measure, a body of hurting people who bind up each other's wounds. It is not a collection of "holier-than-thous," even though some may outwardly give that impression. It has been rightly said that if you find the perfect church, don't join it, for it won't be perfect any more!

One thing that I, as an Englishman, have learned to appreciate in my first two-and-one-half years in the United States is that American society is confrontational. We aren't like that in England—we tend to "let things go." When differences arise here you discuss them "eyeball to eyeball." This is a hurting process, but all cleansing is painful. I've discovered that, when two adults confront each other with mutual respect and are therefore free to "have it out" and really listen to what the other is saying, the former fractured relationship between them is not only mended but strengthened, as a broken bone is stronger when it is healed.

But what about us? What about our striving for professional success as Christian musicians in the church? Success can be very transitory; we can have a wonderful service one Sunday (mountain top) and an awful one the next (valley). We tend to judge ourselves to be only as good as our material: when our choir sings well, we are successful, when it sings badly, we fail.

We like to call our profession a vocation, from the Latin *vocare* "to call." Jesus called his disciples. He said, "You have not chosen me, but I have chosen you, and ordained you [given you gifts/power/authority] to bear much fruit, fruit which will last, so that the Father may give you all that you ask in my Name. This is my commandment: Love one another as I have loved you." And this "Jesus-love" was a hurting, costly love. As the Sunday school question and answer goes: "How much does Jesus love you?" "This much!" stretching wide your arms.

Life is about relationships—relationships between couples: when they are right, life is good, when they go wrong, life is shattered. Life is about relationships with those we love and also with those the Bible calls our "enemies." You know what Jesus told us to do about those relationships—we are to love those who cross us, and to pray for them, as Jesus prayed for those who "crossed" him.

It is impossible to have a one-way relationship. That's why television is so unsatisfactory, for the screen cannot respond to our response to it. A relationship, in order to be living, must be a two-way process. Our vocation, our chosenness, in order to be a living one, must be relational: relational to him who called us, and relational to those to whom we minister, and this must be a two-way process.

It's easy to have a two-way relationship with our choirs; that's what choir practices are all about; the choir responds to the choirmaster, and the choirmaster to the choir. But what about our primary relationship with him who chose us in the first place? (And I'm not talking about the minister!) Is our relationship with him a two-way process? Only you and I can answer that in our hearts. Our relationship with God, in order to be true, must be demonstrated in our relationship with our neighbor.

A Christian lawyer friend in Princeton has pointed out that there's something very personal and very special about being chosen: When God calls us, he calls us by name. "Moses, Moses,"were the words from the burning bush; "Samuel, Samuel," were the words mistaken for Eli's call, and in the blinding light on the road to Damascus, Paul heard, "Saul, Saul!"

"You have searched me out and known me," says the psalmist, "You are acquainted with all my ways." God's call is an ongoing, creative call, not just an impersonal historical fact that does not affect us. "You are the body of Christ," says St. Paul, "and each of you is a different [important] part." This is as true today as it was when these words were written. Each one of us has been chosen, and when God calls us by name he calls not only one part of us, such as our musical expertise, but he calls all of us, wholly. My name represents the whole of me, not just part of me. This chosenness requires a response. There must be communication between the caller and the one who is called: "Lord, what wilt thou have me to do?"

Music is a language of communication. It expresses truths that words cannot. When a player dazzles us only by his technique, he is saying, "Look at me, aren't I clever!" I remember hearing Fernando Germani, many years ago, playing César Franck's third choral at a recital in Liverpool Anglican Cathedral. At the end of the performance I thought, "What a wonderful piece that was—what a marvelous composer!" Germani really communicated what Franck was trying to say. That was true greatness; that was fulfilled vocation. From our communication, our vocation, our chosenness, come fruitfulness. To quote my lawyer friend again: "Fruitfulness is the issuance of that within us that touches others deeply and allows the unexpected to happen."

Last St. Valentine's day, another Princeton friend gave me a small cutglass heart. I hung it in the window of my office where the sun would strike it. Ever since then, at various times of the day, when I've looked up from my desk, I've often seen a beautiful rainbow on the wall in front of me. That is fruitfulness—that is unexpected.

A few months ago I received, out of the blue, a letter from an English composer who was a pupil of mine twenty-five years ago. In it he said,

> I want to say something that has been left unsaid for too long: and that's simply, "Thank you" to you. Thank you for playing *Dieu parmi nous* when I first joined your choir, thank you for transposition, fugue and the line of a descant, the joy of harmony, the revelation of the true function of the leading note, for humanizing music and showing me how to understand it. Well ... just, thank you.

That was the nicest letter I have ever received. That is fruitfulness—that is unexpected.

Fruitfulness may be contrasted with successfulness. To be successful one must achieve results, produce a product. Fruits are not products, for products and results are intentioned, they are things to be reached, things you wish for, things at a distance. Success is always "over there," never "right here"; it is always "to be gained." Seeking success makes you think about getting there first; it's competitive. It can make you hide your course and your ambition from others in order to outsmart them.

Fruit, on the other hand, is born, it breaks forth, it is received, not made. Fruit is a surprise, as the rainbow and the letter were. Success is transitory and it decays. Fruit remains and is living, and it tends to produce more fruit. Fruit comes from broken ground, from hurting, wounded people who 'go on their way weeping, bearing forth good seed' (Psalm 126), and fruit comes when the time is right, in season, and not to order.

Success is essentially lonely; when you win, you're out in front by yourself. (Non-success is even lonelier, for not only are you last, by yourself, but everyone who's ahead of you in the race has his back to you, and, even worse, doesn't even know you're there!). Fruitfulness, on the other hand, is essentially a cooperative venture, such as a husband and wife creating a family. Fruitfulness brings joy; when the sower has sown his seed (as Psalm 126 continues), he shall "doubtless come again with joy, bringing his sheaves with him."

Mother Theresa of Calcutta was interviewed by a brash young reporter recently, who asked her how she felt now that she was getting older and seeing her powers diminishing. She replied, "I am not called to be successful, but to be faithful."

You will remember that St. Paul defines the fruit of the Spirit as "Love, joy, peace, patience, kindness, goodness, *faithfulness,* gentleness and self-control. The first three are for ourselves: Love in our hearts, joy in our hearts, and peace in our hearts. The next three are to our neighbors: Patience towards them, kindness and goodness. The remaining three are to God: Faithfulness (which only God can see), gentleness and self-control. St. John tells us in Revelation that those nearest the King of kings "will be his called, chosen and faithful followers."

Our profession requires us to be successful. Our vocation calls us to be faithful. This needs constant awareness and judgment on our part to enable us to maintain a balance between the two.

May we get the balance right.

American Choral Directors Association (ACDA)
P.O. Box 6310,
Lawton, OK 73506

American Guild of Organists (AGO)
475 Riverside Drive, Suite 1260
New York, NY 10115

Association of Anglican Musicians (AAM),
P.O. Box 164488
Little Rock, AR 72216-4488

Association of Lutheran Church Musicians (ALCM)
c/o Richard Wyble
P.O. Box 16575,
Worcester, MA 01601

Choristers Guild
2834 West Kingsley
Garland, TX 75041-2498

Chorus America—Association of
    Professional Vocal Ensembles
2111 Sansom Street
Philadelphia, PA 19103

Royal Canadian College of Organists
112 St. Clair Ave. West, Suite 302
Toronto, Ontario M4V 2Y3

Royal College of Organists
7 St. Andrew Street
London, EC4A 3LQ
England

Royal School of Church Music in America (RSCM/A)
c/o Robert Quade
St. Paul's Episcopal Church
1361 West Market
Akron, OH 44313

Royal School of Church Music (Headquarters)
Addington Palace
Croydon, Surrey
CR9 5AD
England

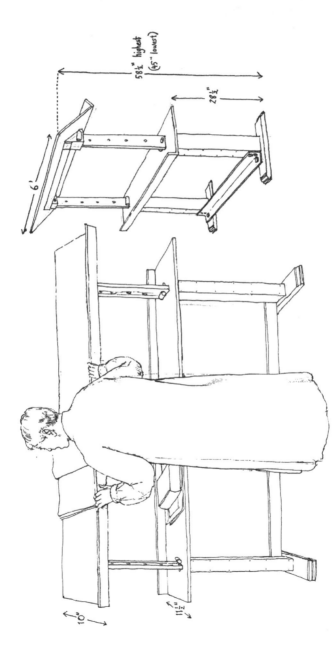

Music desks, as used in the practice room of Trinity Church, Princeton, New Jersey. Drawn by Eberhard Froehlich